ORCHID ™

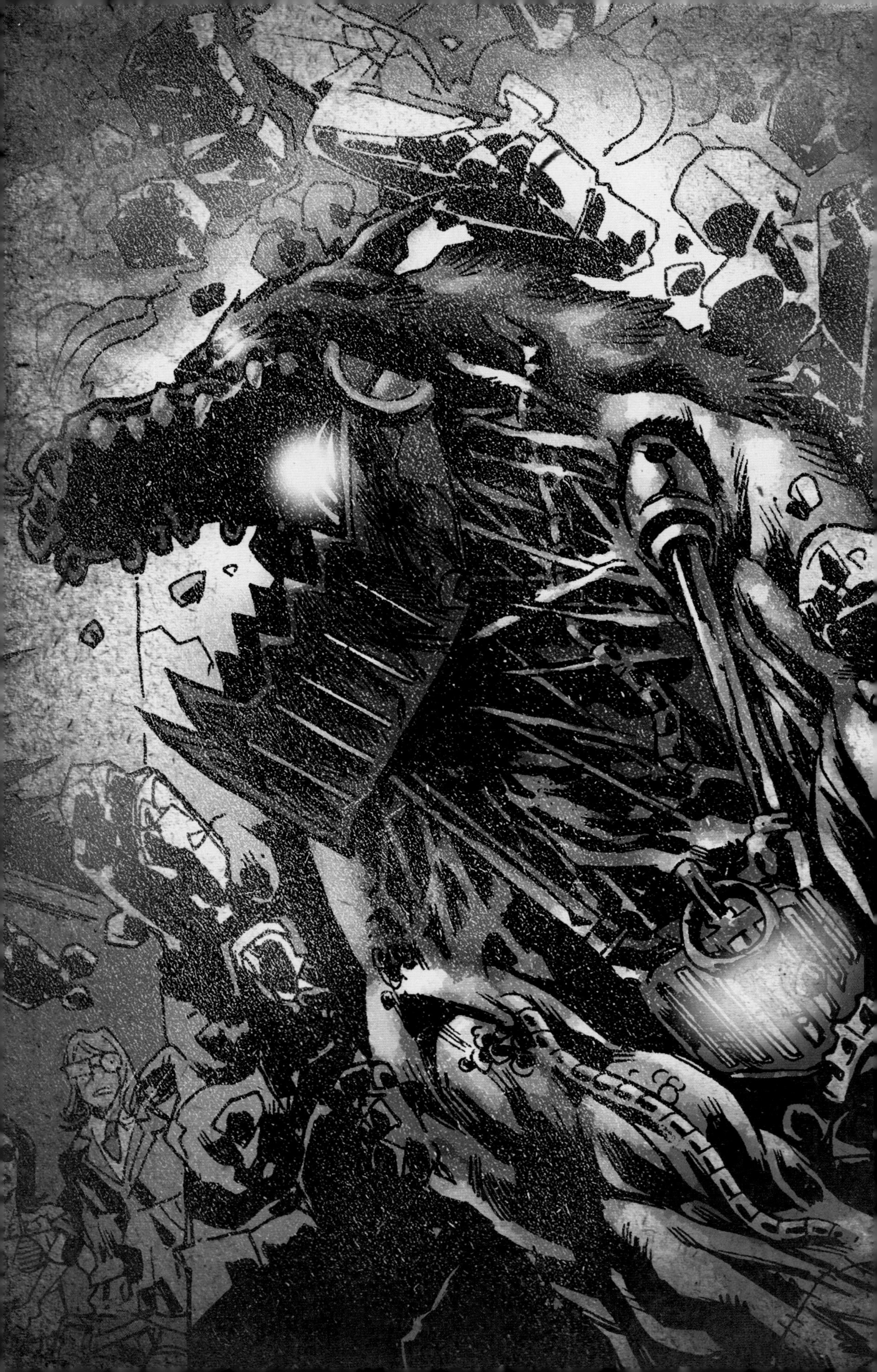

ORCHID™

VOLUME 2

SCRIPT
TOM MORELLO

ART
SCOTT HEPBURN

COLORS
DAN JACKSON

LETTERS
NATE PIEKOS OF BLAMBOT®

COVER ART
MASSIMO CARNEVALE

DARK HORSE BOOKS

PRESIDENT & PUBLISHER
MIKE RICHARDSON

EDITOR
SIERRA HAHN

ASSISTANT EDITOR
JIM GIBBONS

COLLECTION DESIGNER
DAVID NESTELLE

SPECIAL THANKS TO DAVE LAND AND MICHELE FISHER.

Neil Hankerson Executive Vice President • Tom Weddle Chief Financial Officer • Randy Stradley Vice President of Publishing • Michael Martens Vice President of Book Trade Sales • Anita Nelson Vice President of Business Affairs • Matt Parkinson Vice President of Marketing • David Scroggy Vice President of Product Development • Dale LaFountain Vice President of Information Technology • Darlene Vogel Senior Director of Print, Design, and Production • Ken Lizzi General Counsel • Davey Estrada Editorial Director • Scott Allie Senior Managing Editor • Chris Warner Senior Books Editor • Diana Schutz Executive Editor • Cary Grazzini Director of Print and Development • Lia Ribacchi Art Director • Cara Niece Director of Scheduling • Tim Wiesch Director of International Licensing

This volume reprints the comic-book series *Orchid* #5–#8 from Dark Horse Comics.

Published by Dark Horse Books
A division of Dark Horse Comics, Inc.
10956 SE Main Street
Milwaukie, OR 97222

DarkHorse.com
NightwatchmanMusic.com

To find a comics shop in your area, call the Comic Shop Locator Service toll-free at (888) 266-4226.

First edition: December 2012
ISBN 978-1-59582-966-5

10 9 8 7 6 5 4 3 2 1
Printed by Midas Printing International, Ltd., Huizhou, China.

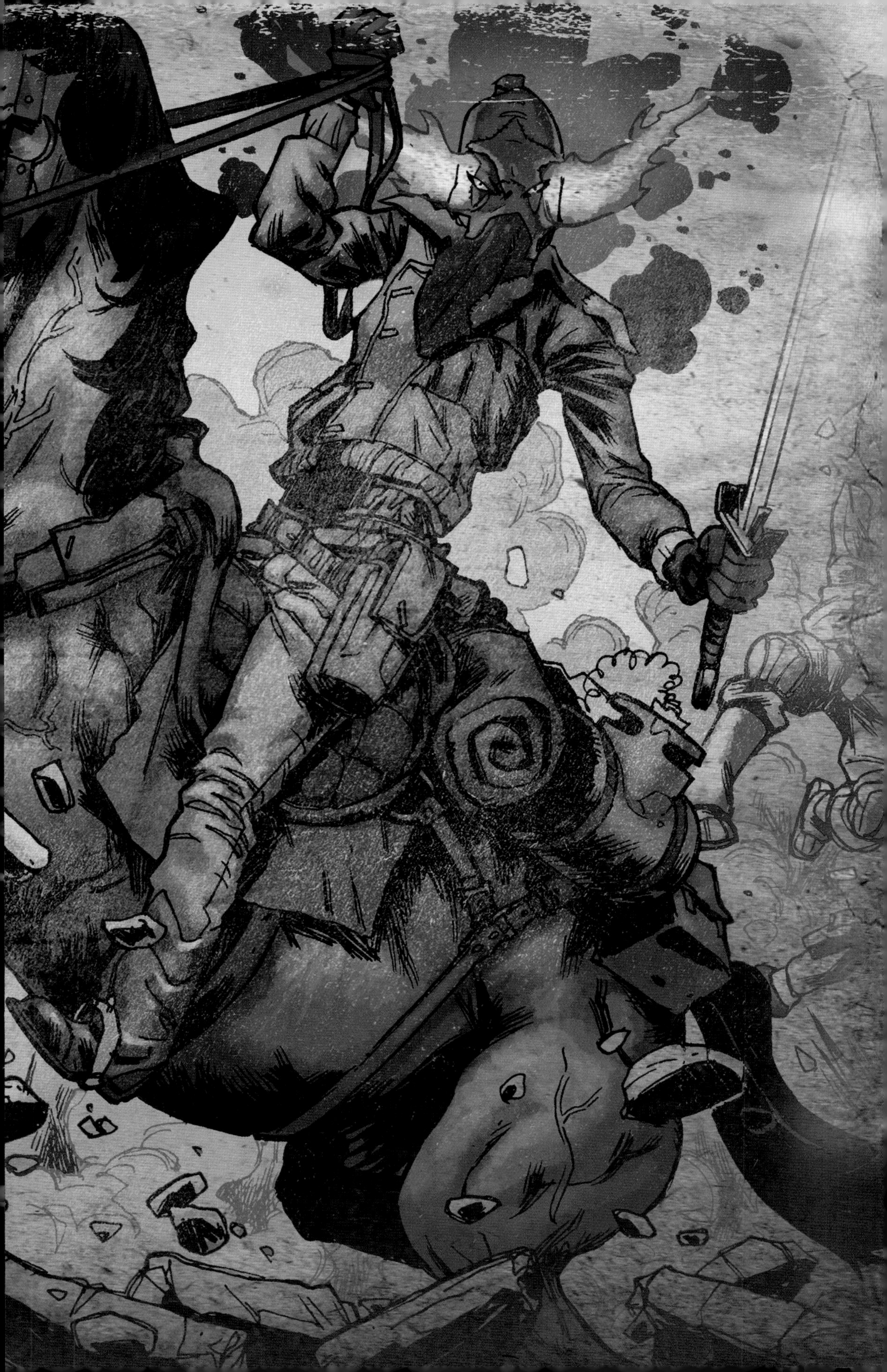

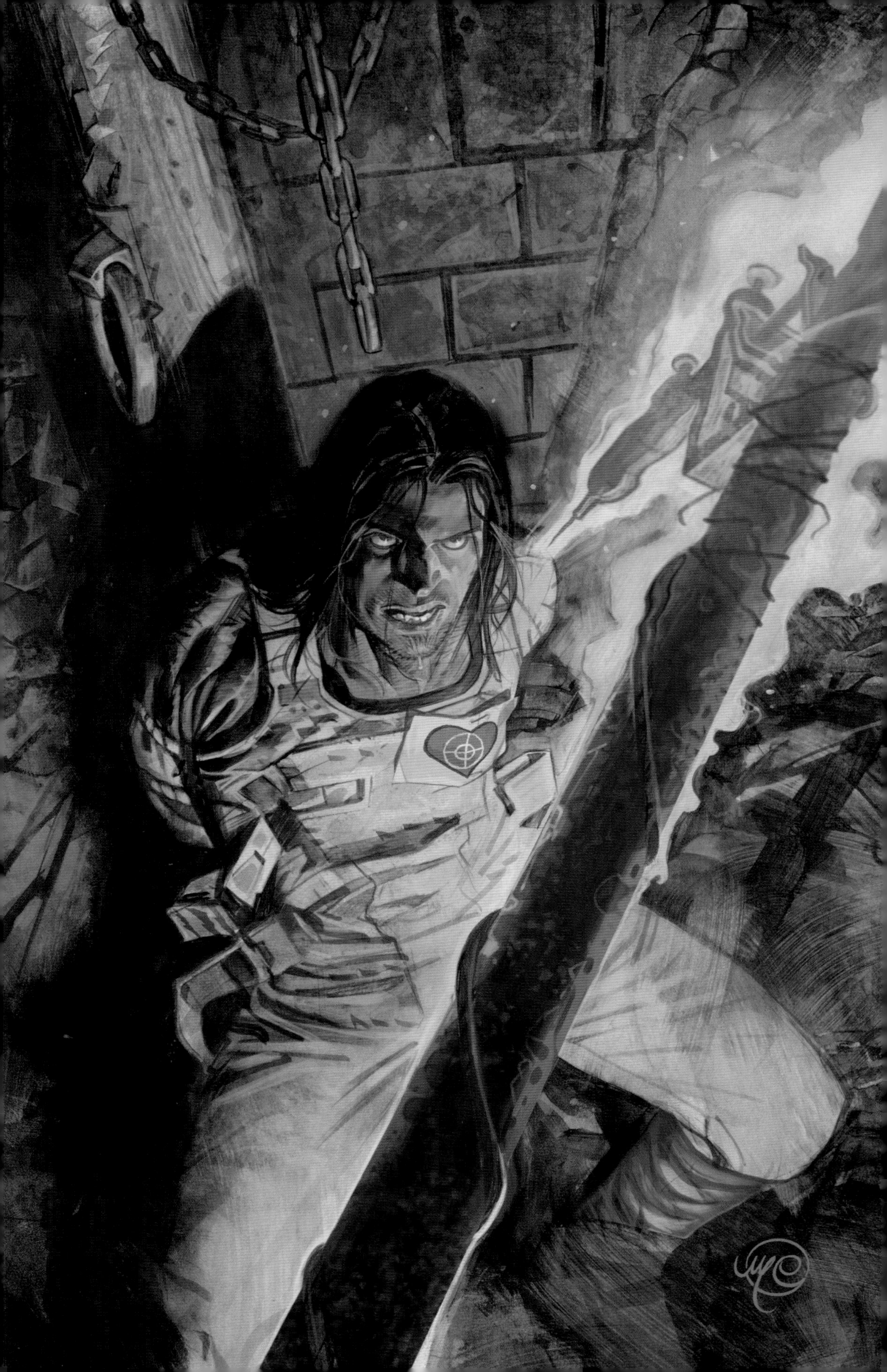

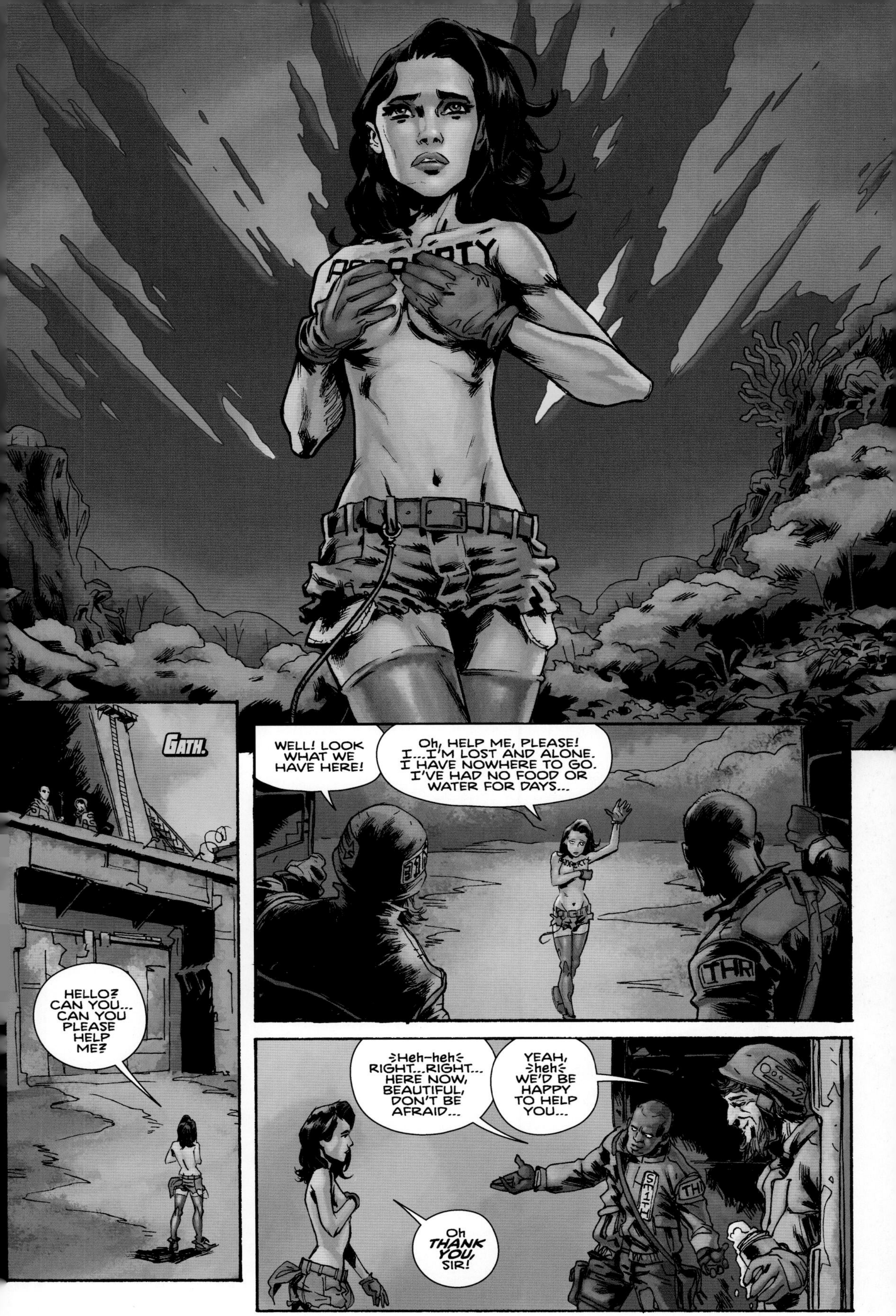
GATH.
HELLO? CAN YOU... CAN YOU PLEASE HELP ME?
WELL! LOOK WHAT WE HAVE HERE!
Oh, HELP ME, PLEASE! I...I'M LOST AND ALONE. I HAVE NOWHERE TO GO. I'VE HAD NO FOOD OR WATER FOR DAYS...
THR
Heh-heh RIGHT...RIGHT... HERE NOW, BEAUTIFUL, DON'T BE AFRAID...
YEAH, heh WE'D BE HAPPY TO HELP YOU...
Oh THANK YOU, SIR!

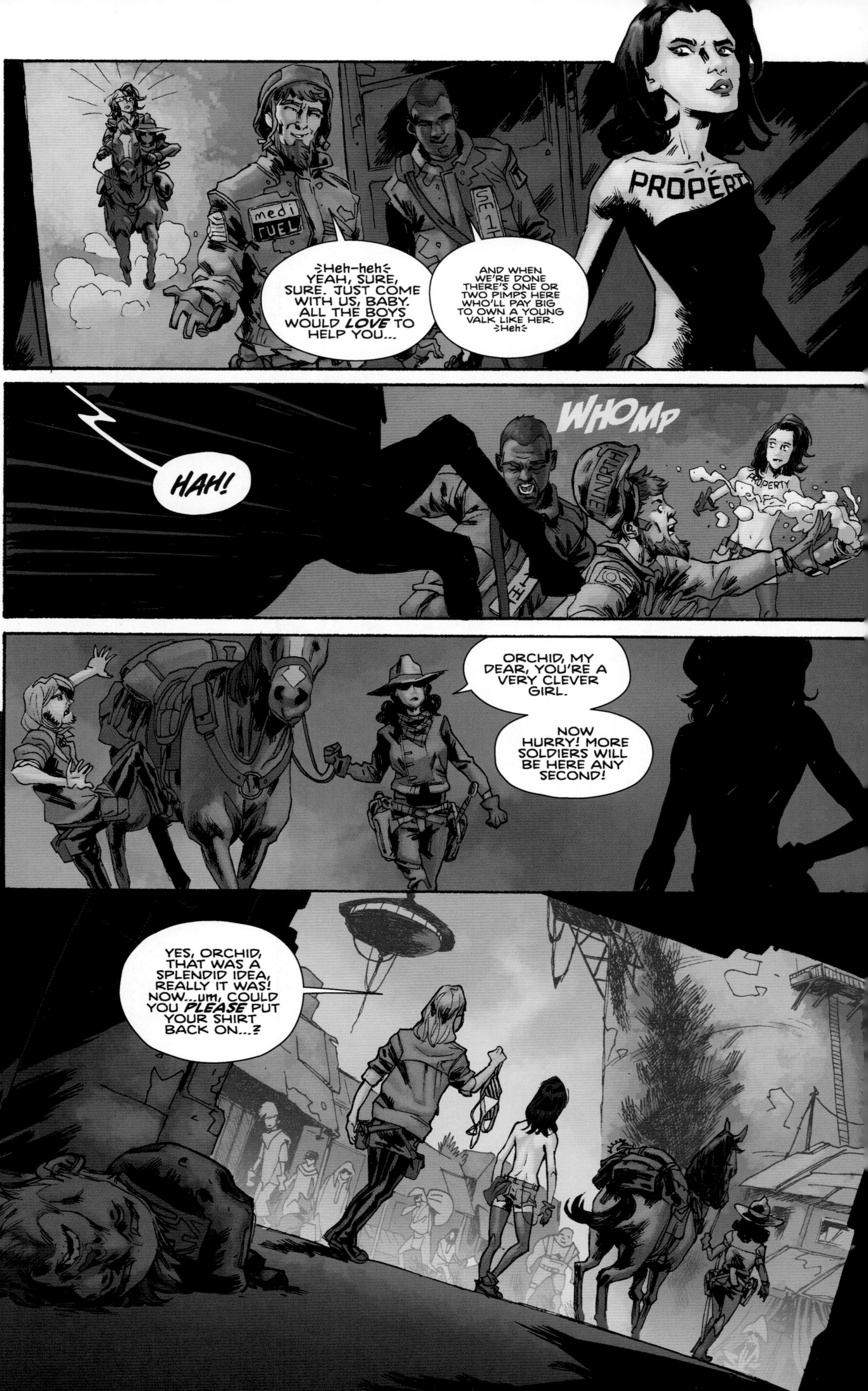
PROPERTY
Heh-heh YEAH, SURE, SURE. JUST COME WITH US, BABY. ALL THE BOYS WOULD LOVE TO HELP YOU...
AND WHEN WE'RE DONE THERE'S ONE OR TWO PIMPS HERE WHO'LL PAY BIG TO OWN A YOUNG VALK LIKE HER. Heh
WHOMP
HAH!
ORCHID, MY DEAR, YOU'RE A VERY CLEVER GIRL.
NOW HURRY! MORE SOLDIERS WILL BE HERE ANY SECOND!
YES, ORCHID, THAT WAS A SPLENDID IDEA, REALLY IT WAS! NOW...um, COULD YOU PLEASE PUT YOUR SHIRT BACK ON...?

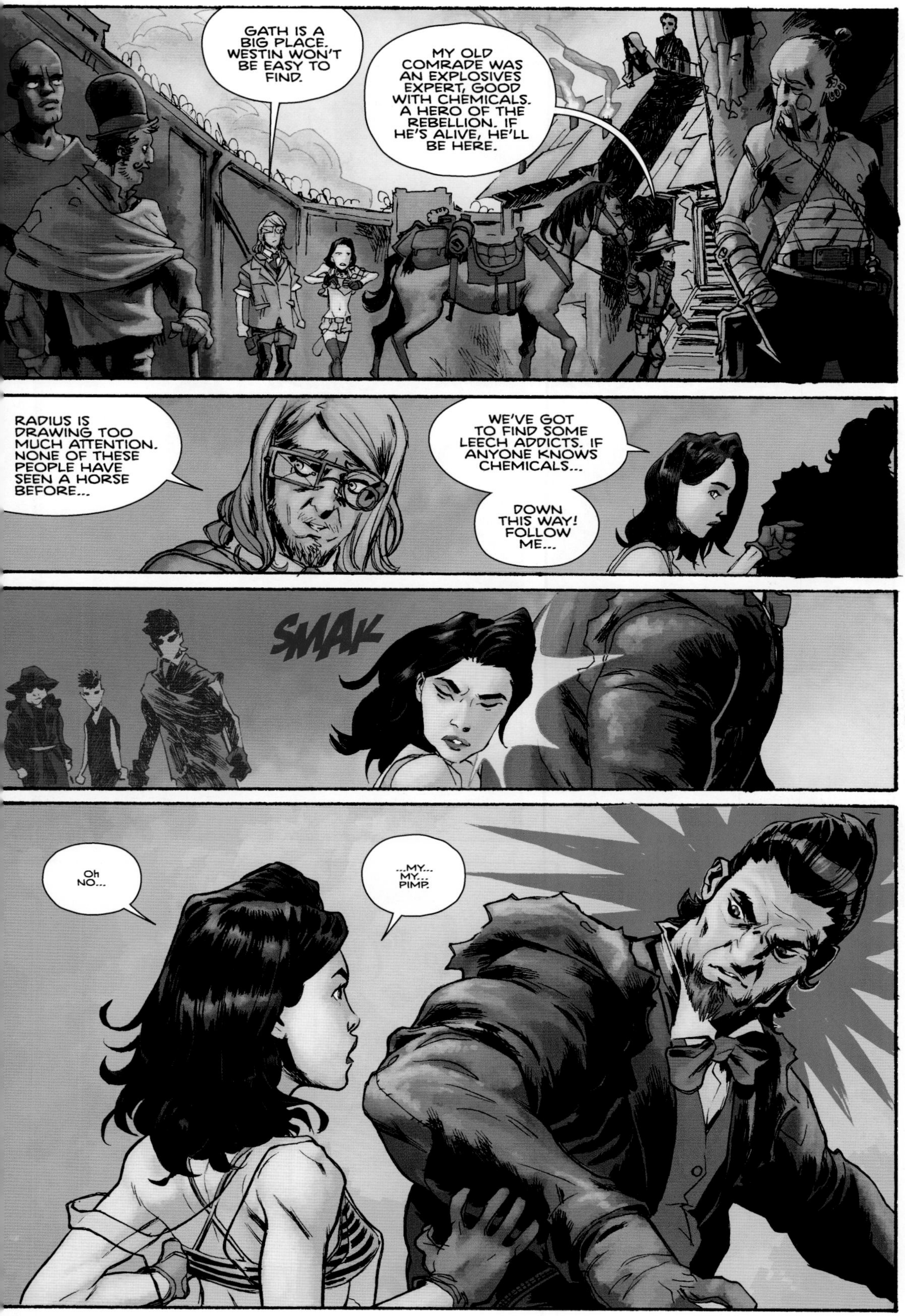
GATH IS A BIG PLACE. WESTIN WON'T BE EASY TO FIND.
MY OLD COMRADE WAS AN EXPLOSIVES EXPERT, GOOD WITH CHEMICALS. A HERO OF THE REBELLION. IF HE'S ALIVE, HE'LL BE HERE.
RADIUS IS DRAWING TOO MUCH ATTENTION. NONE OF THESE PEOPLE HAVE SEEN A HORSE BEFORE...
WE'VE GOT TO FIND SOME LEECH ADDICTS. IF ANYONE KNOWS CHEMICALS...
DOWN THIS WAY! FOLLOW ME...
SMAK
Oh NO...
...MY... MY... PIMP.

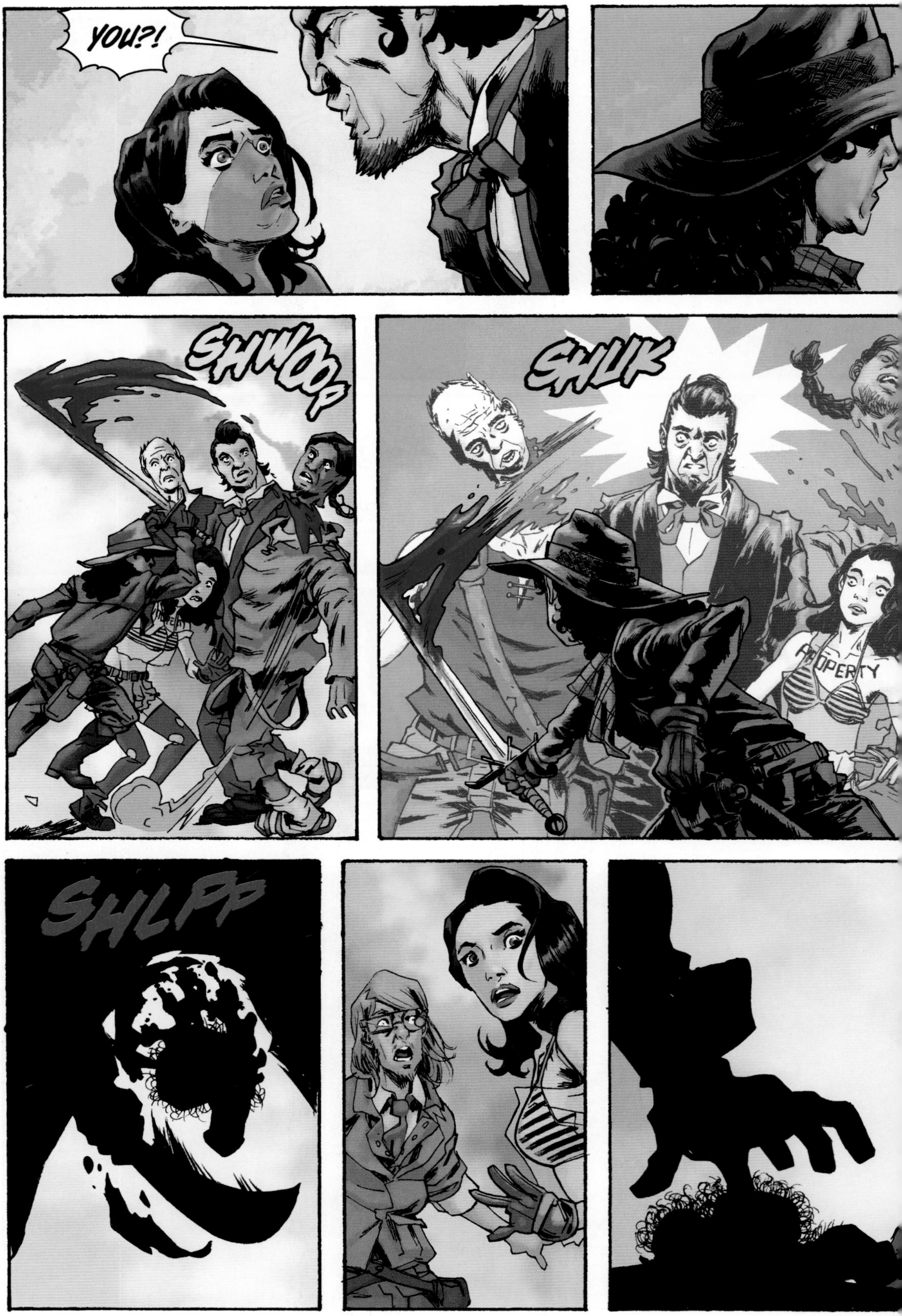
YOU?!
SHWOOP
SHUK
PROPERTY
SHLPP

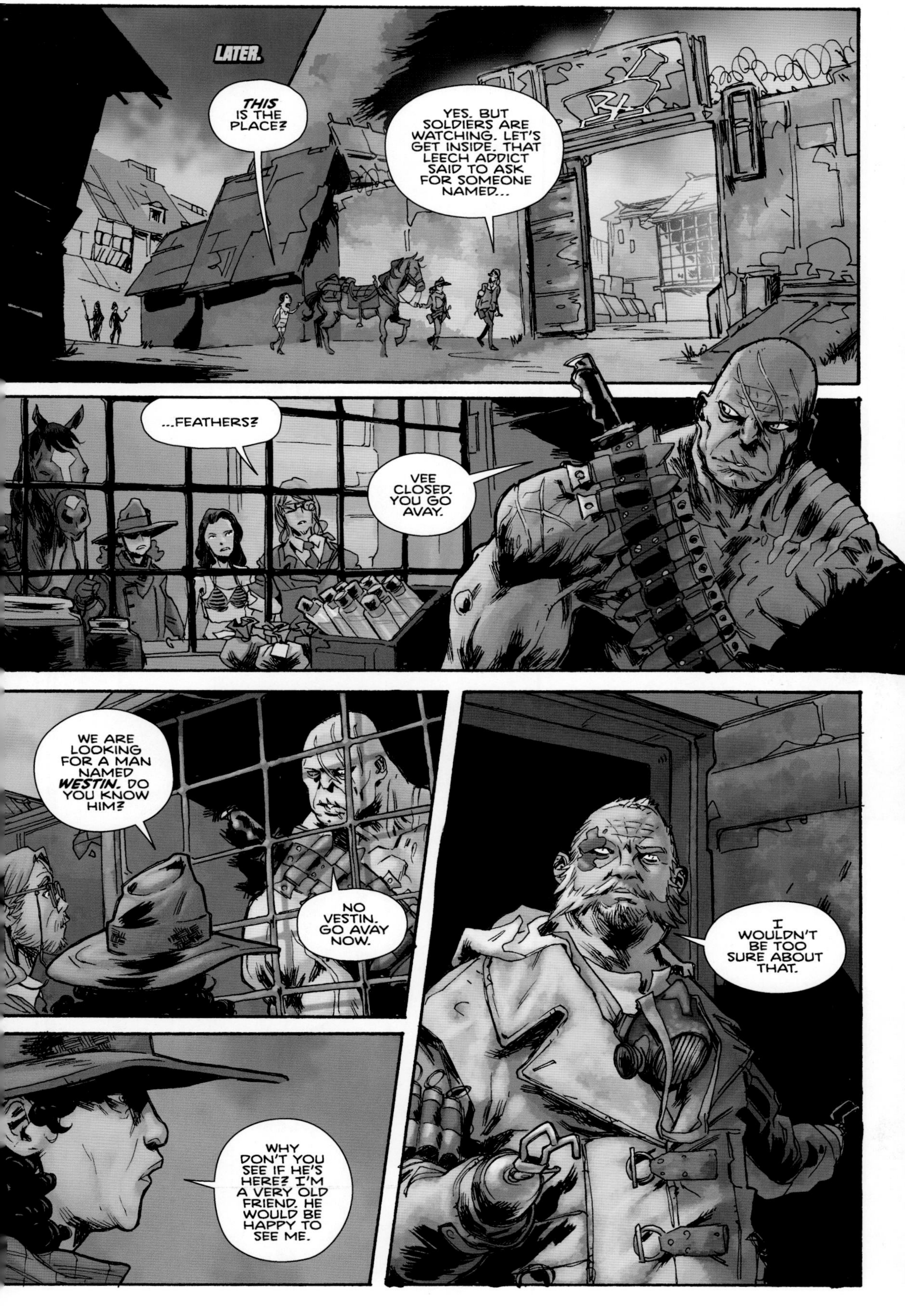
LATER.
THIS IS THE PLACE?
YES. BUT SOLDIERS ARE WATCHING. LET'S GET INSIDE. THAT LEECH ADDICT SAID TO ASK FOR SOMEONE NAMED...
...FEATHERS?
VEE CLOSED. YOU GO AVAY.
WE ARE LOOKING FOR A MAN NAMED WESTIN. DO YOU KNOW HIM?
NO VESTIN. GO AVAY NOW.
I WOULDN'T BE TOO SURE ABOUT THAT.
WHY DON'T YOU SEE IF HE'S HERE? I'M A VERY OLD FRIEND. HE WOULD BE HAPPY TO SEE ME.

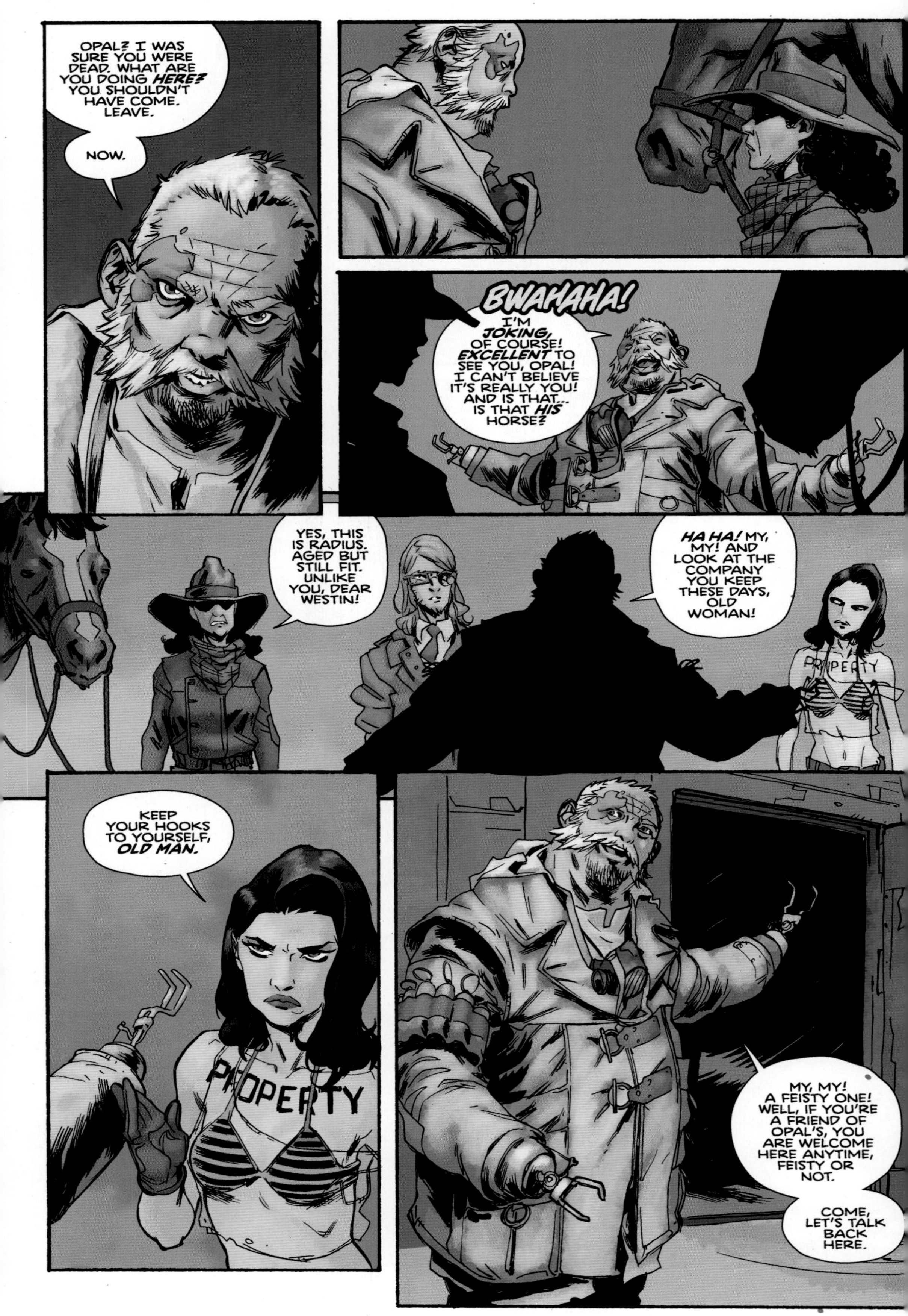
OPAL? I WAS SURE YOU WERE DEAD. WHAT ARE YOU DOING HERE? YOU SHOULDN'T HAVE COME. LEAVE.
NOW.
BWAHAHA!
I'M JOKING, OF COURSE! EXCELLENT TO SEE YOU, OPAL! I CAN'T BELIEVE IT'S REALLY YOU! AND IS THAT... IS THAT HIS HORSE?
YES, THIS IS RADIUS. AGED BUT STILL FIT. UNLIKE YOU, DEAR WESTIN!
HA HA! MY, MY! AND LOOK AT THE COMPANY YOU KEEP THESE DAYS, OLD WOMAN!
PROPERTY
KEEP YOUR HOOKS TO YOURSELF, OLD MAN.
PROPERTY
MY, MY! A FEISTY ONE! WELL, IF YOU'RE A FRIEND OF OPAL'S, YOU ARE WELCOME HERE ANYTIME, FEISTY OR NOT.
COME, LET'S TALK BACK HERE.

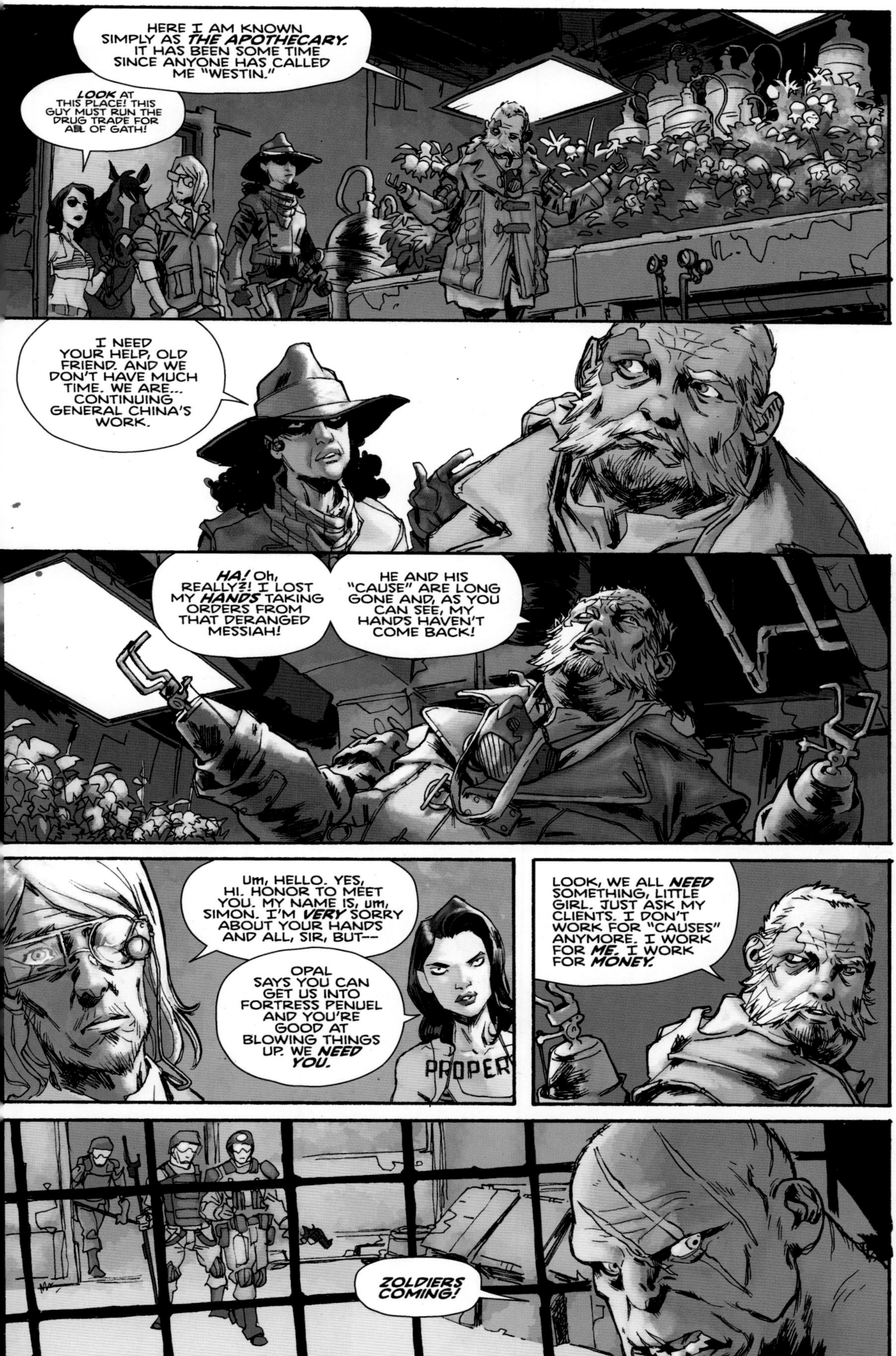
HERE I AM KNOWN SIMPLY AS *THE APOTHECARY.* IT HAS BEEN SOME TIME SINCE ANYONE HAS CALLED ME "WESTIN."
LOOK AT THIS PLACE! THIS GUY MUST RUN THE DRUG TRADE FOR ALL OF GATH!
I NEED YOUR HELP, OLD FRIEND. AND WE DON'T HAVE MUCH TIME. WE ARE... CONTINUING GENERAL CHINA'S WORK.
HA! OH, REALLY?! I LOST MY *HANDS* TAKING ORDERS FROM THAT DERANGED MESSIAH!
HE AND HIS "CAUSE" ARE LONG GONE AND, AS YOU CAN SEE, MY HANDS HAVEN'T COME BACK!
UM, HELLO. YES, HI. HONOR TO MEET YOU. MY NAME IS, UM, SIMON. I'M *VERY* SORRY ABOUT YOUR HANDS AND ALL, SIR, BUT--
OPAL SAYS YOU CAN GET US INTO FORTRESS PENUEL AND YOU'RE GOOD AT BLOWING THINGS UP. WE *NEED YOU.*
PROPER
LOOK, WE ALL *NEED* SOMETHING, LITTLE GIRL. JUST ASK MY CLIENTS. I DON'T WORK FOR "CAUSES" ANYMORE. I WORK FOR *ME.* I WORK FOR *MONEY.*
ZOLDIERS COMING!

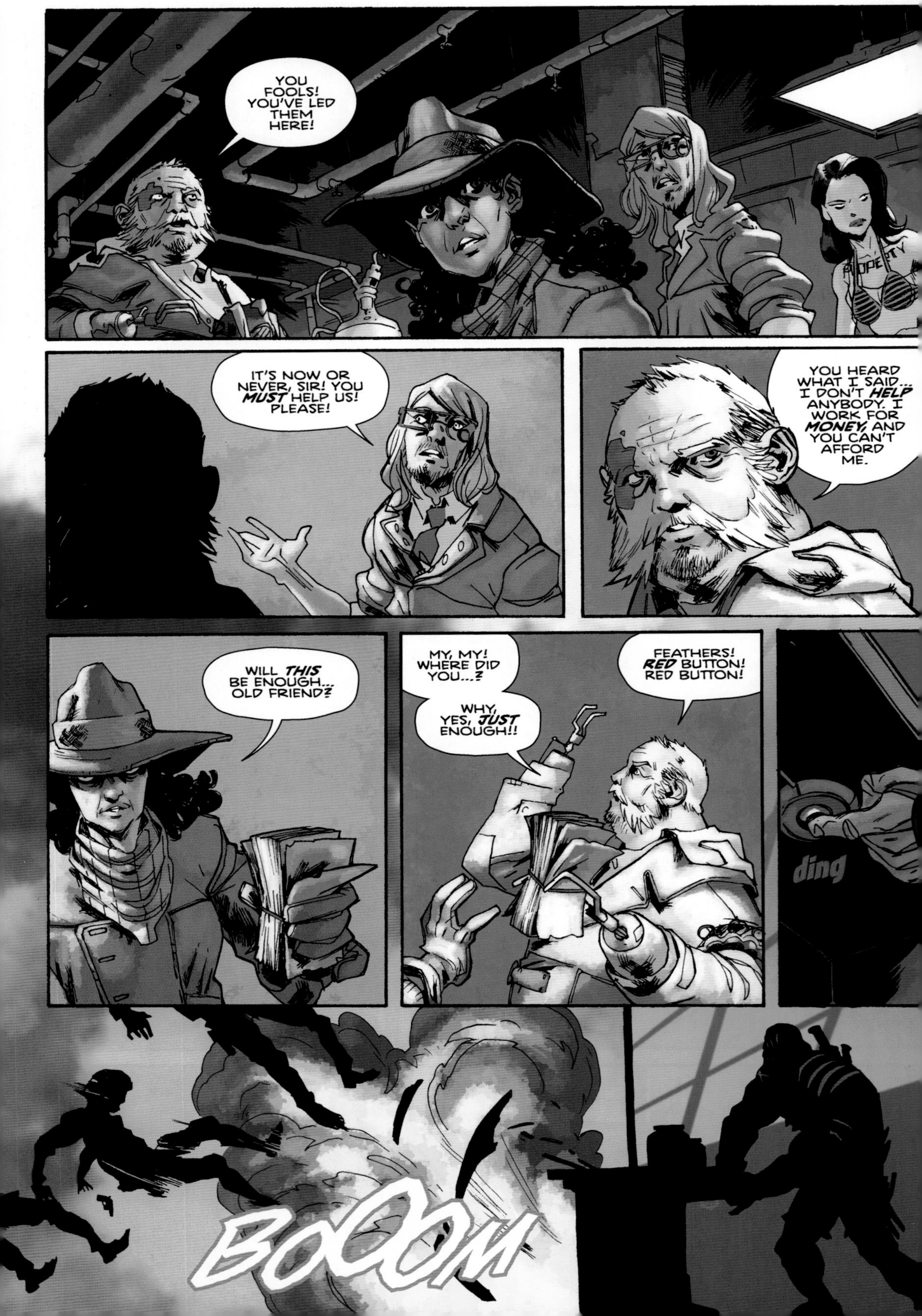
YOU FOOLS! YOU'VE LED THEM HERE!
IT'S NOW OR NEVER, SIR! YOU MUST HELP US! PLEASE!
YOU HEARD WHAT I SAID... I DON'T HELP ANYBODY. I WORK FOR MONEY, AND YOU CAN'T AFFORD ME.
WILL THIS BE ENOUGH... OLD FRIEND?
MY, MY! WHERE DID YOU...?
WHY, YES, JUST ENOUGH!!
FEATHERS! RED BUTTON! RED BUTTON!
ding
BOOOM

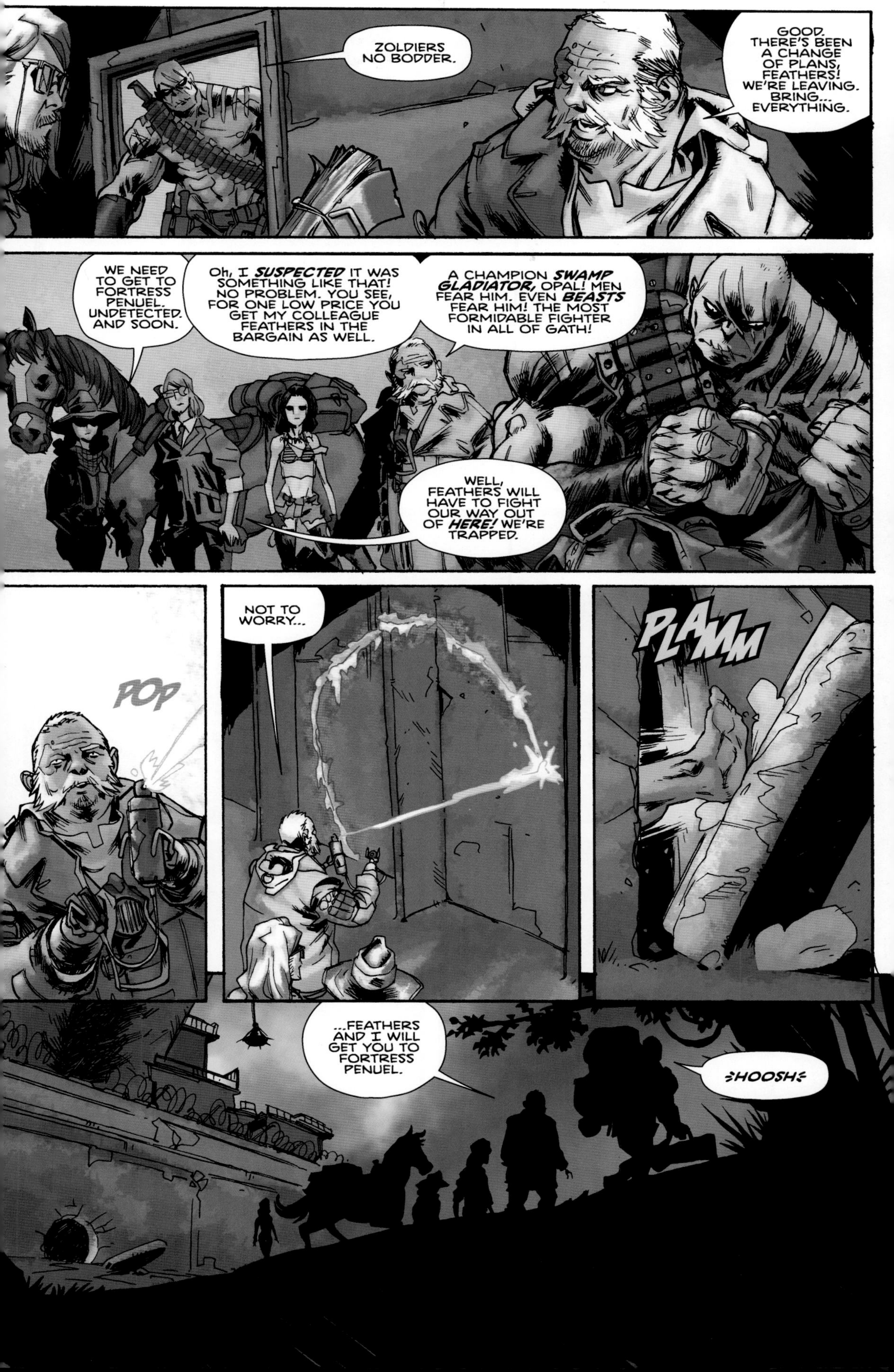
ZOLDIERS NO BODDER.
GOOD. THERE'S BEEN A CHANGE OF PLANS, FEATHERS! WE'RE LEAVING. BRING... EVERYTHING.
WE NEED TO GET TO FORTRESS PENUEL. UNDETECTED. AND SOON.
Oh, I SUSPECTED IT WAS SOMETHING LIKE THAT! NO PROBLEM. YOU SEE, FOR ONE LOW PRICE YOU GET MY COLLEAGUE FEATHERS IN THE BARGAIN AS WELL.
A CHAMPION SWAMP GLADIATOR, OPAL! MEN FEAR HIM. EVEN BEASTS FEAR HIM! THE MOST FORMIDABLE FIGHTER IN ALL OF GATH!
WELL, FEATHERS WILL HAVE TO FIGHT OUR WAY OUT OF HERE! WE'RE TRAPPED.
POP
NOT TO WORRY...
PLAMM
...FEATHERS AND I WILL GET YOU TO FORTRESS PENUEL.
HOOSH

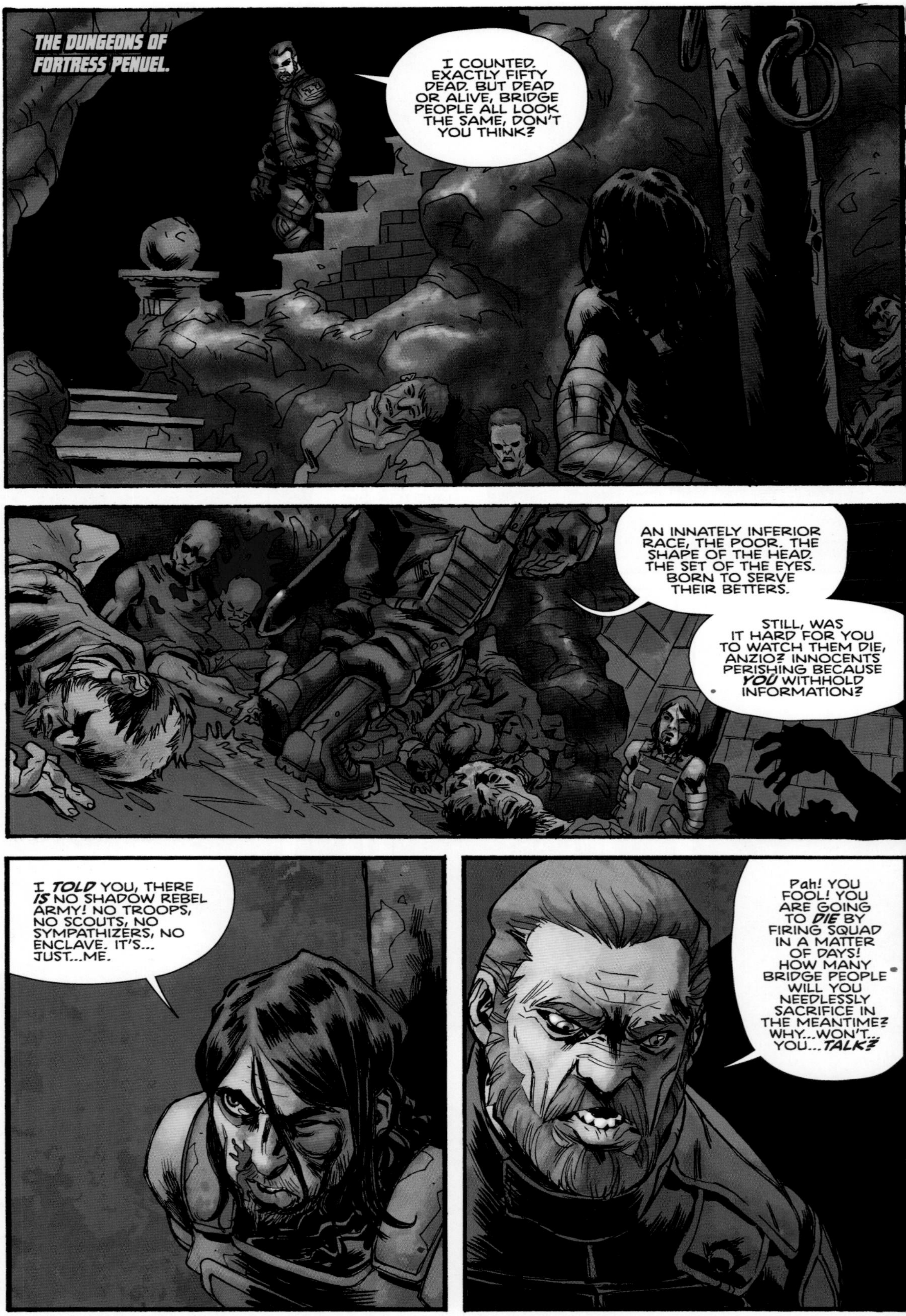
THE DUNGEONS OF FORTRESS PENUEL.
I COUNTED. EXACTLY FIFTY DEAD. BUT DEAD OR ALIVE, BRIDGE PEOPLE ALL LOOK THE SAME, DON'T YOU THINK?
AN INNATELY INFERIOR RACE, THE POOR. THE SHAPE OF THE HEAD. THE SET OF THE EYES. BORN TO SERVE THEIR BETTERS.
STILL, WAS IT HARD FOR YOU TO WATCH THEM DIE, ANZIO? INNOCENTS PERISHING BECAUSE YOU WITHHOLD INFORMATION?
I TOLD YOU, THERE IS NO SHADOW REBEL ARMY! NO TROOPS, NO SCOUTS, NO SYMPATHIZERS, NO ENCLAVE. IT'S... JUST...ME.
Pah! YOU FOOL! YOU ARE GOING TO DIE BY FIRING SQUAD IN A MATTER OF DAYS! HOW MANY BRIDGE PEOPLE WILL YOU NEEDLESSLY SACRIFICE IN THE MEANTIME? WHY...WON'T... YOU...TALK?

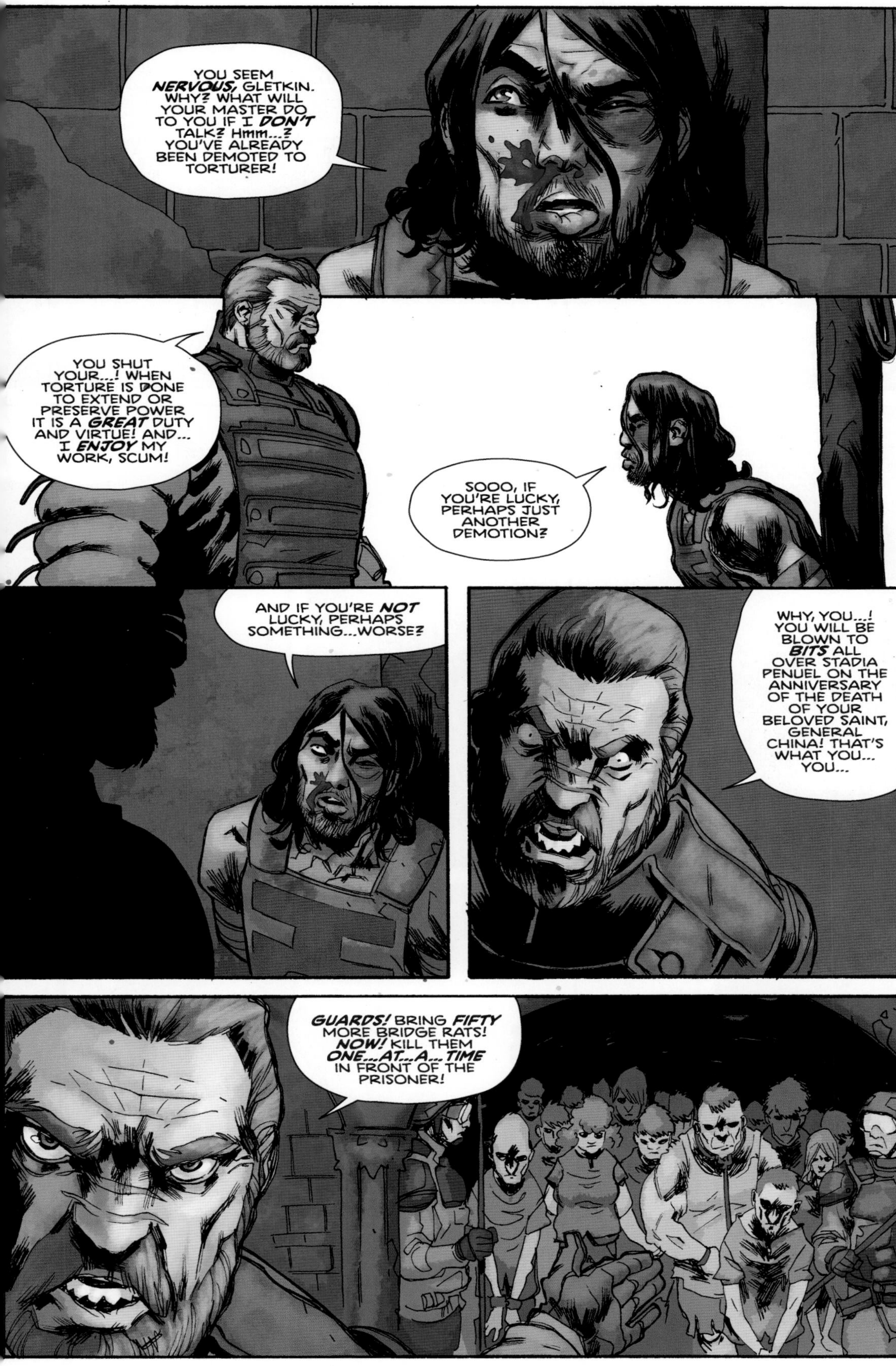
YOU SEEM NERVOUS, GLETKIN. WHY? WHAT WILL YOUR MASTER DO TO YOU IF I DON'T TALK? Hmm...? YOU'VE ALREADY BEEN DEMOTED TO TORTURER!
YOU SHUT YOUR...! WHEN TORTURE IS DONE TO EXTEND OR PRESERVE POWER IT IS A GREAT DUTY AND VIRTUE! AND... I ENJOY MY WORK, SCUM!
SOOO, IF YOU'RE LUCKY, PERHAPS JUST ANOTHER DEMOTION?
AND IF YOU'RE NOT LUCKY, PERHAPS SOMETHING...WORSE?
WHY, YOU...! YOU WILL BE BLOWN TO BITS ALL OVER STADIA PENUEL ON THE ANNIVERSARY OF THE DEATH OF YOUR BELOVED SAINT, GENERAL CHINA! THAT'S WHAT YOU... YOU...
GUARDS! BRING FIFTY MORE BRIDGE RATS! NOW! KILL THEM ONE...AT...A...TIME IN FRONT OF THE PRISONER!

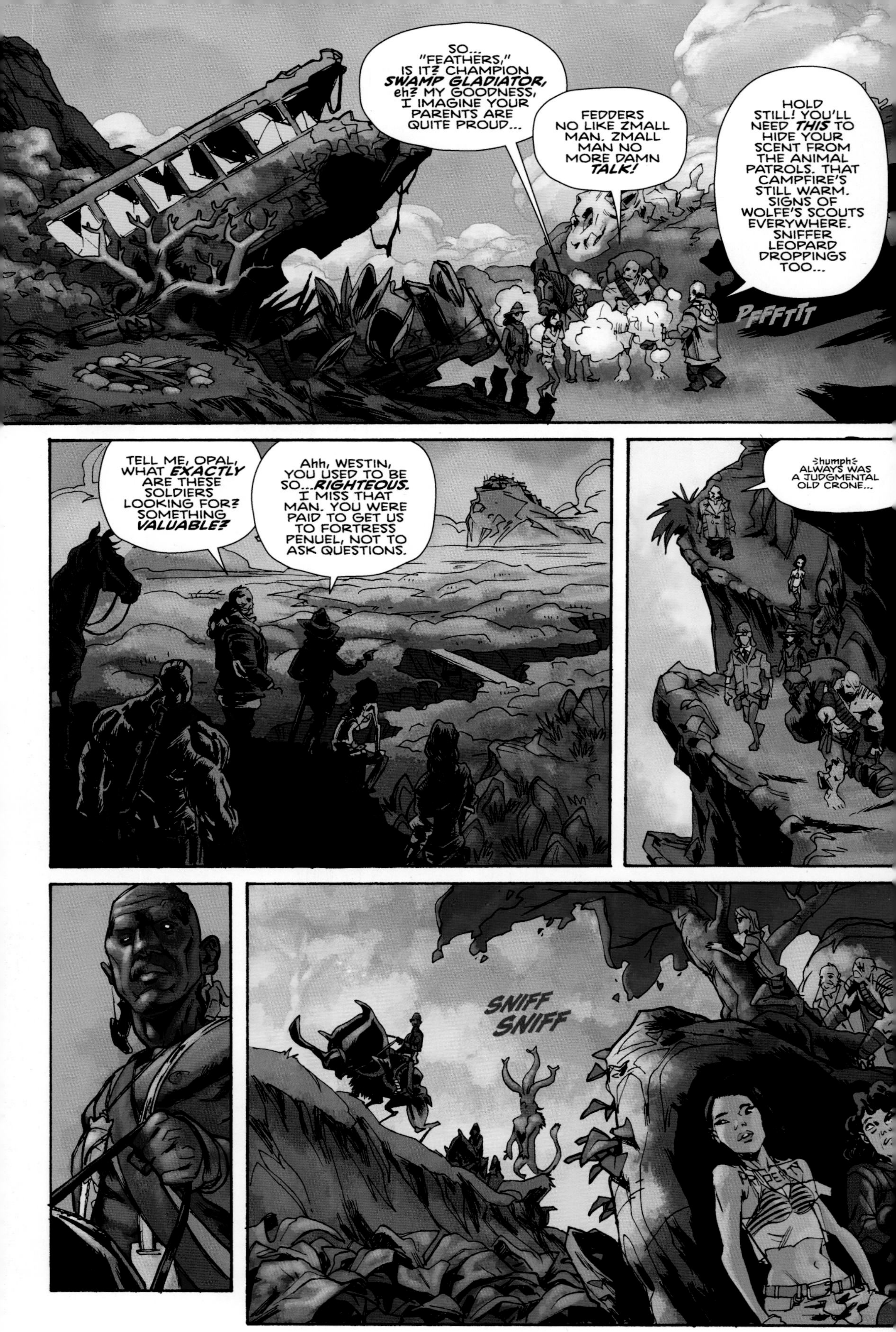
SO... "FEATHERS," IS IT? CHAMPION SWAMP GLADIATOR, eh? MY GOODNESS, I IMAGINE YOUR PARENTS ARE QUITE PROUD...
FEDDERS NO LIKE ZMALL MAN. ZMALL MAN NO MORE DAMN TALK!
HOLD STILL! YOU'LL NEED THIS TO HIDE YOUR SCENT FROM THE ANIMAL PATROLS. THAT CAMPFIRE'S STILL WARM. SIGNS OF WOLFE'S SCOUTS EVERYWHERE. SNIFFER LEOPARD DROPPINGS TOO...
PFFFTTT
TELL ME, OPAL, WHAT EXACTLY ARE THESE SOLDIERS LOOKING FOR? SOMETHING VALUABLE?
Ahh, WESTIN, YOU USED TO BE SO...RIGHTEOUS. I MISS THAT MAN. YOU WERE PAID TO GET US TO FORTRESS PENUEL, NOT TO ASK QUESTIONS.
humph ALWAYS WAS A JUDGMENTAL OLD CRONE...
SNIFF SNIFF

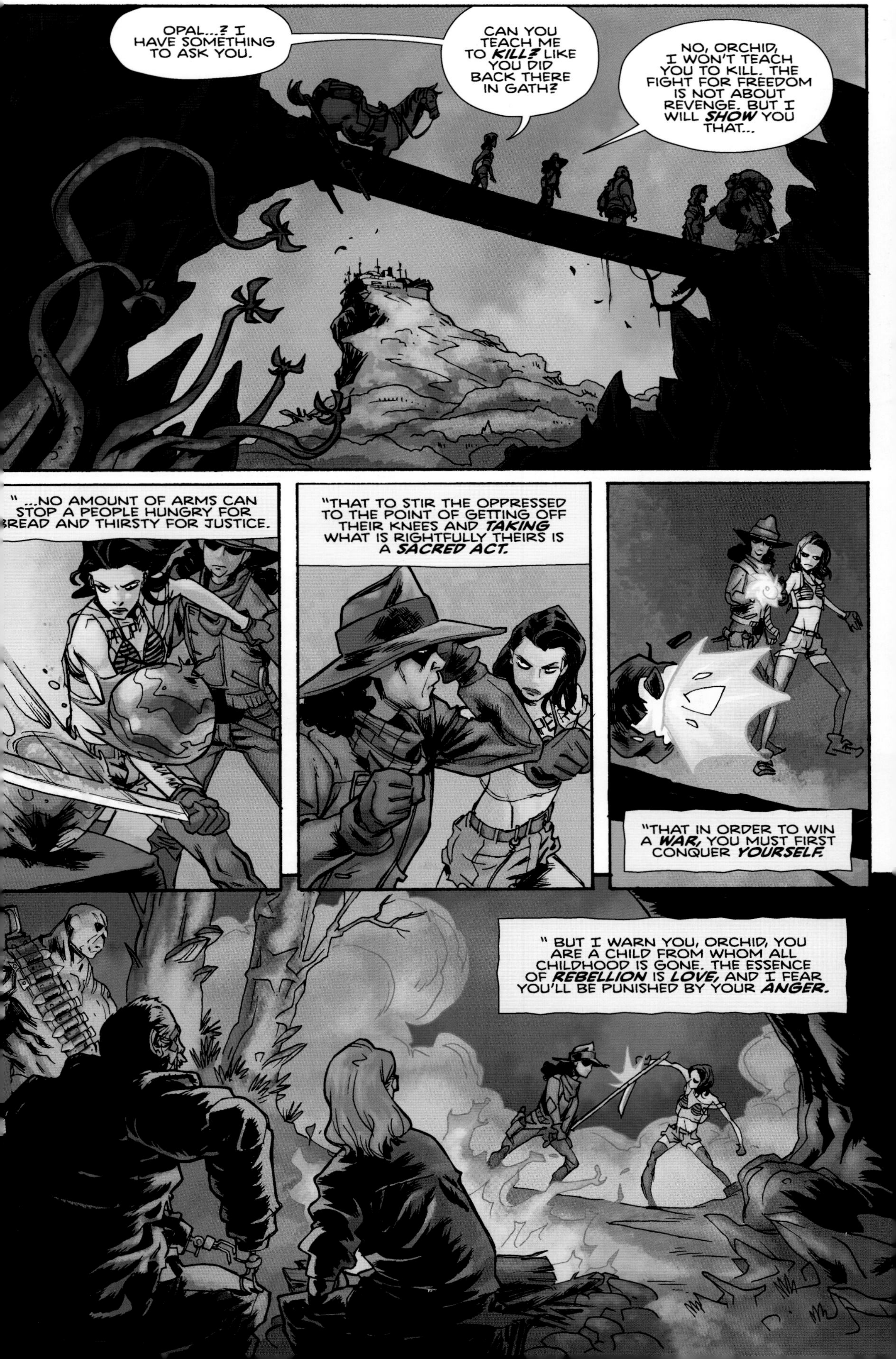

OPAL...? I HAVE SOMETHING TO ASK YOU.
CAN YOU TEACH ME TO KILL? LIKE YOU DID BACK THERE IN GATH?
NO, ORCHID, I WON'T TEACH YOU TO KILL. THE FIGHT FOR FREEDOM IS NOT ABOUT REVENGE. BUT I WILL SHOW YOU THAT...
"...NO AMOUNT OF ARMS CAN STOP A PEOPLE HUNGRY FOR BREAD AND THIRSTY FOR JUSTICE.
"THAT TO STIR THE OPPRESSED TO THE POINT OF GETTING OFF THEIR KNEES AND TAKING WHAT IS RIGHTFULLY THEIRS IS A SACRED ACT.
"THAT IN ORDER TO WIN A WAR, YOU MUST FIRST CONQUER YOURSELF.
" BUT I WARN YOU, ORCHID, YOU ARE A CHILD FROM WHOM ALL CHILDHOOD IS GONE. THE ESSENCE OF REBELLION IS LOVE, AND I FEAR YOU'LL BE PUNISHED BY YOUR ANGER.

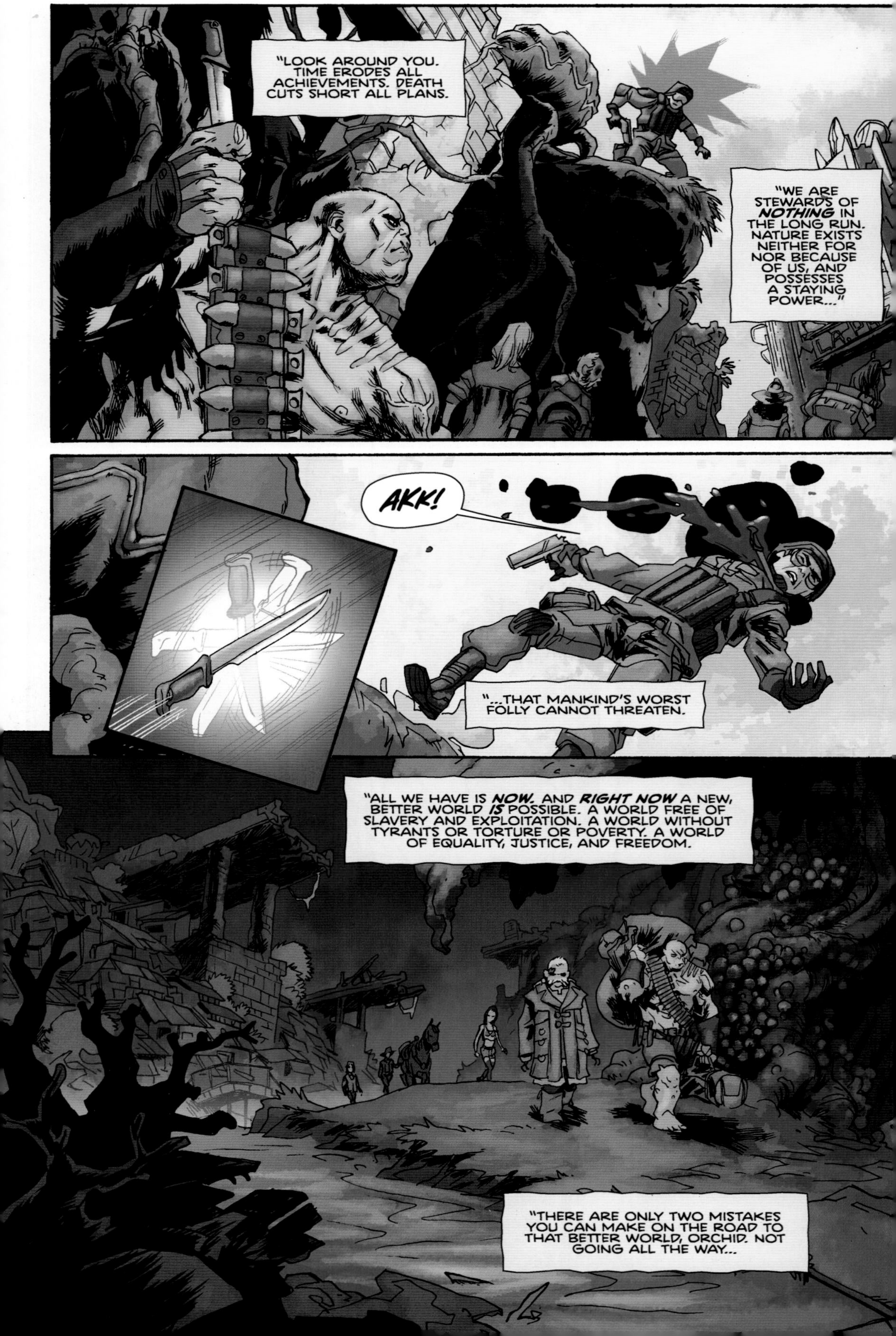
"LOOK AROUND YOU. TIME ERODES ALL ACHIEVEMENTS. DEATH CUTS SHORT ALL PLANS.
"WE ARE STEWARDS OF NOTHING IN THE LONG RUN. NATURE EXISTS NEITHER FOR NOR BECAUSE OF US, AND POSSESSES A STAYING POWER..."
AKK!
"...THAT MANKIND'S WORST FOLLY CANNOT THREATEN.
"ALL WE HAVE IS NOW. AND RIGHT NOW A NEW, BETTER WORLD IS POSSIBLE. A WORLD FREE OF SLAVERY AND EXPLOITATION. A WORLD WITHOUT TYRANTS OR TORTURE OR POVERTY. A WORLD OF EQUALITY, JUSTICE, AND FREEDOM.
"THERE ARE ONLY TWO MISTAKES YOU CAN MAKE ON THE ROAD TO THAT BETTER WORLD, ORCHID. NOT GOING ALL THE WAY...

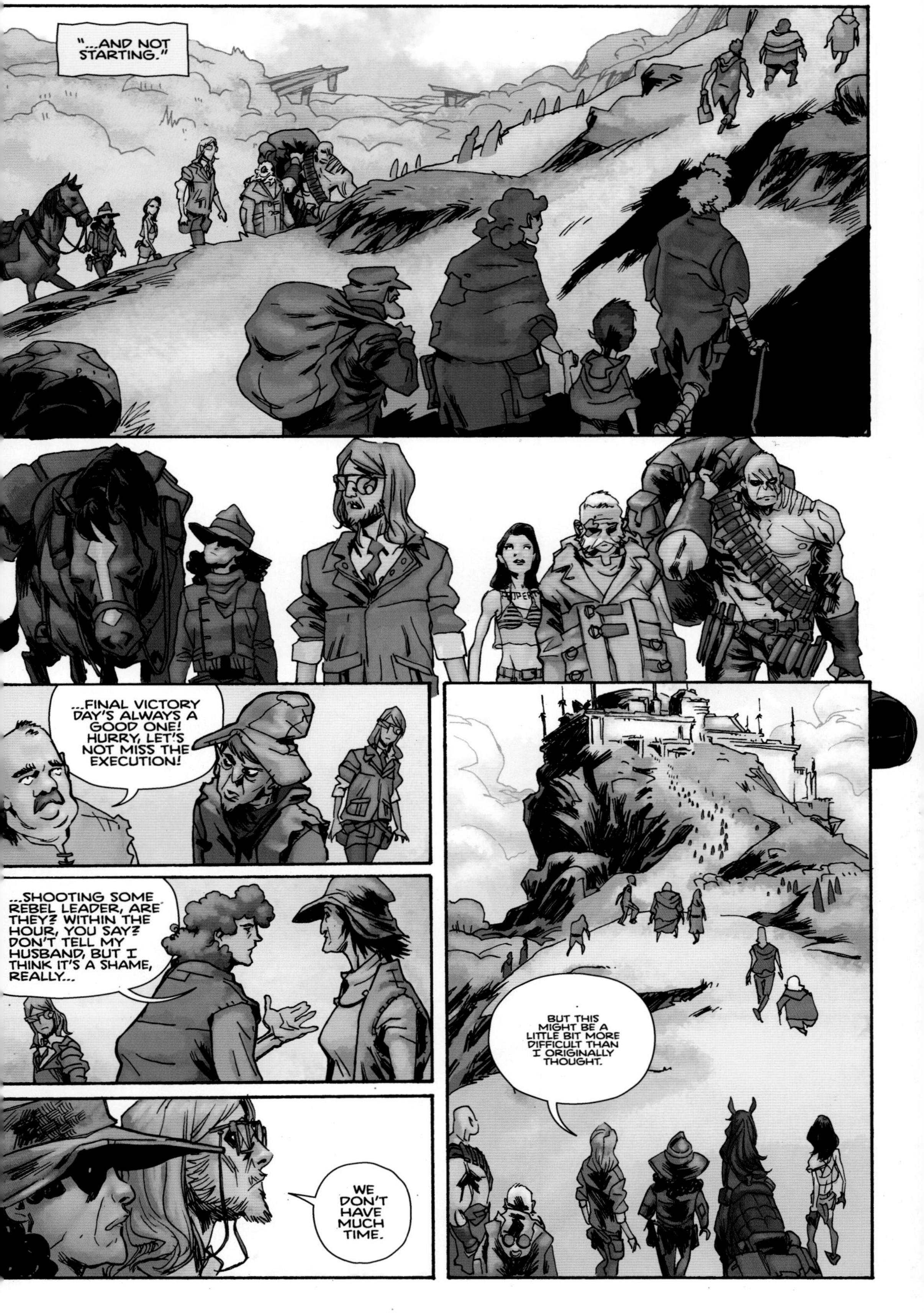
"...AND NOT STARTING."
...FINAL VICTORY DAY'S ALWAYS A GOOD ONE! HURRY, LET'S NOT MISS THE EXECUTION!
...SHOOTING SOME REBEL LEADER, ARE THEY? WITHIN THE HOUR, YOU SAY? DON'T TELL MY HUSBAND, BUT I THINK IT'S A SHAME, REALLY...
WE DON'T HAVE MUCH TIME.
BUT THIS MIGHT BE A LITTLE BIT MORE DIFFICULT THAN I ORIGINALLY THOUGHT.

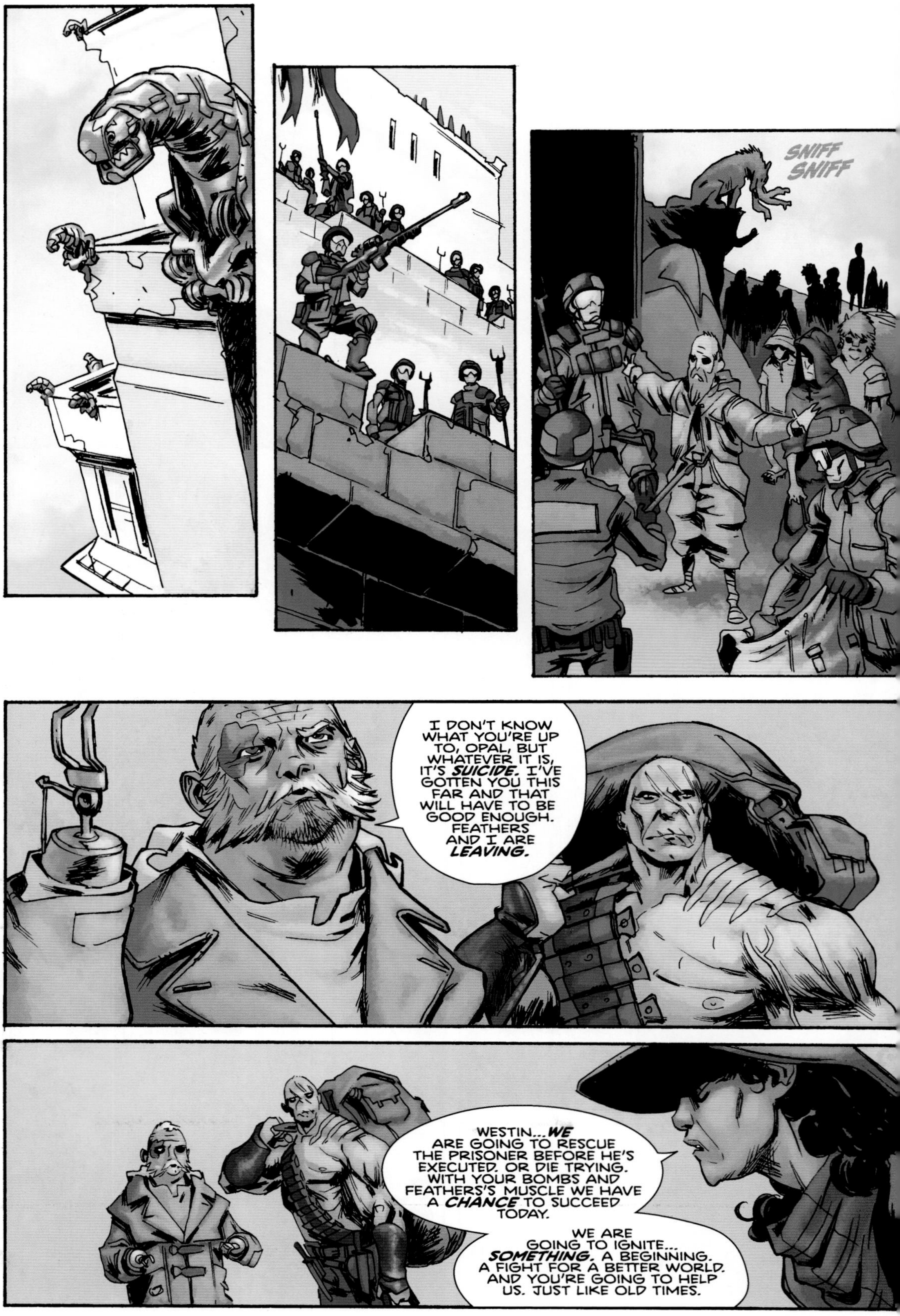

SNIFF SNIFF
I DON'T KNOW WHAT YOU'RE UP TO, OPAL, BUT WHATEVER IT IS, IT'S SUICIDE. I'VE GOTTEN YOU THIS FAR AND THAT WILL HAVE TO BE GOOD ENOUGH. FEATHERS AND I ARE LEAVING.
WESTIN... WE ARE GOING TO RESCUE THE PRISONER BEFORE HE'S EXECUTED. OR DIE TRYING. WITH YOUR BOMBS AND FEATHERS'S MUSCLE WE HAVE A CHANCE TO SUCCEED TODAY.
WE ARE GOING TO IGNITE... SOMETHING. A BEGINNING. A FIGHT FOR A BETTER WORLD. AND YOU'RE GOING TO HELP US. JUST LIKE OLD TIMES.

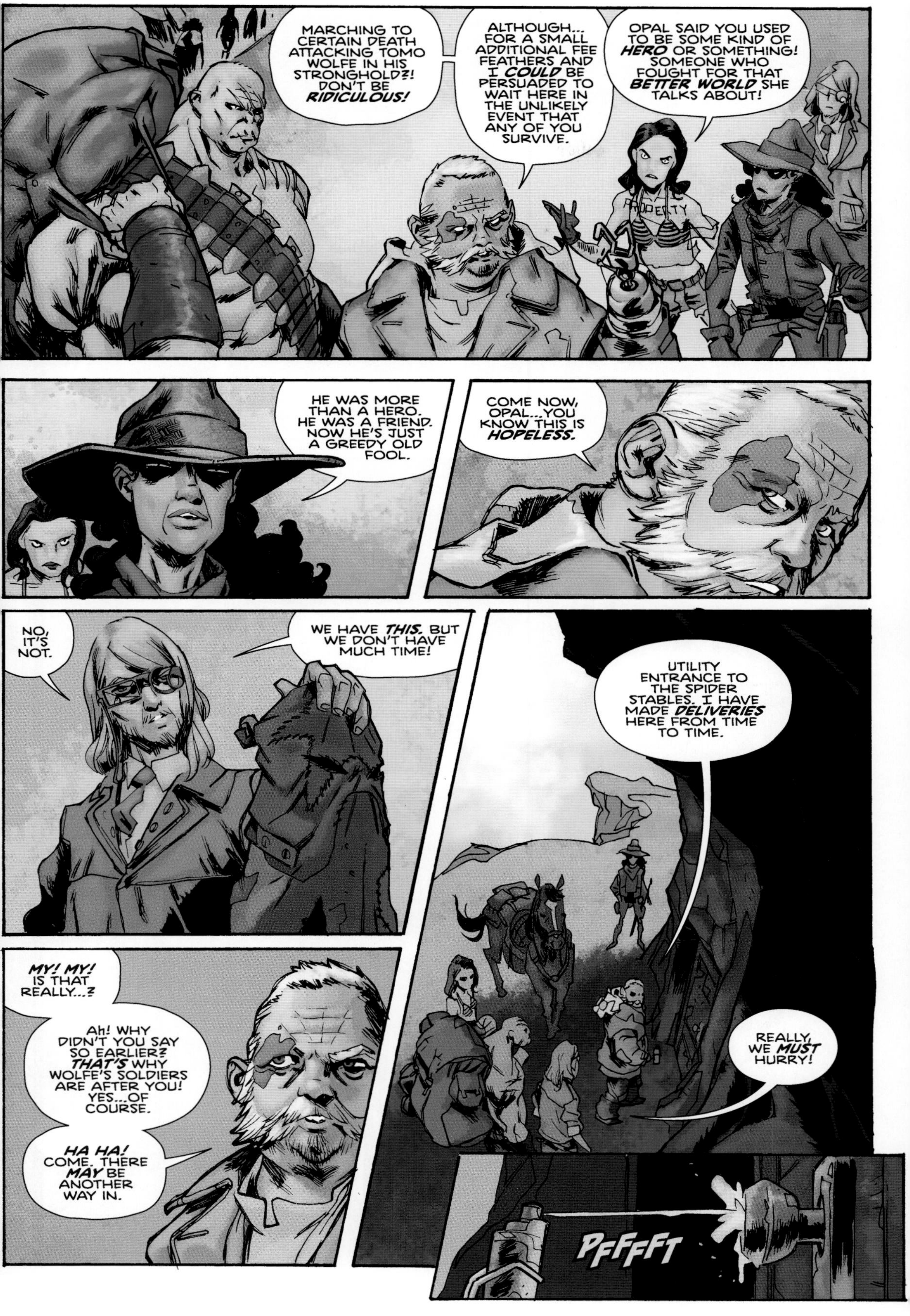
MARCHING TO CERTAIN DEATH ATTACKING TOMO WOLFE IN HIS STRONGHOLD?! DON'T BE RIDICULOUS!
ALTHOUGH... FOR A SMALL ADDITIONAL FEE FEATHERS AND I COULD BE PERSUADED TO WAIT HERE IN THE UNLIKELY EVENT THAT ANY OF YOU SURVIVE.
OPAL SAID YOU USED TO BE SOME KIND OF HERO OR SOMETHING! SOMEONE WHO FOUGHT FOR THAT BETTER WORLD SHE TALKS ABOUT!
PROPERTY
HE WAS MORE THAN A HERO. HE WAS A FRIEND. NOW HE'S JUST A GREEDY OLD FOOL.
COME NOW, OPAL...YOU KNOW THIS IS HOPELESS.
NO, IT'S NOT.
WE HAVE THIS. BUT WE DON'T HAVE MUCH TIME!
MY! MY! IS THAT REALLY...?
AH! WHY DIDN'T YOU SAY SO EARLIER? THAT'S WHY WOLFE'S SOLDIERS ARE AFTER YOU! YES...OF COURSE.
HA HA! COME. THERE MAY BE ANOTHER WAY IN.
UTILITY ENTRANCE TO THE SPIDER STABLES. I HAVE MADE DELIVERIES HERE FROM TIME TO TIME.
REALLY, WE MUST HURRY!
PFFFFT

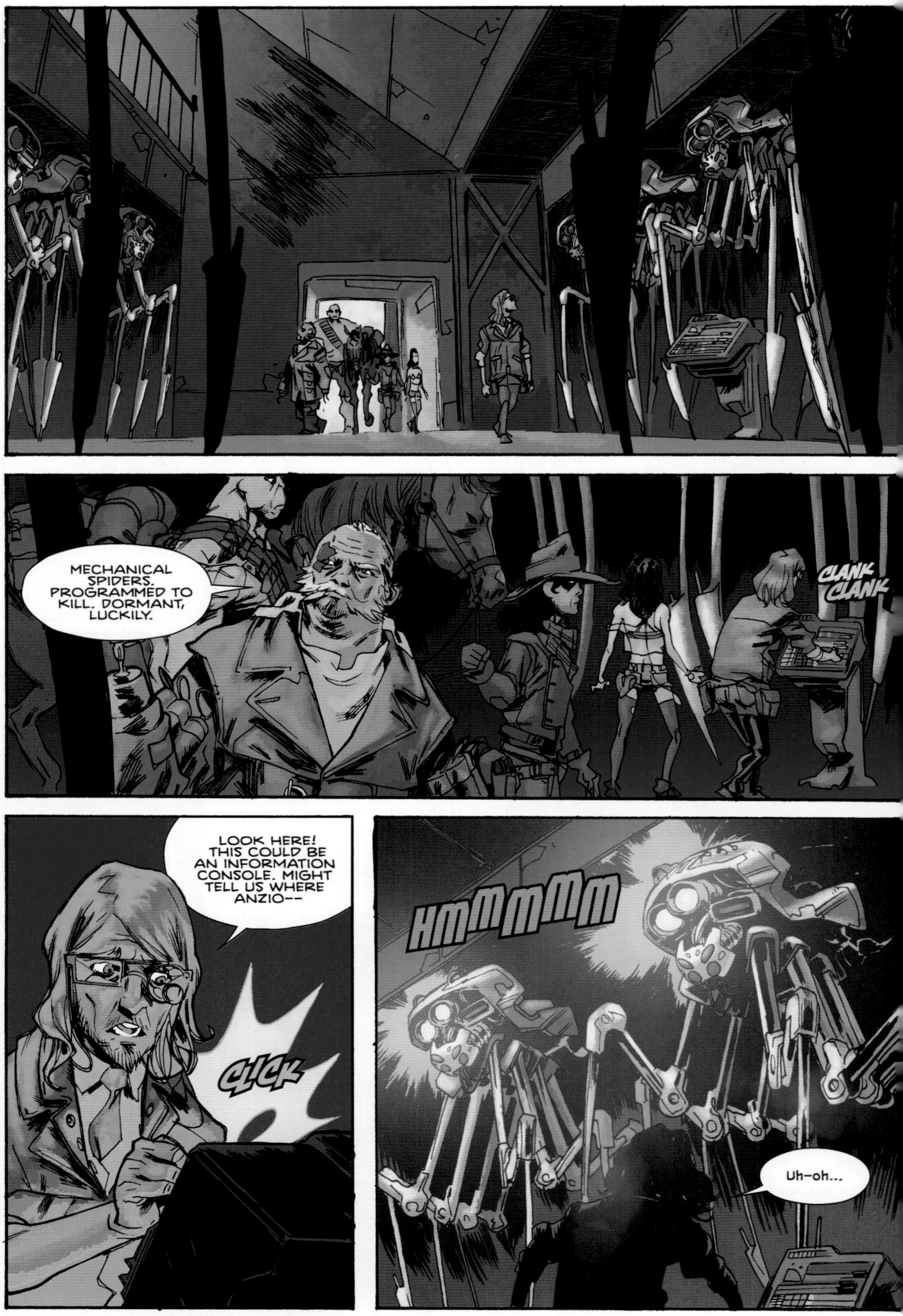
MECHANICAL SPIDERS. PROGRAMMED TO KILL. DORMANT, LUCKILY.
CLANK CLANK
LOOK HERE! THIS COULD BE AN INFORMATION CONSOLE. MIGHT TELL US WHERE ANZIO--
CLICK
HMMMMMM
Uh-oh...

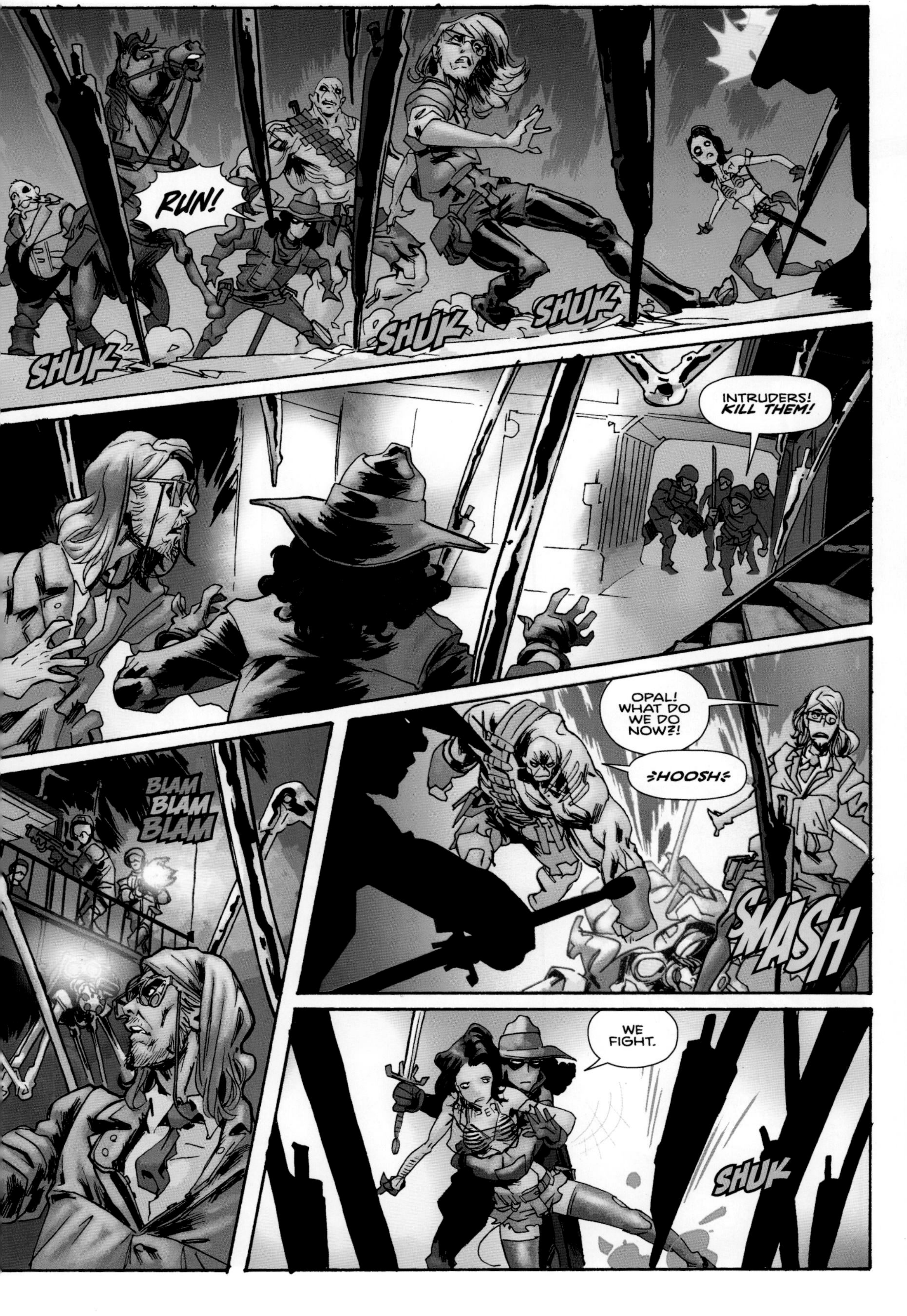
RUN!
SHUK
SHUK
SHUK
SHUK
INTRUDERS! KILL THEM!
OPAL! WHAT DO WE DO NOW?!
HOOSH
BLAM BLAM BLAM
SMASH
WE FIGHT.
SHUK

KLANK

KLIK

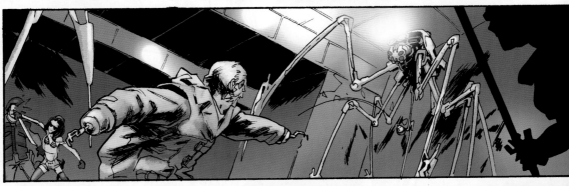

BOOM

MY! MY! JUST LIKE OLD TIMES INDEED! *HA HA!*

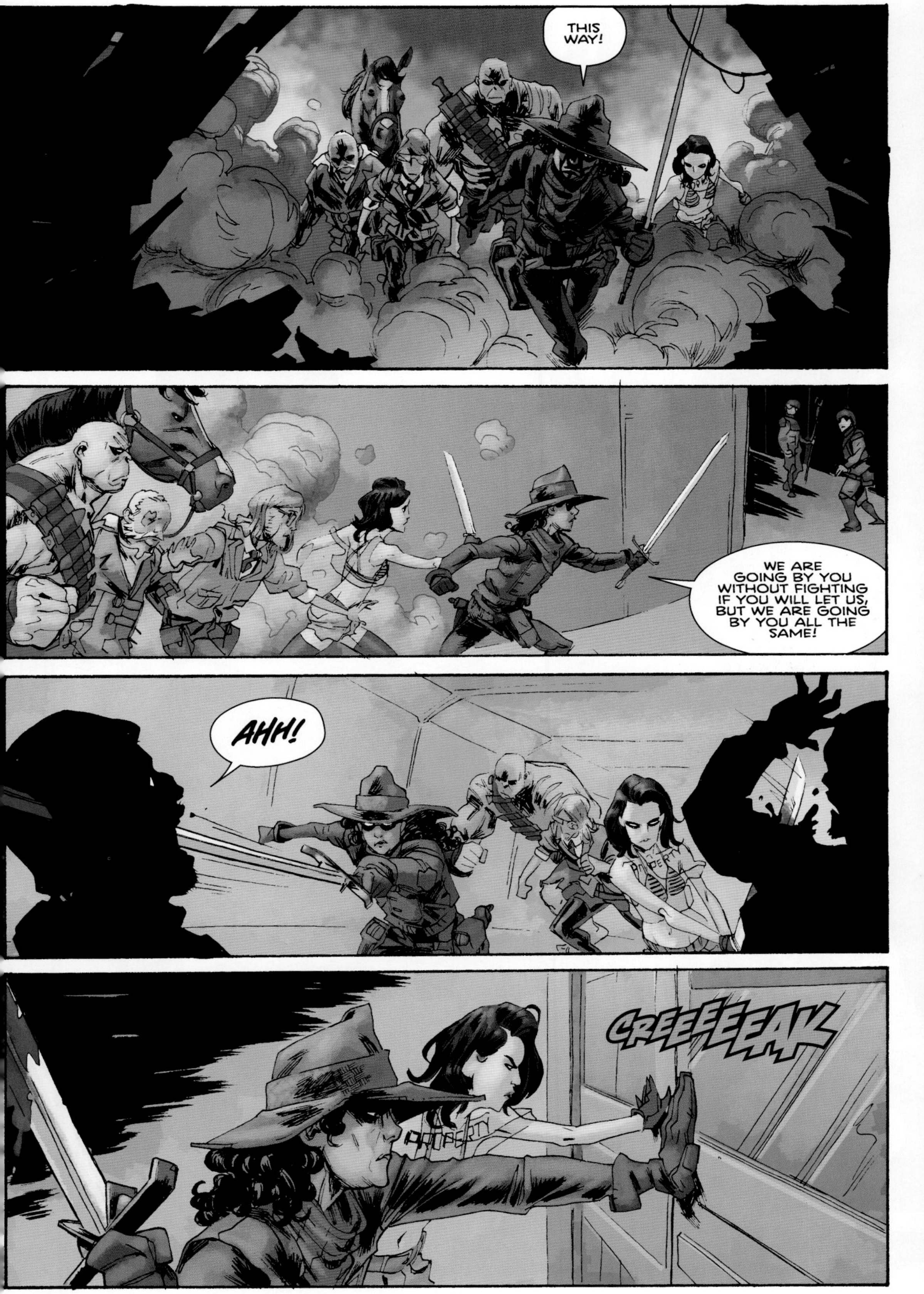
THIS WAY!
WE ARE GOING BY YOU WITHOUT FIGHTING IF YOU WILL LET US, BUT WE ARE GOING BY YOU ALL THE SAME!
AHH!
CREEEEEAK

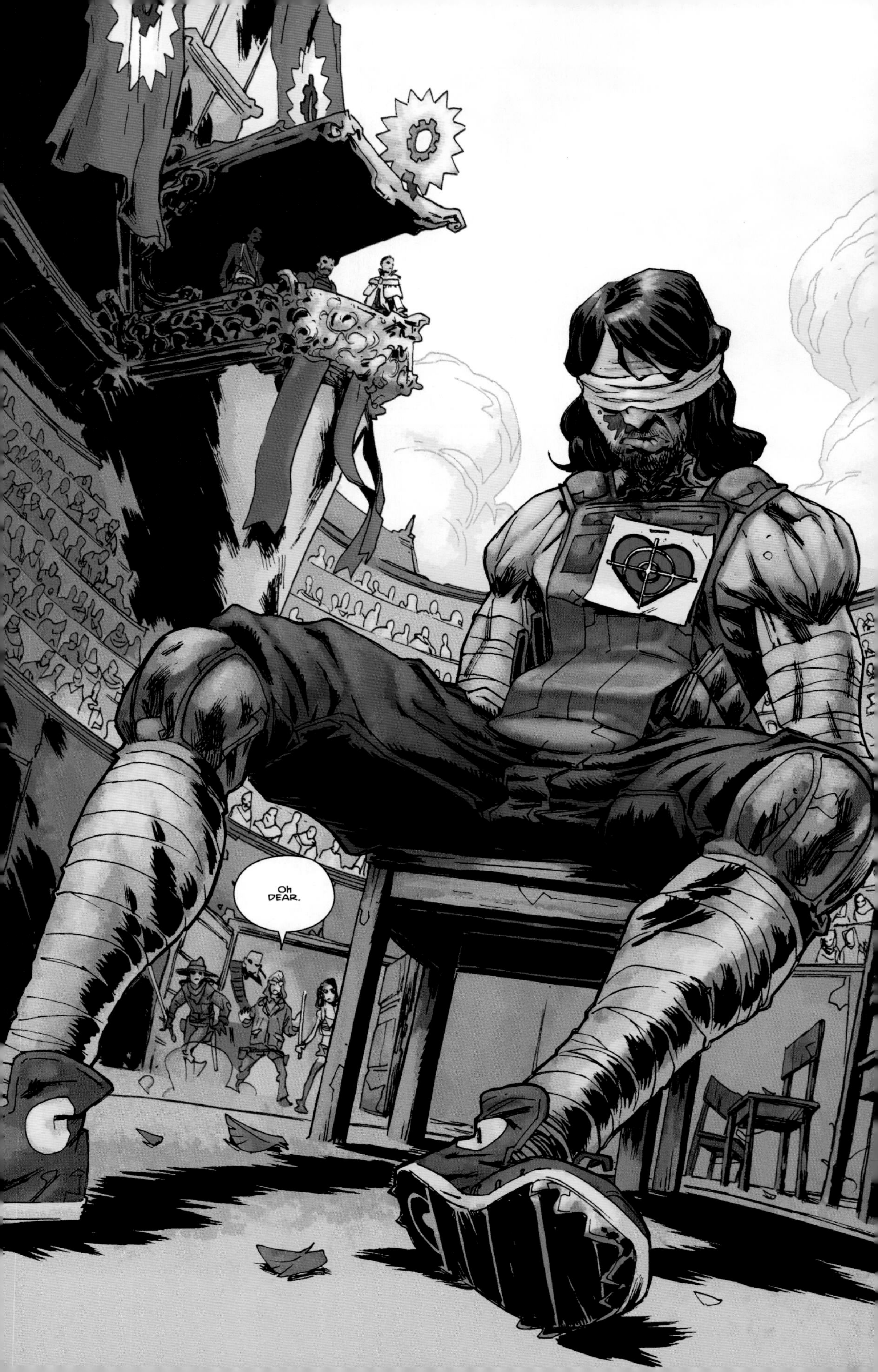
Oh DEAR.

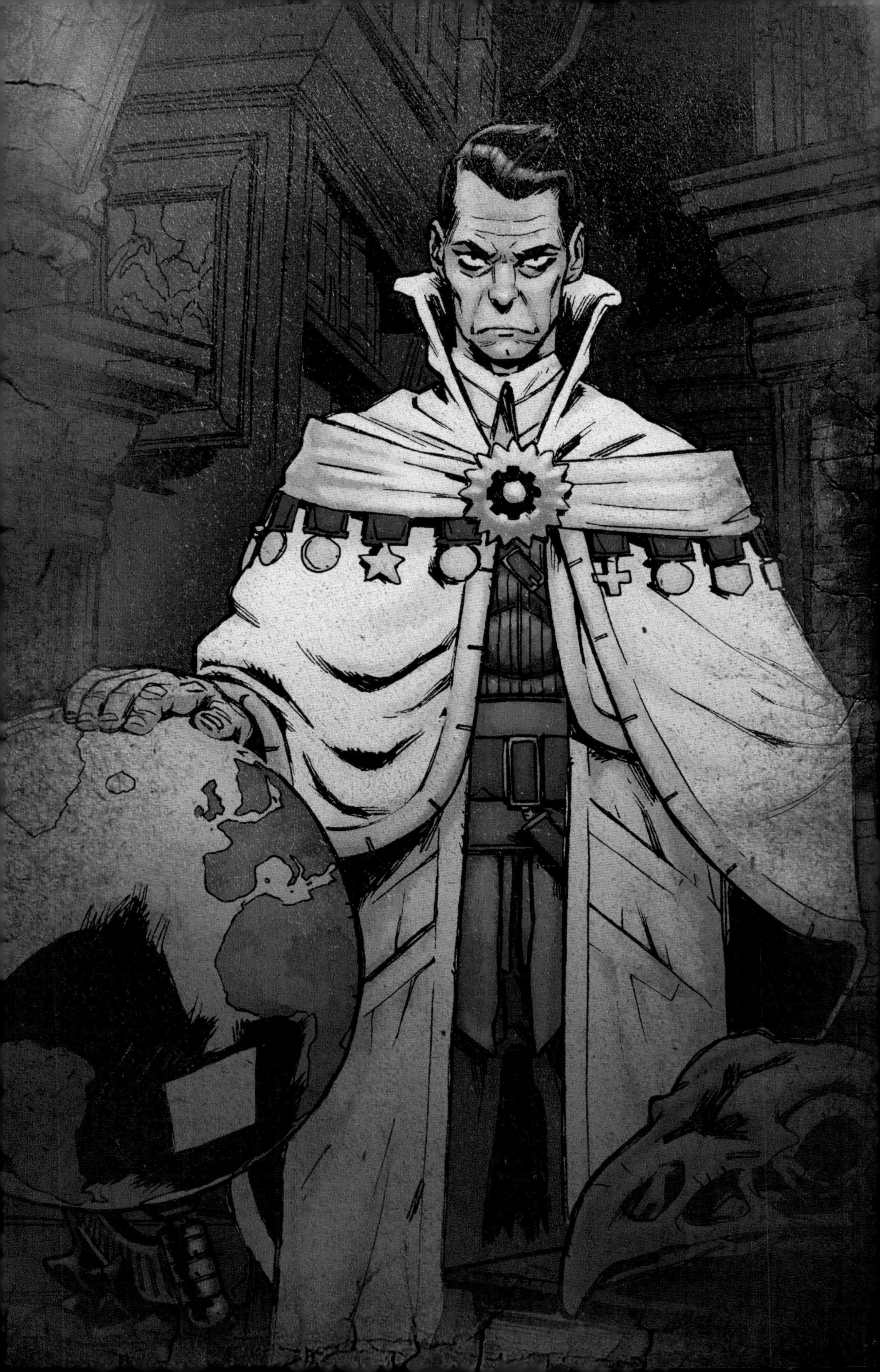

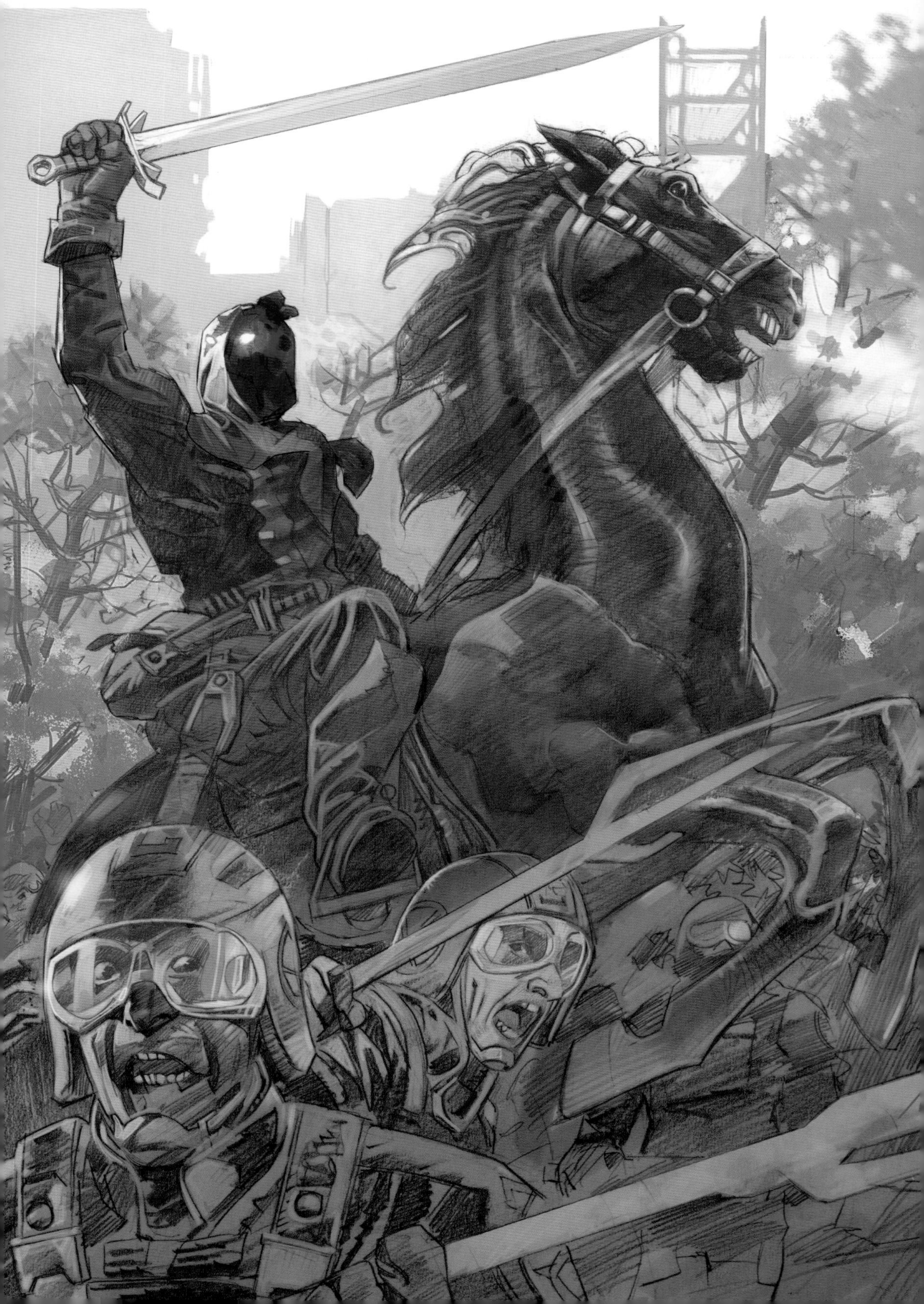

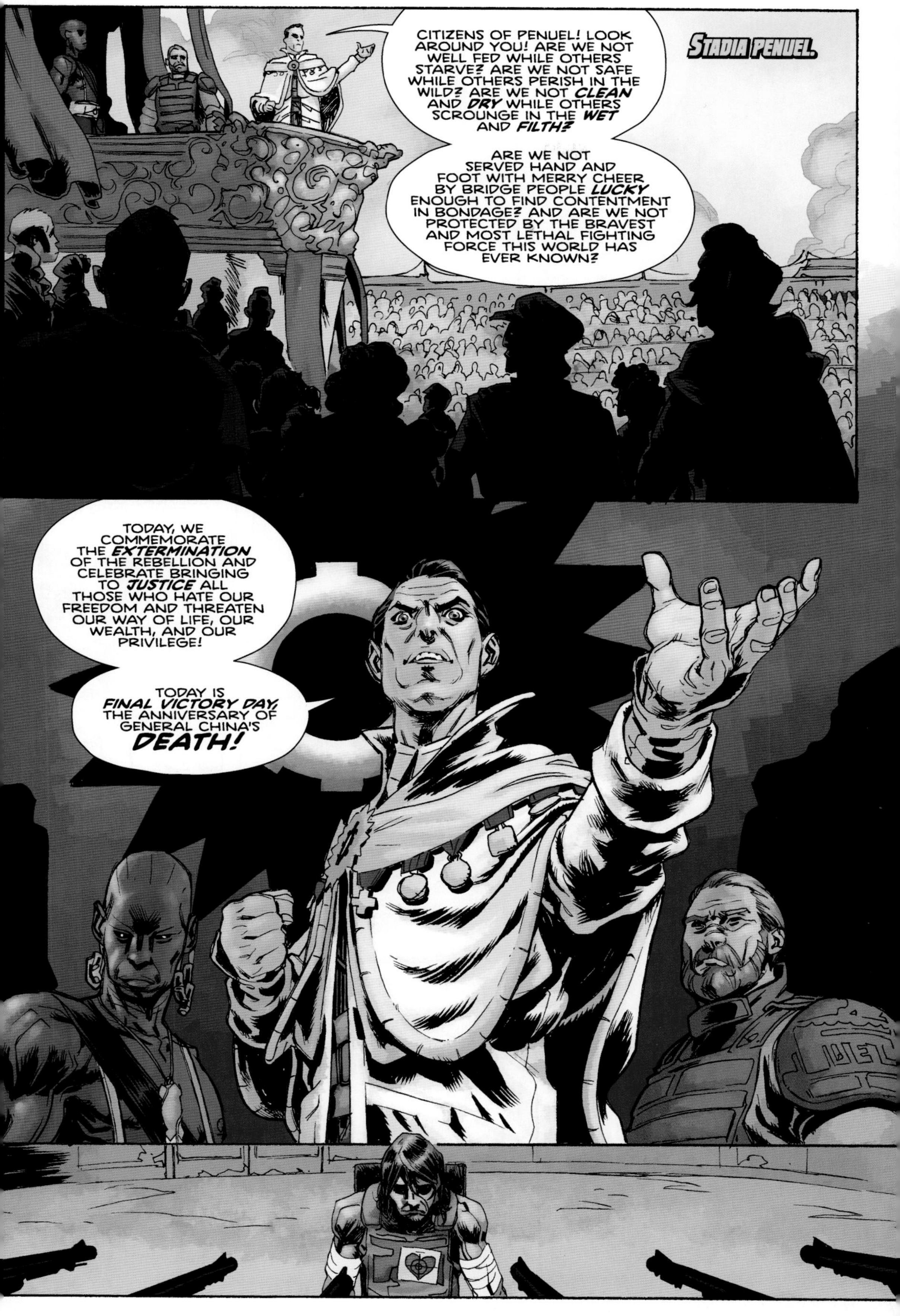

STADIA PENUEL.
CITIZENS OF PENUEL! LOOK AROUND YOU! ARE WE NOT WELL FED WHILE OTHERS STARVE? ARE WE NOT SAFE WHILE OTHERS PERISH IN THE WILD? ARE WE NOT CLEAN AND DRY WHILE OTHERS SCROUNGE IN THE WET AND FILTH?
ARE WE NOT SERVED HAND AND FOOT WITH MERRY CHEER BY BRIDGE PEOPLE LUCKY ENOUGH TO FIND CONTENTMENT IN BONDAGE? AND ARE WE NOT PROTECTED BY THE BRAVEST AND MOST LETHAL FIGHTING FORCE THIS WORLD HAS EVER KNOWN?
TODAY, WE COMMEMORATE THE EXTERMINATION OF THE REBELLION AND CELEBRATE BRINGING TO JUSTICE ALL THOSE WHO HATE OUR FREEDOM AND THREATEN OUR WAY OF LIFE, OUR WEALTH, AND OUR PRIVILEGE!
TODAY IS FINAL VICTORY DAY, THE ANNIVERSARY OF GENERAL CHINA'S DEATH!

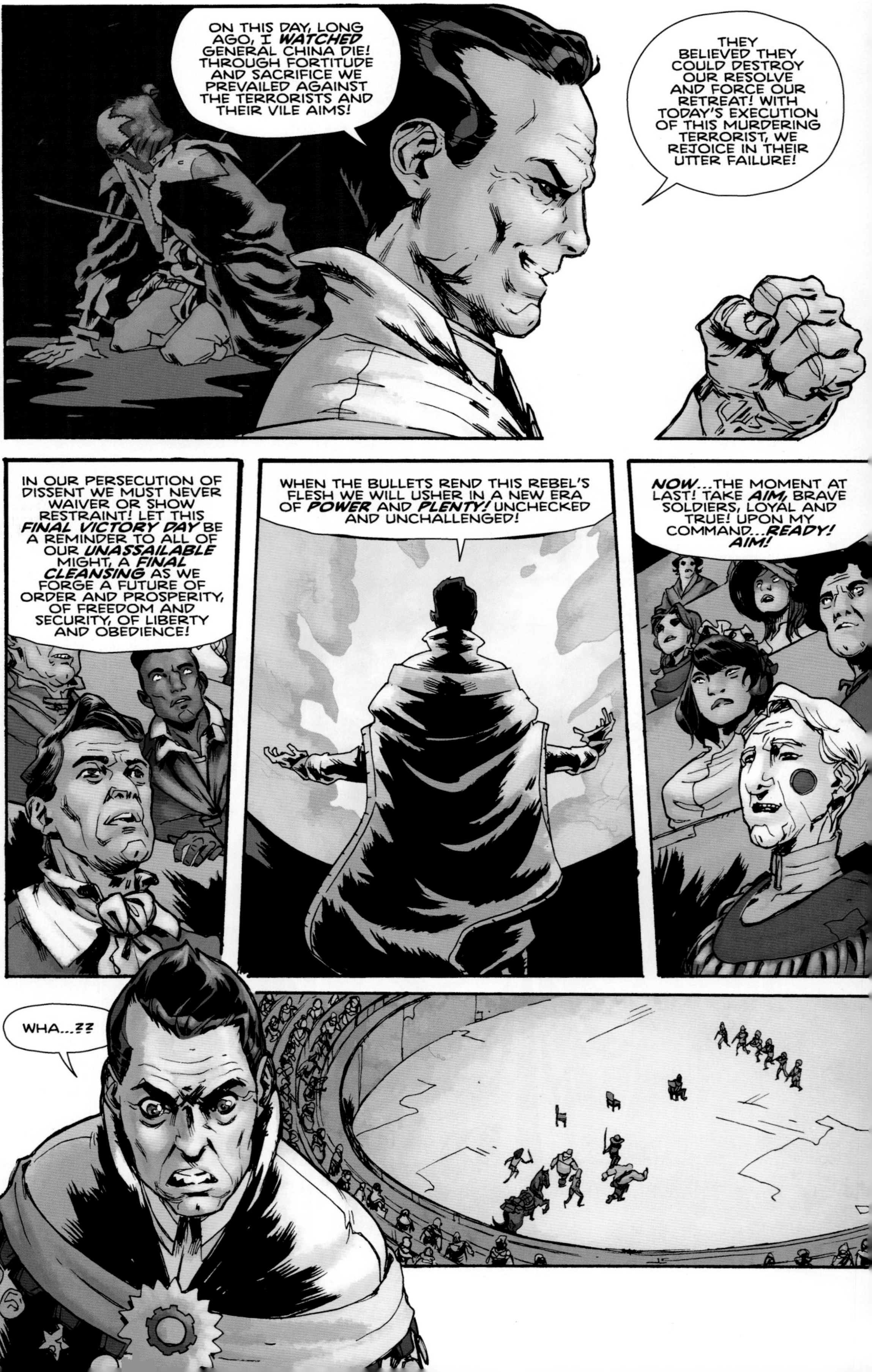
ON THIS DAY, LONG AGO, I WATCHED GENERAL CHINA DIE! THROUGH FORTITUDE AND SACRIFICE WE PREVAILED AGAINST THE TERRORISTS AND THEIR VILE AIMS!
THEY BELIEVED THEY COULD DESTROY OUR RESOLVE AND FORCE OUR RETREAT! WITH TODAY'S EXECUTION OF THIS MURDERING TERRORIST, WE REJOICE IN THEIR UTTER FAILURE!
IN OUR PERSECUTION OF DISSENT WE MUST NEVER WAIVER OR SHOW RESTRAINT! LET THIS FINAL VICTORY DAY BE A REMINDER TO ALL OF OUR UNASSAILABLE MIGHT, A FINAL CLEANSING AS WE FORGE A FUTURE OF ORDER AND PROSPERITY, OF FREEDOM AND SECURITY, OF LIBERTY AND OBEDIENCE!
WHEN THE BULLETS REND THIS REBEL'S FLESH WE WILL USHER IN A NEW ERA OF POWER AND PLENTY! UNCHECKED AND UNCHALLENGED!
NOW...THE MOMENT AT LAST! TAKE AIM, BRAVE SOLDIERS, LOYAL AND TRUE! UPON MY COMMAND...READY! AIM!
WHA...??

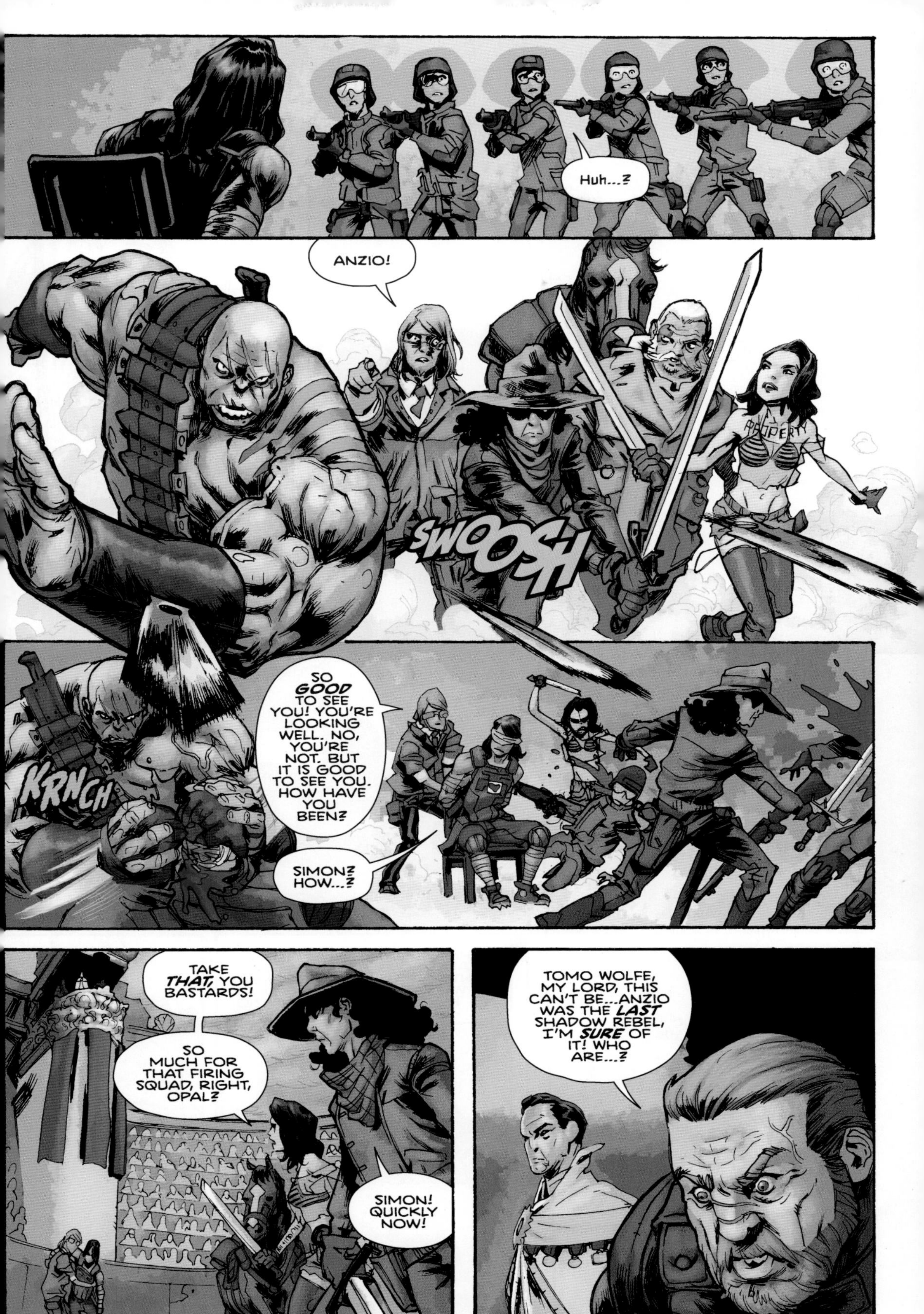

Huh...?
ANZIO!
SWOOSH
SO GOOD TO SEE YOU! YOU'RE LOOKING WELL. NO, YOU'RE NOT. BUT IT IS GOOD TO SEE YOU. HOW HAVE YOU BEEN?
KRNCH
SIMON? HOW...?
TAKE THAT, YOU BASTARDS!
SO MUCH FOR THAT FIRING SQUAD, RIGHT, OPAL?
SIMON! QUICKLY NOW!
TOMO WOLFE, MY LORD, THIS CAN'T BE...ANZIO WAS THE LAST SHADOW REBEL, I'M SURE OF IT! WHO ARE...?

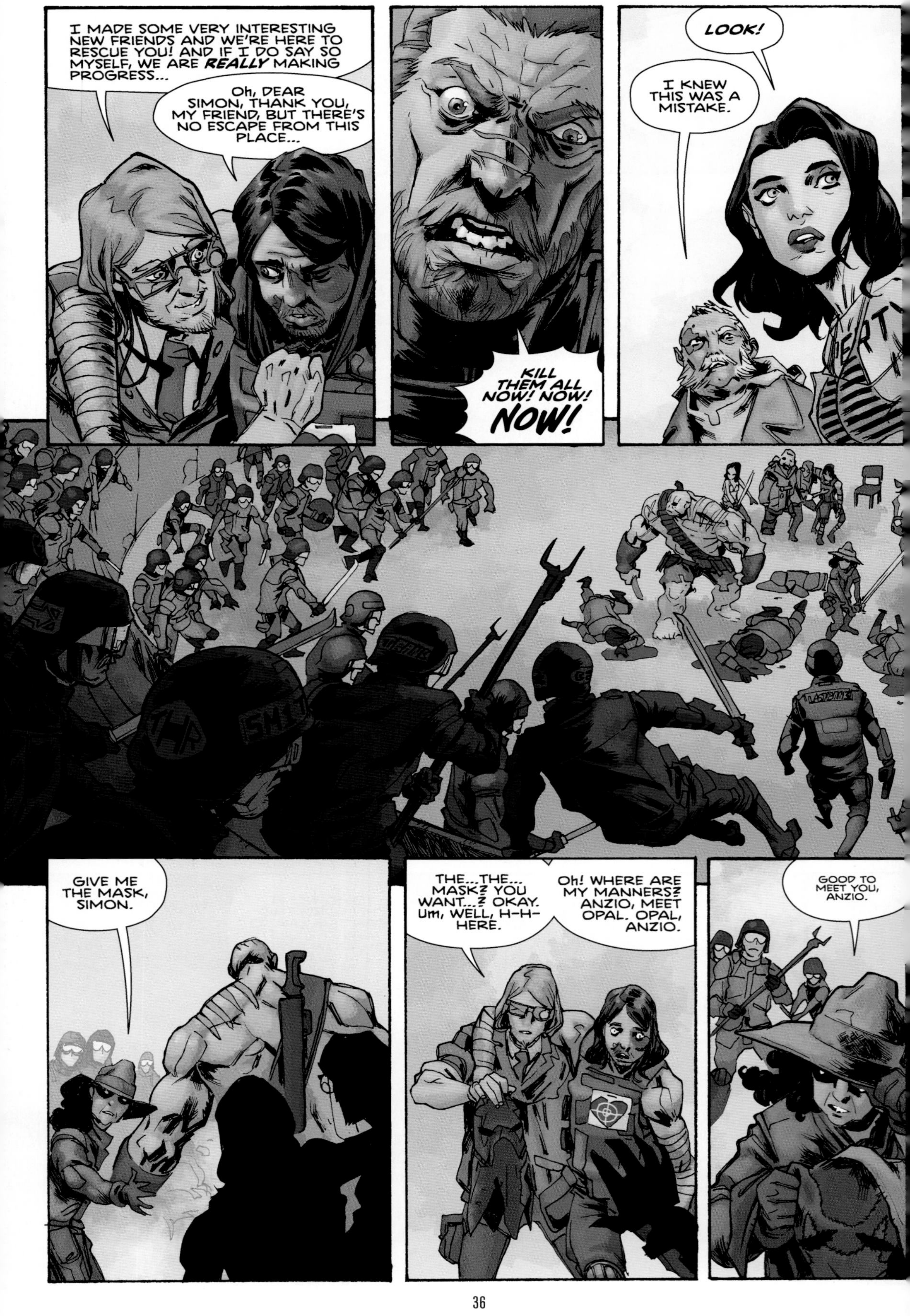

I MADE SOME VERY INTERESTING NEW FRIENDS AND WE'RE HERE TO RESCUE YOU! AND IF I DO SAY SO MYSELF, WE ARE REALLY MAKING PROGRESS...
Oh, DEAR SIMON, THANK YOU, MY FRIEND, BUT THERE'S NO ESCAPE FROM THIS PLACE...
KILL THEM ALL NOW! NOW! NOW!
LOOK!
I KNEW THIS WAS A MISTAKE.
GIVE ME THE MASK, SIMON.
THE...THE... MASK? YOU WANT...? OKAY. Um, WELL, H-H-HERE.
Oh! WHERE ARE MY MANNERS? ANZIO, MEET OPAL. OPAL, ANZIO.
GOOD TO MEET YOU, ANZIO.

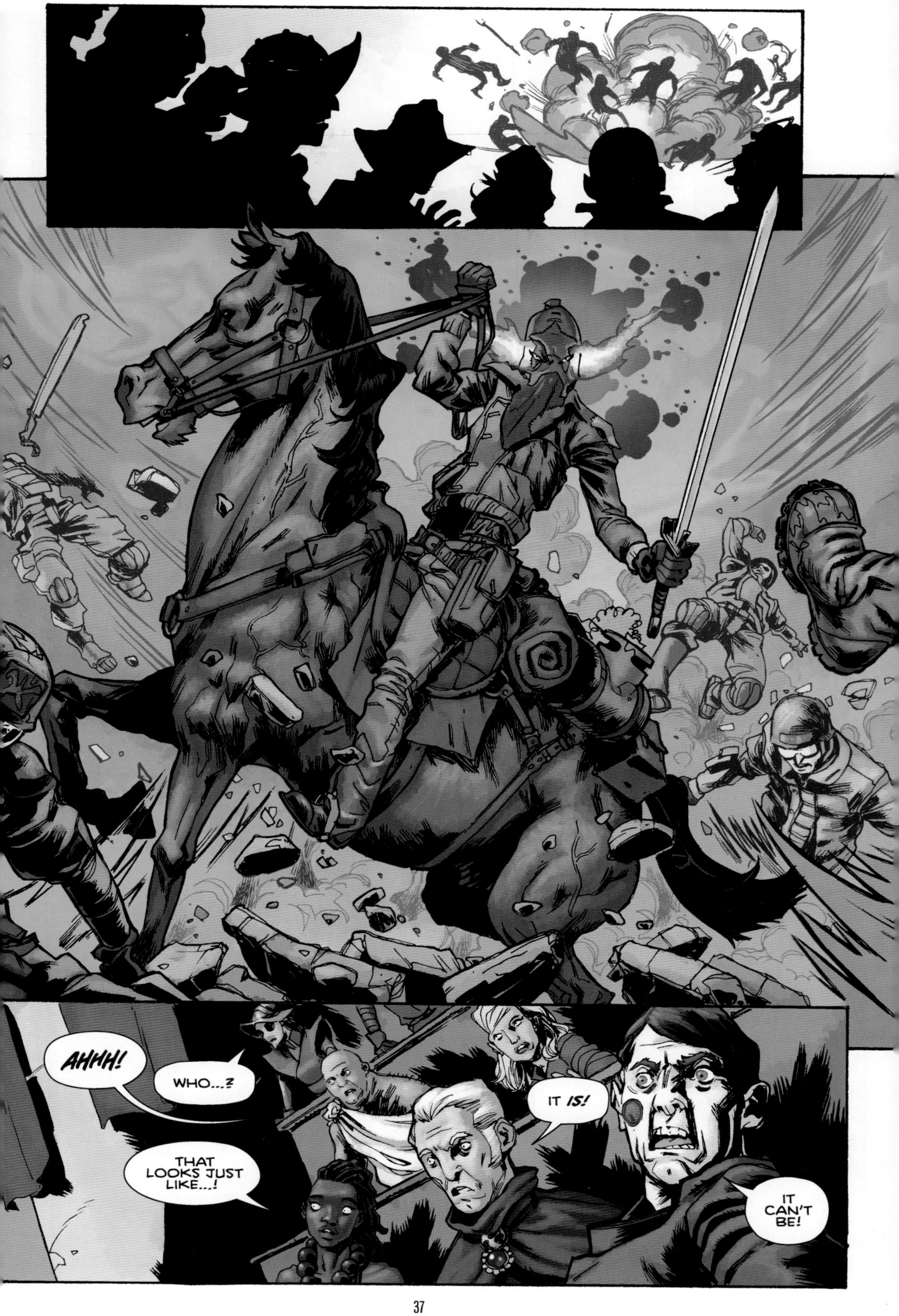
AHHH!
WHO...?
THAT LOOKS JUST LIKE...!
IT IS!
IT CAN'T BE!

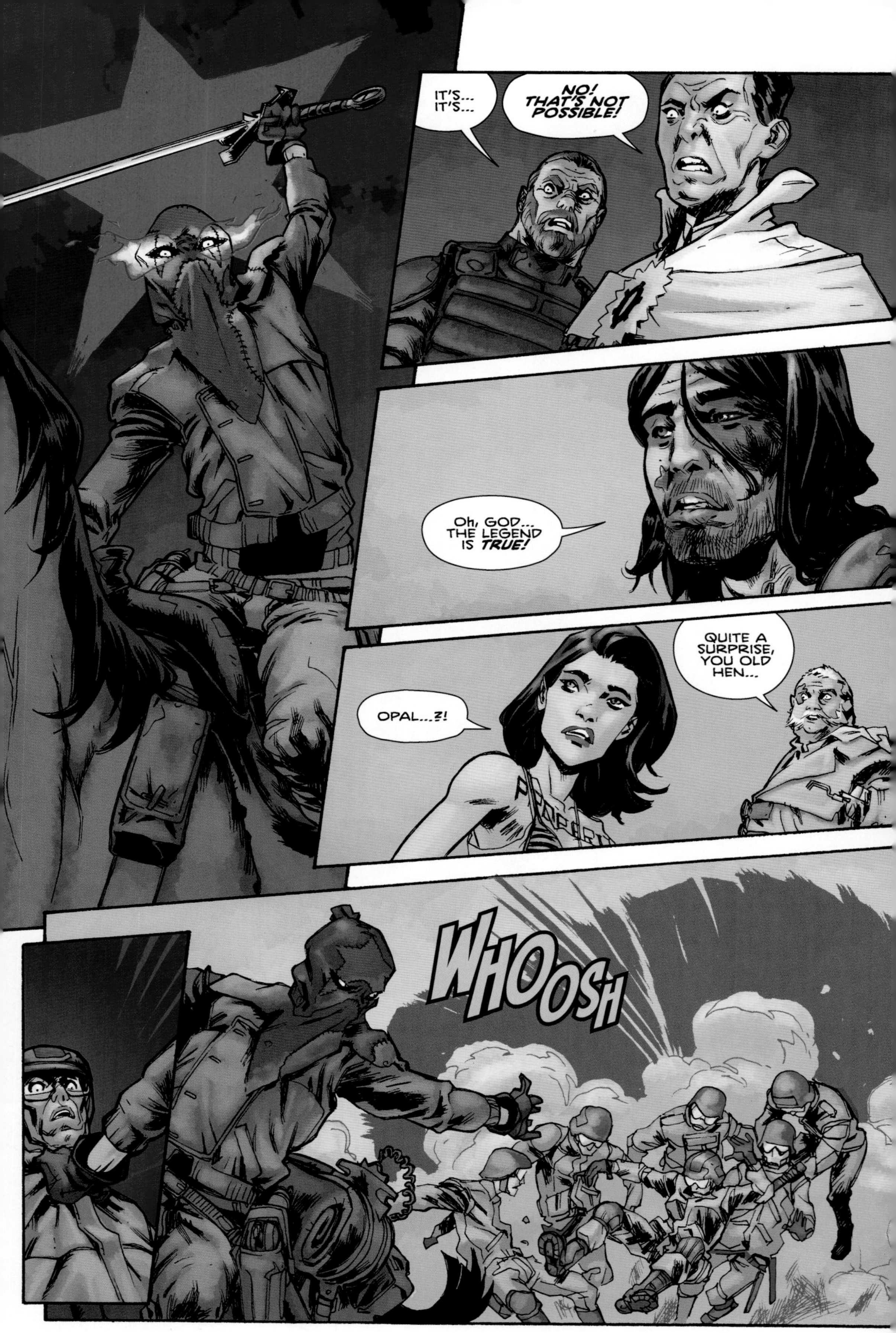
IT'S... IT'S...
NO! THAT'S NOT POSSIBLE!
Oh, GOD... THE LEGEND IS TRUE!
QUITE A SURPRISE, YOU OLD HEN...
OPAL...?!
WHOOSH

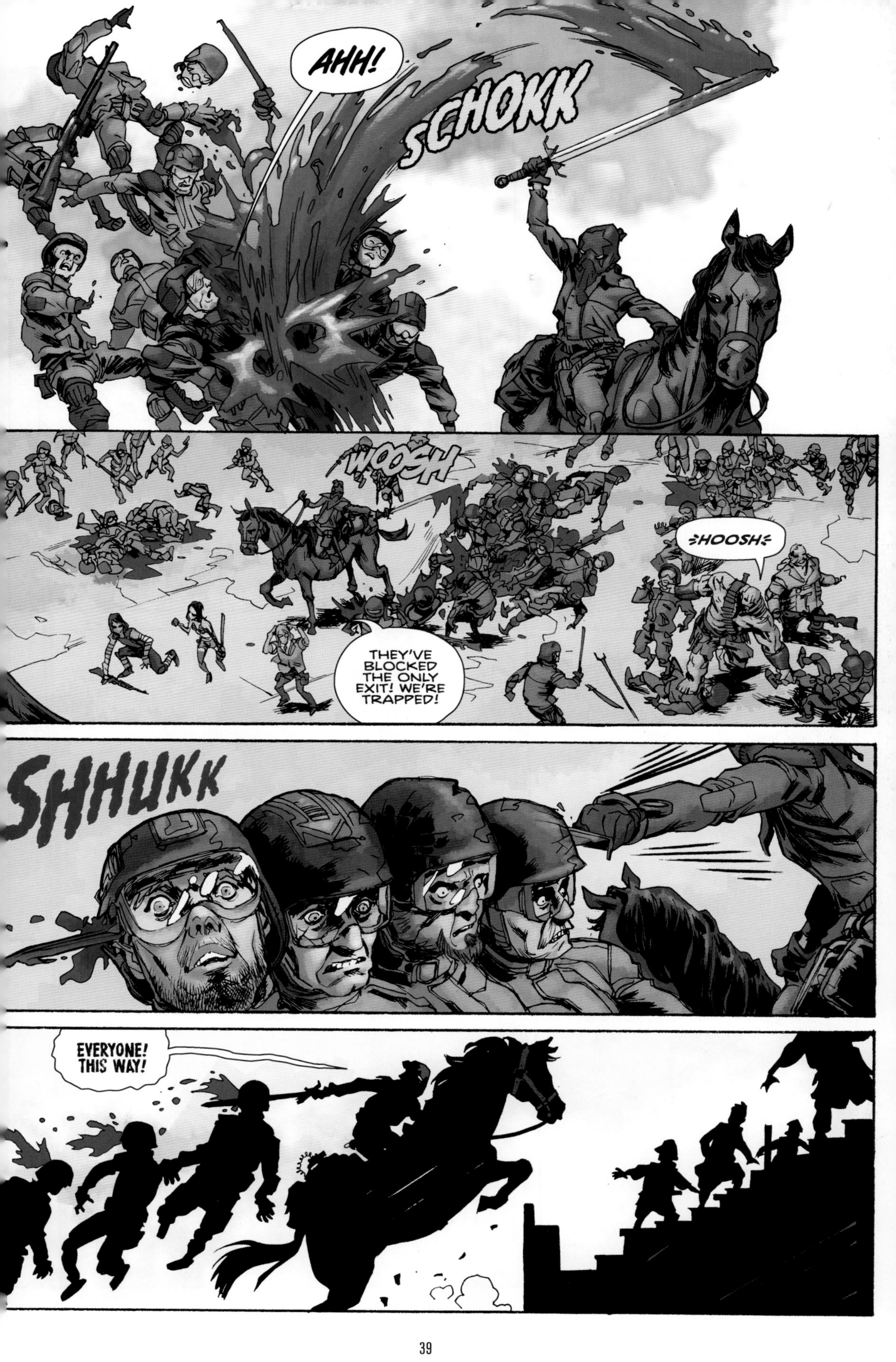
AHH!
SCHOKK
WOOSH
HOOSH
THEY'VE BLOCKED THE ONLY EXIT! WE'RE TRAPPED!
SHHUKK
EVERYONE! THIS WAY!

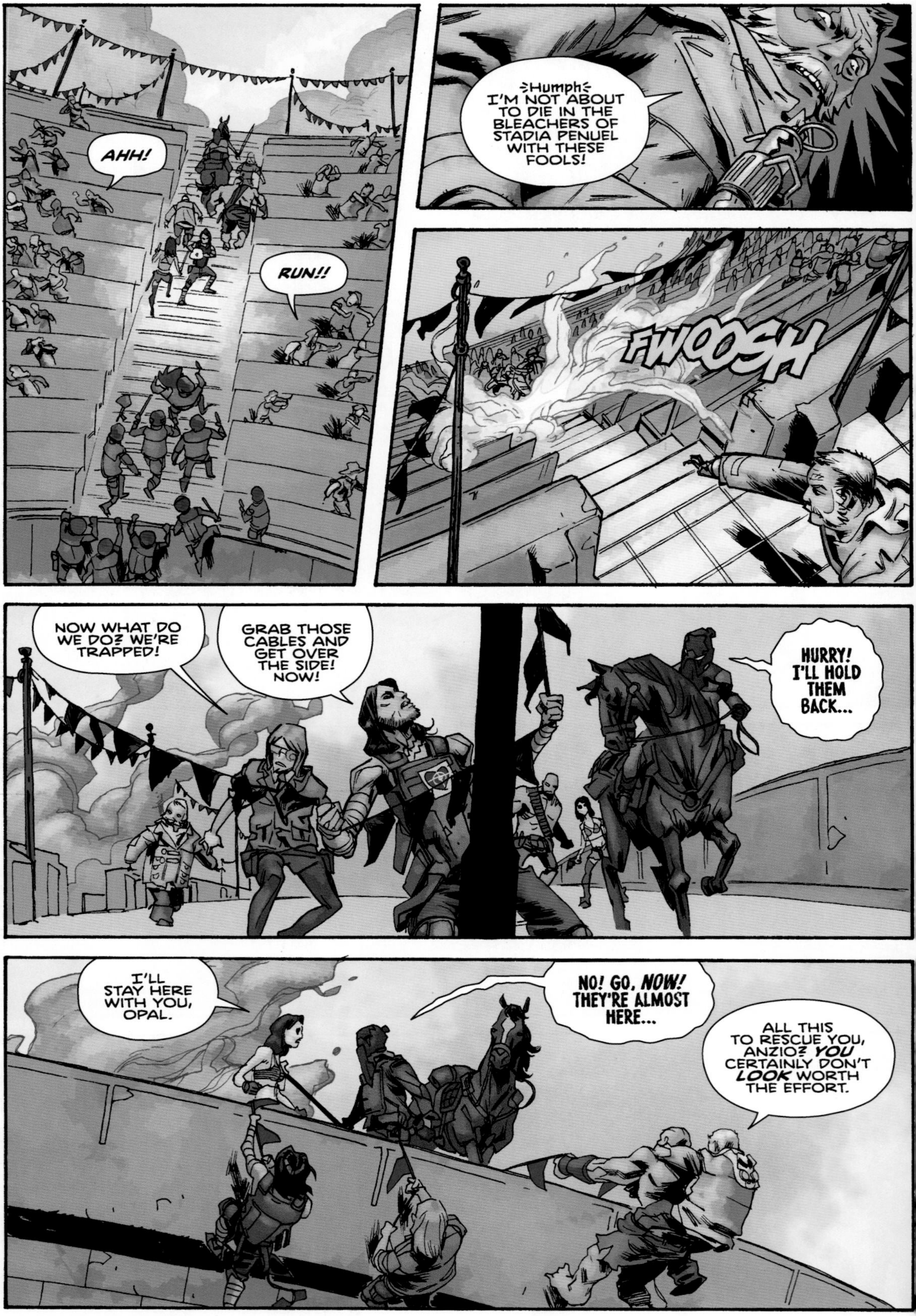
AHH!
RUN!!
Humph
I'M NOT ABOUT TO DIE IN THE BLEACHERS OF STADIA PENUEL WITH THESE FOOLS!
FWOOSH
NOW WHAT DO WE DO? WE'RE TRAPPED!
GRAB THOSE CABLES AND GET OVER THE SIDE! NOW!
HURRY! I'LL HOLD THEM BACK...
I'LL STAY HERE WITH YOU, OPAL.
NO! GO, NOW! THEY'RE ALMOST HERE...
ALL THIS TO RESCUE YOU, ANZIO? YOU CERTAINLY DON'T LOOK WORTH THE EFFORT.

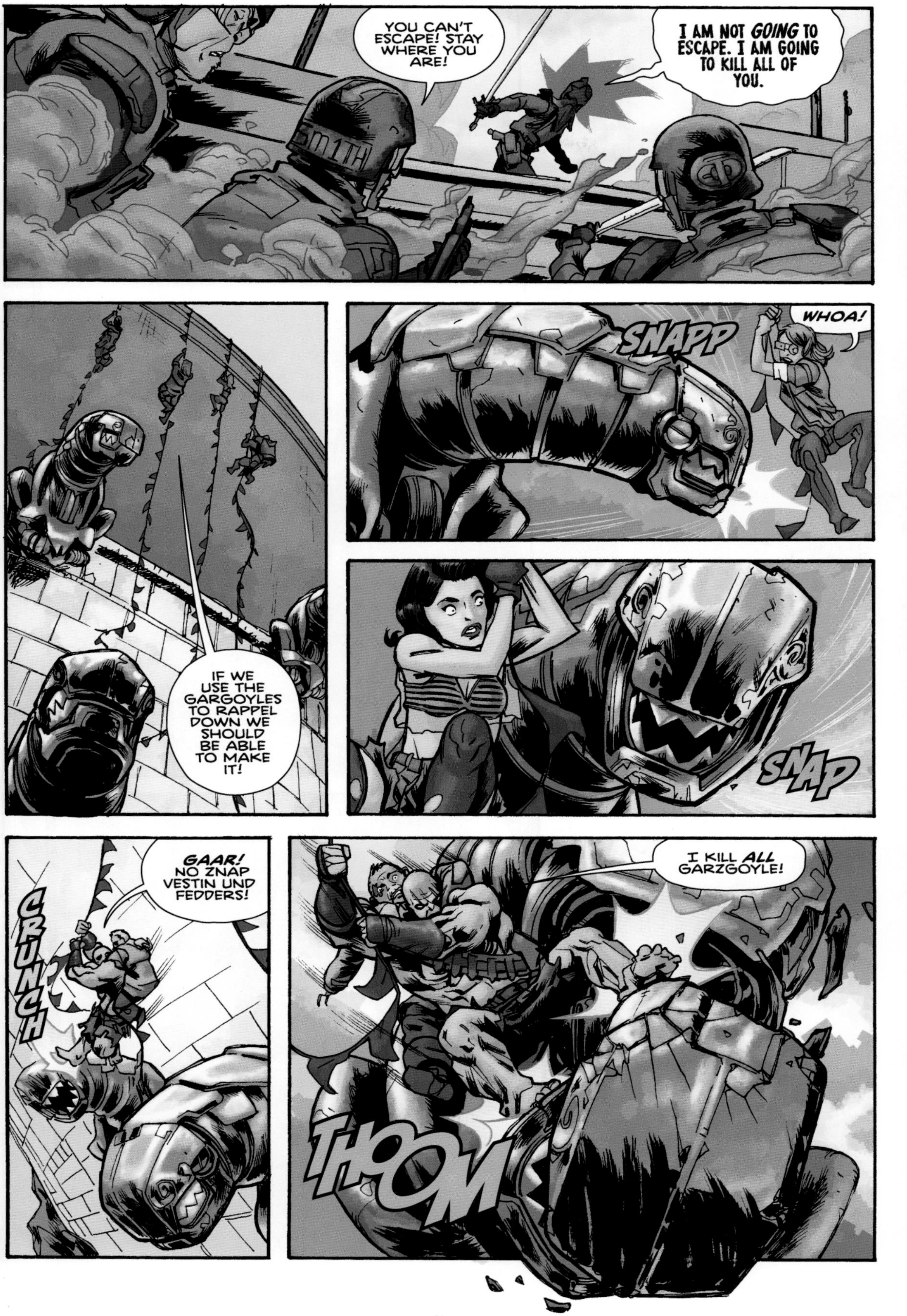
YOU CAN'T ESCAPE! STAY WHERE YOU ARE!
I AM NOT *GOING* TO ESCAPE. I AM GOING TO KILL ALL OF YOU.
IF WE USE THE GARGOYLES TO RAPPEL DOWN WE SHOULD BE ABLE TO MAKE IT!
SNAPP
WHOA!
SNAP
CRUNCH
GAAR! NO ZNAP VESTIN UND FEDDERS!
I KILL *ALL* GARZGOYLE!
THOOM

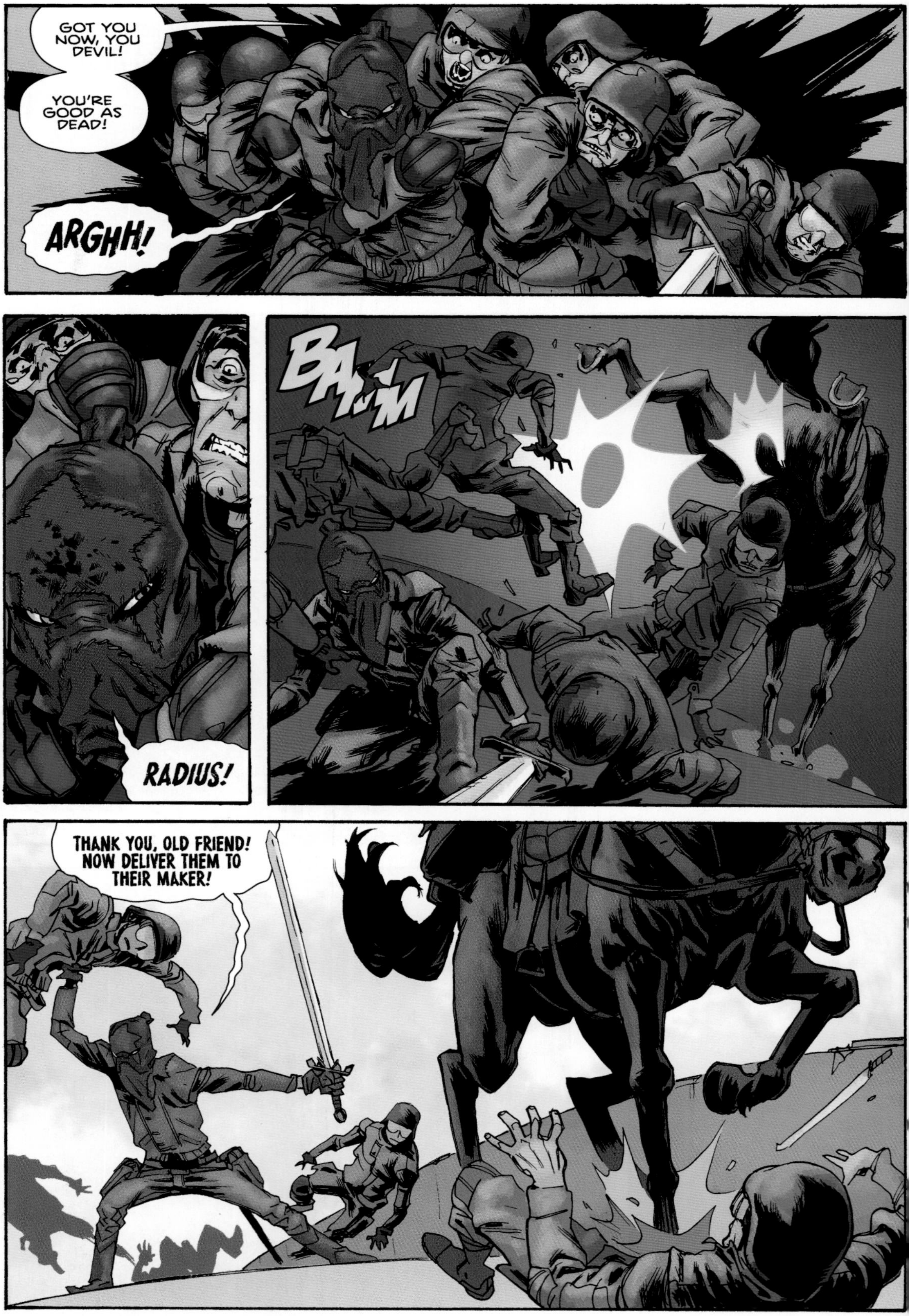
GOT YOU NOW, YOU DEVIL!
YOU'RE GOOD AS DEAD!
ARGHH!
RADIUS!
BAM
THANK YOU, OLD FRIEND! NOW DELIVER THEM TO THEIR MAKER!

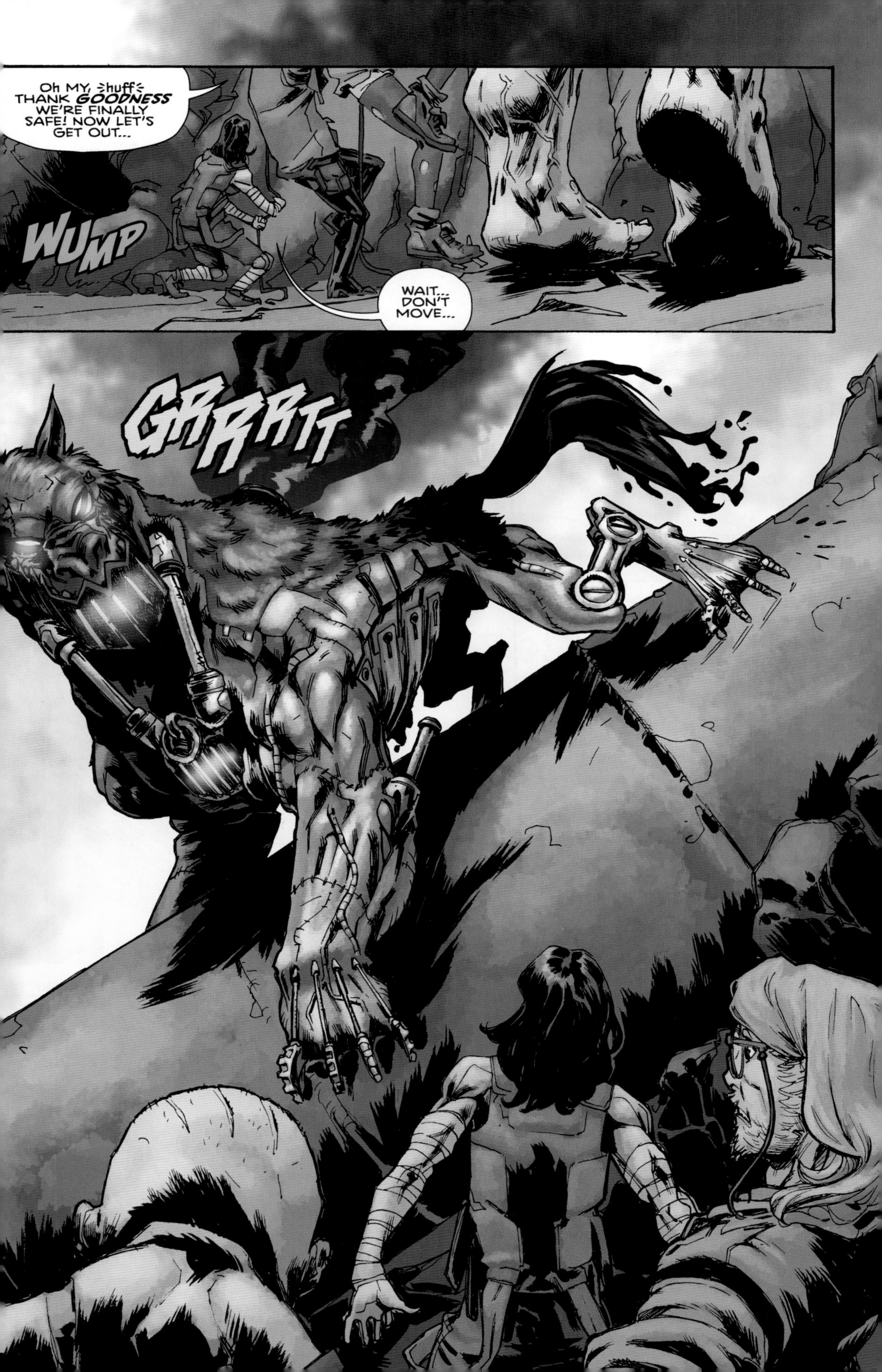
Oh MY, ≥huff≤ THANK GOODNESS WE'RE FINALLY SAFE! NOW LET'S GET OUT...
WUMP
WAIT... DON'T MOVE...
GRRRTT

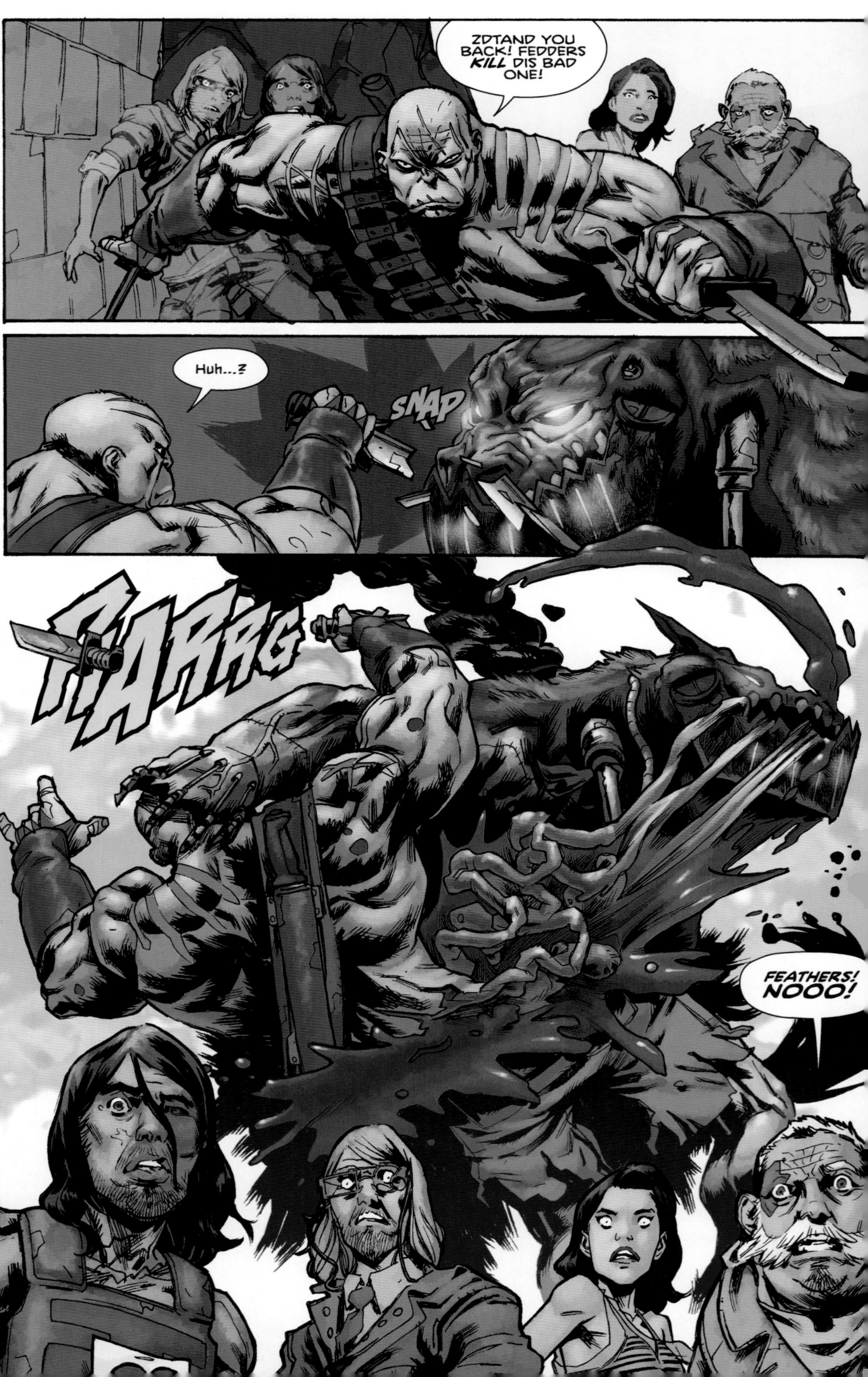
ZDTAND YOU BACK! FEDDERS KILL DIS BAD ONE!
Huh...?
SNAP
PARRG
FEATHERS! NOOO!

GLLUKK

NO, NO, NO...POOR FEATHERS...

RRGGG

THAT *THING* TORE HIM APART... HOW...?

PULL YOURSELF TOGETHER!

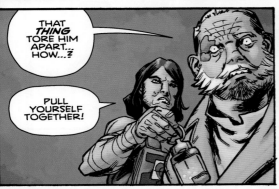

HSSHH

ARRK-KK-KK

THANK YOU, DEAR RADIUS. THANK YOU FOR ALL YOU HAVE BEEN TO ME, ALL YOU'VE MEANT TO ME.

...I DON'T WANT TO LEAVE YOU, OLD FRIEND. I'M SORRY...

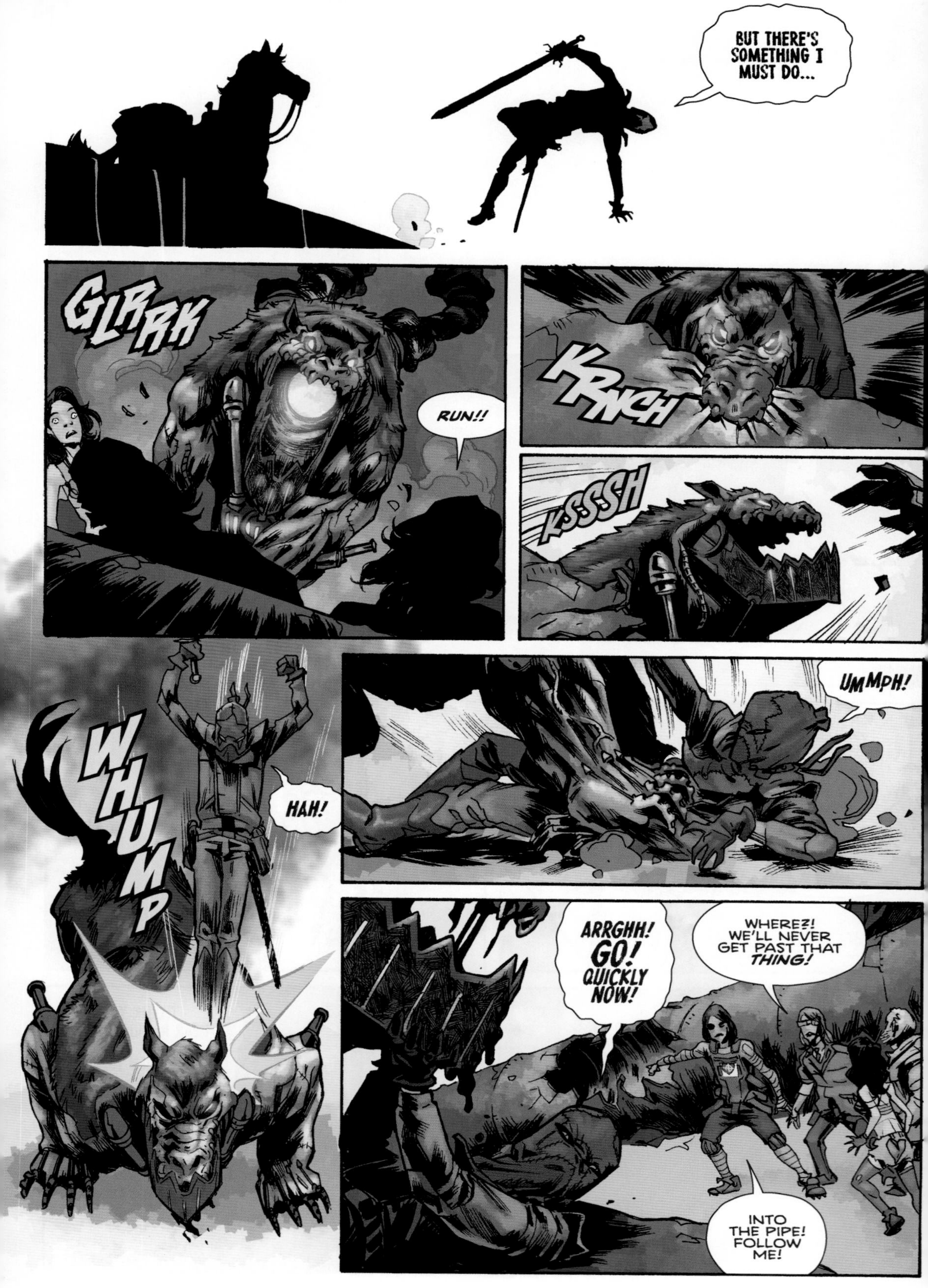
BUT THERE'S SOMETHING I MUST DO...
GLRRK
RUN!!
KRNCH
KSSSH
WHUMP
HAH!
UMMPH!
ARRGHH! GO! QUICKLY NOW!
WHERE?! WE'LL NEVER GET PAST THAT THING!
INTO THE PIPE! FOLLOW ME!

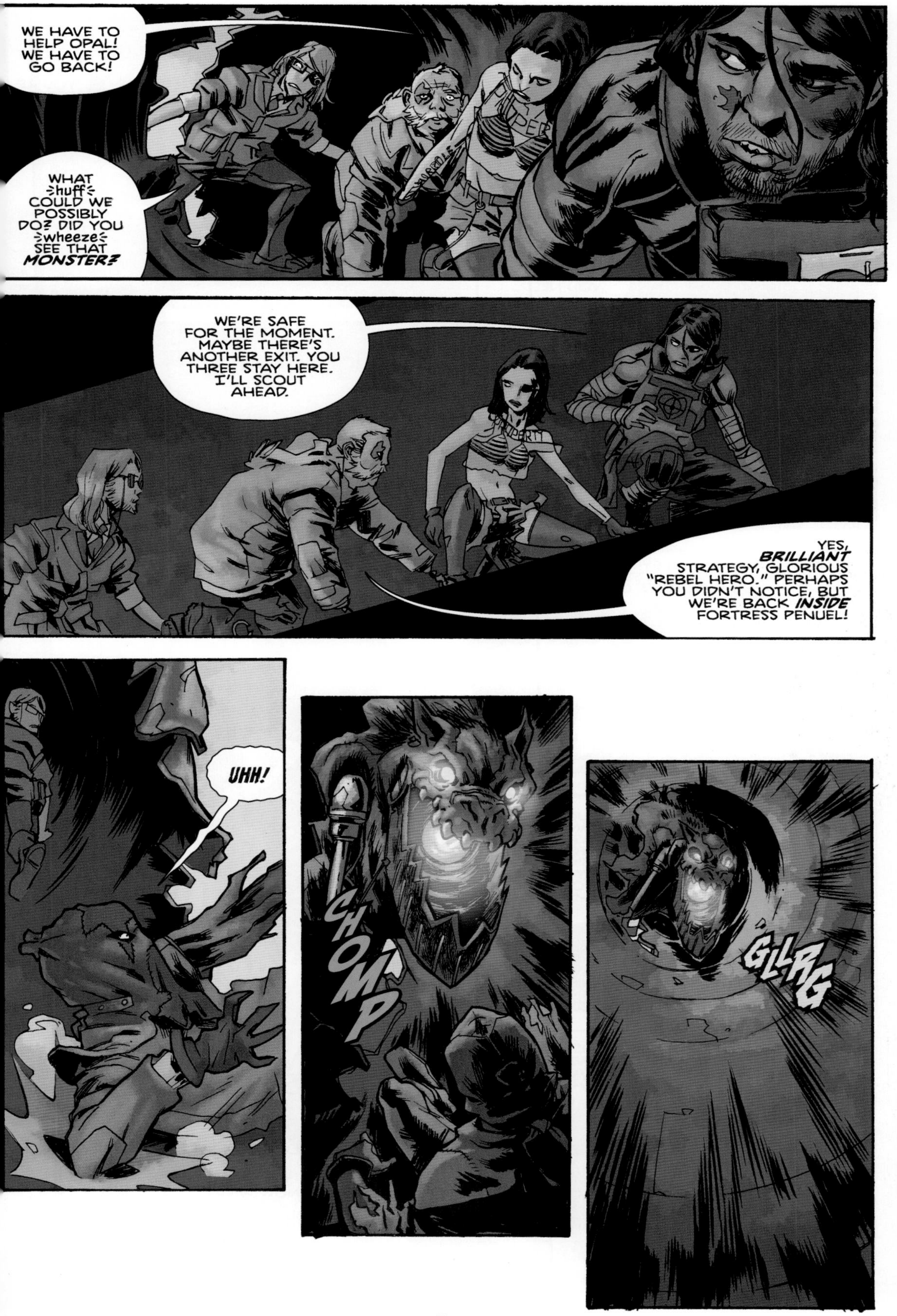
WE HAVE TO HELP OPAL! WE HAVE TO GO BACK!
WHAT ~huff~ COULD WE POSSIBLY DO? DID YOU ~wheeze~ SEE THAT MONSTER?
WE'RE SAFE FOR THE MOMENT. MAYBE THERE'S ANOTHER EXIT. YOU THREE STAY HERE. I'LL SCOUT AHEAD.
YES, BRILLIANT STRATEGY, GLORIOUS "REBEL HERO." PERHAPS YOU DIDN'T NOTICE, BUT WE'RE BACK INSIDE FORTRESS PENUEL!
UHH!
CHOMP
GLLRG

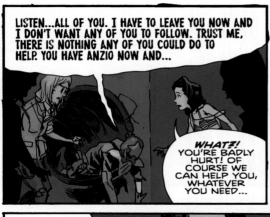

LISTEN...ALL OF YOU. I HAVE TO LEAVE YOU NOW AND I DON'T WANT ANY OF YOU TO FOLLOW. TRUST ME, THERE IS NOTHING ANY OF YOU COULD DO TO HELP. YOU HAVE ANZIO NOW AND...

WHAT?! YOU'RE BADLY HURT! OF COURSE WE CAN HELP YOU, WHATEVER YOU NEED...

ORCHID, YOU HAVE ALREADY HELPED ME MORE THAN YOU KNOW. BUT YOU CANNOT SAVE ME. WHAT LITTLE CHANCE THERE IS OF THAT...I MUST FIND OUT FOR MYSELF.

NO! WE'LL STAY HERE TILL YOU'RE BETTER AND...

ORCHID, I HAVE TO DO...WHAT I CAME HERE...TO... DO...❄

OPAL!

SHE PASSED OUT!

I SAW IT WITH MY OWN EYES! GENERAL CHINA RUNNING *AMUCK* IN STADIA PENUEL! DOZENS, MAYBE *HUNDREDS* OF SOLDIERS WERE...

...SLAUGHTERED LIKE ANTS! AND IT WAS *SURELY* THE LEGENDARY MASK. THEY SAY THAT TOMO WOLFE HIMSELF...

...WAS SPEECHLESS AS THE REBEL PRISONER ESCAPED AND *THE GHOST OF GENERAL CHINA* FLEW OUT OF THE STADIUM AND *DISAPPEARED!*

THANK YOU, MY DEAR FRIEND. YOUR PRESENCE IS ALWAYS A GREAT COMFORT.

I DON'T KNOW WHAT TRICKERY IS AFOOT, BUT THAT WAS *NOT* A SUPERNATURAL SPECTER IN THE STADIUM TODAY. JUST THE *IDEA* THAT SOMEONE WOULD *DARE*...

I HAVE COME *TOO FAR* TO HAVE *MY* DAY MARRED BY SOME CHARLATAN IN A PAINTED HOOD!

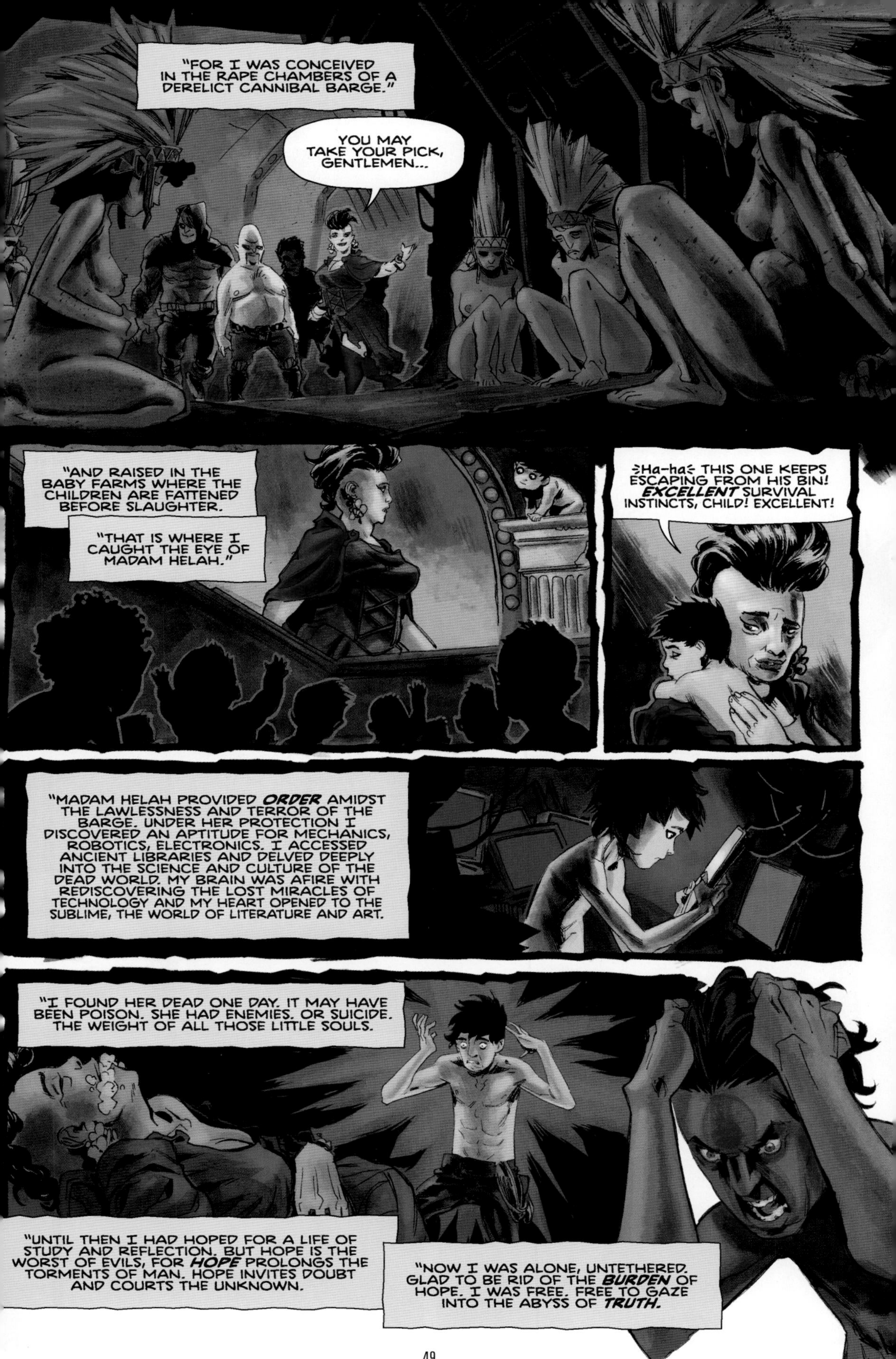
"FOR I WAS CONCEIVED IN THE RAPE CHAMBERS OF A DERELICT CANNIBAL BARGE."
YOU MAY TAKE YOUR PICK, GENTLEMEN...
"AND RAISED IN THE BABY FARMS WHERE THE CHILDREN ARE FATTENED BEFORE SLAUGHTER.
"THAT IS WHERE I CAUGHT THE EYE OF MADAM HELAH."
Ha-ha THIS ONE KEEPS ESCAPING FROM HIS BIN! EXCELLENT SURVIVAL INSTINCTS, CHILD! EXCELLENT!
"MADAM HELAH PROVIDED ORDER AMIDST THE LAWLESSNESS AND TERROR OF THE BARGE. UNDER HER PROTECTION I DISCOVERED AN APTITUDE FOR MECHANICS, ROBOTICS, ELECTRONICS. I ACCESSED ANCIENT LIBRARIES AND DELVED DEEPLY INTO THE SCIENCE AND CULTURE OF THE DEAD WORLD. MY BRAIN WAS AFIRE WITH REDISCOVERING THE LOST MIRACLES OF TECHNOLOGY AND MY HEART OPENED TO THE SUBLIME, THE WORLD OF LITERATURE AND ART.
"I FOUND HER DEAD ONE DAY. IT MAY HAVE BEEN POISON. SHE HAD ENEMIES. OR SUICIDE. THE WEIGHT OF ALL THOSE LITTLE SOULS.
"UNTIL THEN I HAD HOPED FOR A LIFE OF STUDY AND REFLECTION. BUT HOPE IS THE WORST OF EVILS, FOR HOPE PROLONGS THE TORMENTS OF MAN. HOPE INVITES DOUBT AND COURTS THE UNKNOWN.
"NOW I WAS ALONE, UNTETHERED. GLAD TO BE RID OF THE BURDEN OF HOPE. I WAS FREE. FREE TO GAZE INTO THE ABYSS OF TRUTH.

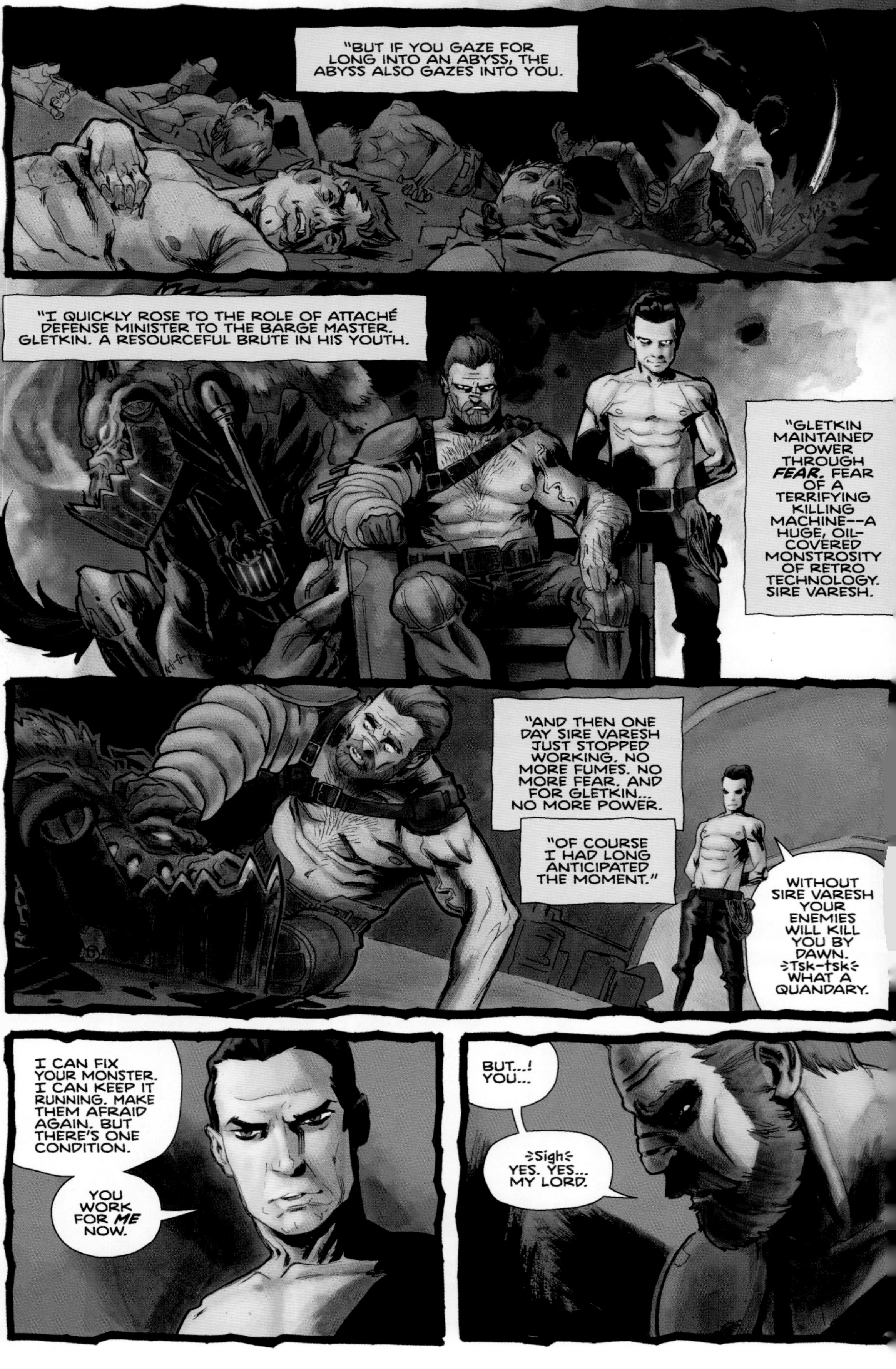
"BUT IF YOU GAZE FOR LONG INTO AN ABYSS, THE ABYSS ALSO GAZES INTO YOU.
"I QUICKLY ROSE TO THE ROLE OF ATTACHÉ DEFENSE MINISTER TO THE BARGE MASTER. GLETKIN. A RESOURCEFUL BRUTE IN HIS YOUTH.
"GLETKIN MAINTAINED POWER THROUGH FEAR. FEAR OF A TERRIFYING KILLING MACHINE--A HUGE, OIL-COVERED MONSTROSITY OF RETRO TECHNOLOGY. SIRE VARESH.
"AND THEN ONE DAY SIRE VARESH JUST STOPPED WORKING. NO MORE FUMES. NO MORE FEAR. AND FOR GLETKIN... NO MORE POWER.
"OF COURSE I HAD LONG ANTICIPATED THE MOMENT."
WITHOUT SIRE VARESH YOUR ENEMIES WILL KILL YOU BY DAWN. Tsk-tsk WHAT A QUANDARY.
I CAN FIX YOUR MONSTER. I CAN KEEP IT RUNNING. MAKE THEM AFRAID AGAIN. BUT THERE'S ONE CONDITION.
YOU WORK FOR ME NOW.
BUT...! YOU...
Sigh YES. YES... MY LORD.

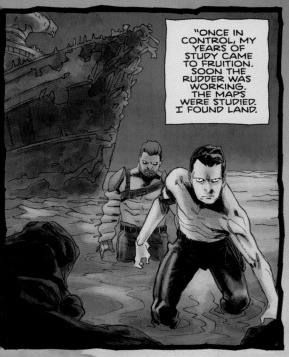

"ONCE IN CONTROL, MY YEARS OF STUDY CAME TO FRUITION. SOON THE RUDDER WAS WORKING. THE MAPS WERE STUDIED. I FOUND LAND.

"AND THEN I FOUND A HOME.

"IT WAS DRY, EASILY DEFENDED. THE ROCKY OUTCROP THAT WOULD BECOME HOME TO *THIS* IMPREGNABLE FORTRESS. I NAMED IT 'PENUEL' AFTER THE BIBLICAL SITE WHERE JAKE VIED WITH THE LORD'S ANGEL...AND THE ANGEL WAS OVERTHROWN.

"NEXT, THE ROBOTICS FACTORY.

"THE TECHNOLOGY WAS RUDIMENTARY REALLY, THE WATERLOGGED PIECES ALL JUST WAITING FOR SOMEONE WHO KNEW HOW TO TURN ON THE POWER. SOON I HAD AN ARMY OF MECHANICAL SERVANTS AND WEAPONS TO TAME WHATEVER I ENCOUNTERED.

"IT WAS A SIMPLE MATTER TO BUY OFF, OR DESTROY, THE LOCAL WARLORDS. THEIR SUBJECTS BECAME *MY* SUBJECTS. MY LEGIONS GREW. THE REFUSE DRAINED INTO THE SCUM CULTURE BENEATH THE BRIDGES.

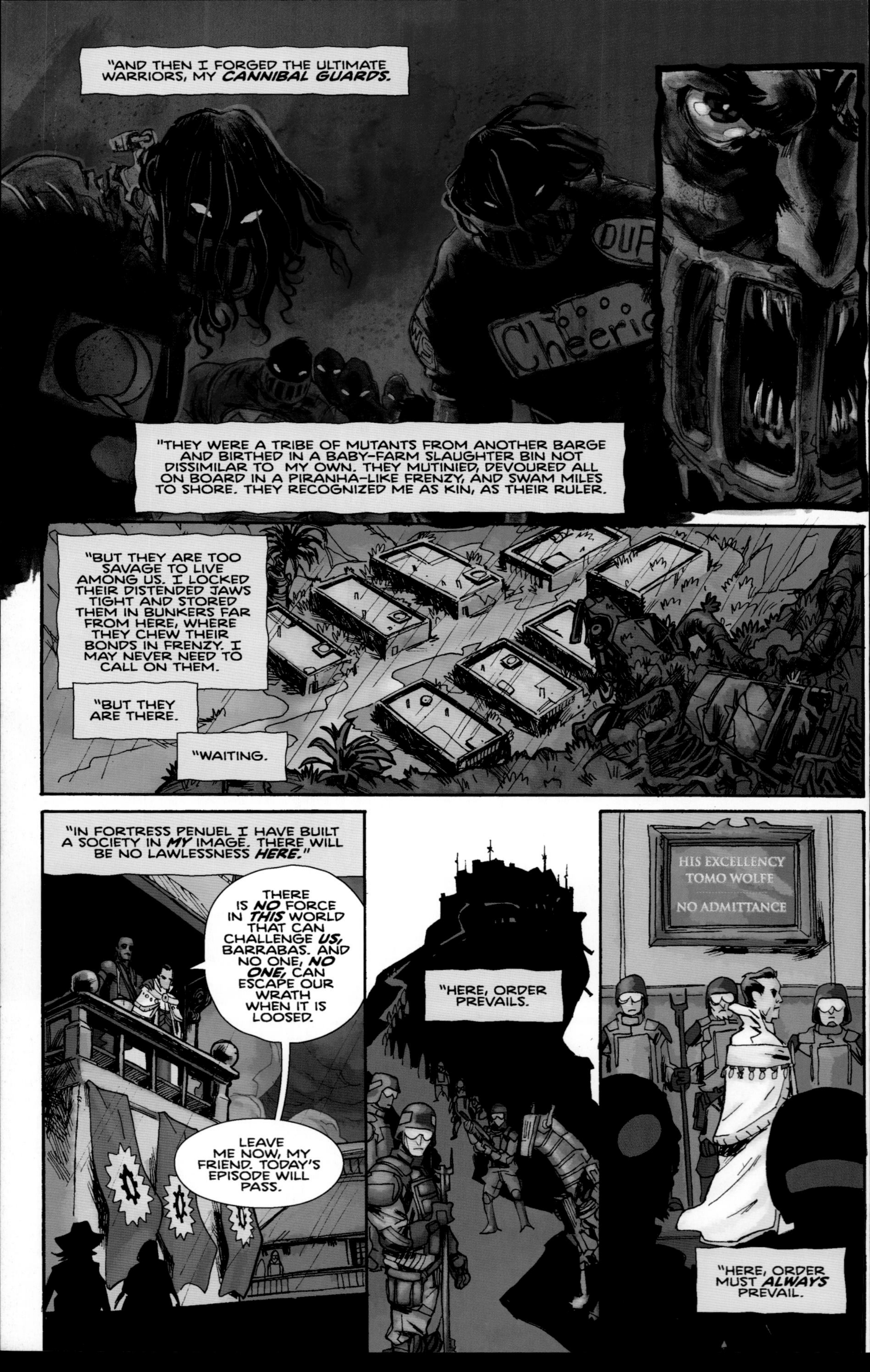
"AND THEN I FORGED THE ULTIMATE WARRIORS, MY *CANNIBAL GUARDS.*
"THEY WERE A TRIBE OF MUTANTS FROM ANOTHER BARGE AND BIRTHED IN A BABY-FARM SLAUGHTER BIN NOT DISSIMILAR TO MY OWN. THEY MUTINIED, DEVOURED ALL ON BOARD IN A PIRANHA-LIKE FRENZY, AND SWAM MILES TO SHORE. THEY RECOGNIZED ME AS KIN, AS THEIR RULER.
"BUT THEY ARE TOO SAVAGE TO LIVE AMONG US. I LOCKED THEIR DISTENDED JAWS TIGHT AND STORED THEM IN BUNKERS FAR FROM HERE, WHERE THEY CHEW THEIR BONDS IN FRENZY. I MAY NEVER NEED TO CALL ON THEM.
"BUT THEY ARE THERE.
"WAITING.
"IN FORTRESS PENUEL I HAVE BUILT A SOCIETY IN *MY* IMAGE. THERE WILL BE NO LAWLESSNESS *HERE.*"
THERE IS ***NO*** FORCE IN ***THIS*** WORLD THAT CAN CHALLENGE ***US,*** BARRABAS. AND NO ONE, ***NO ONE,*** CAN ESCAPE OUR WRATH WHEN IT IS LOOSED.
LEAVE ME NOW, MY FRIEND. TODAY'S EPISODE WILL PASS.
"HERE, ORDER PREVAILS.
HIS EXCELLENCY
TOMO WOLFE
NO ADMITTANCE
"HERE, ORDER MUST ***ALWAYS*** PREVAIL.

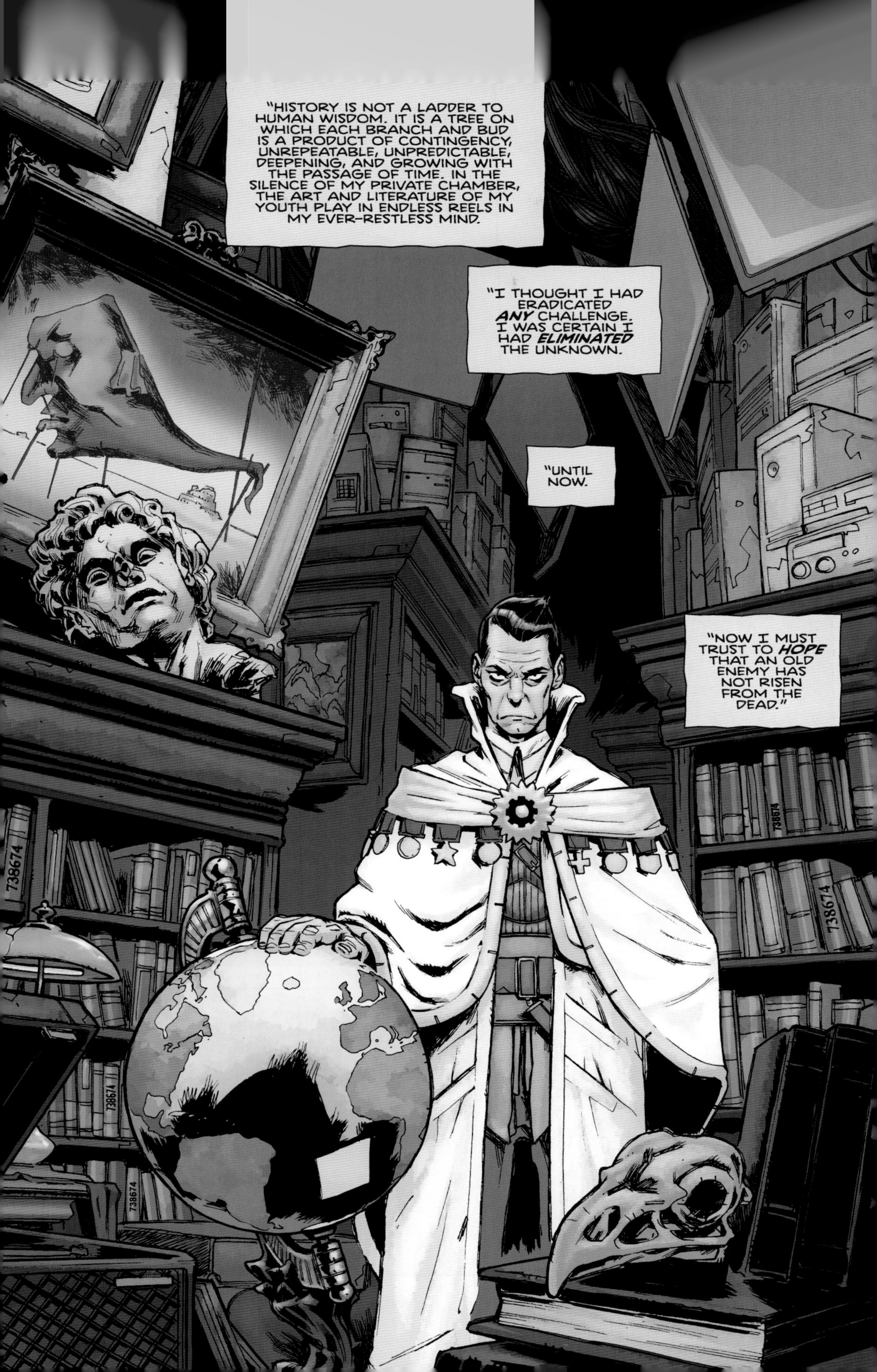
"HISTORY IS NOT A LADDER TO HUMAN WISDOM. IT IS A TREE ON WHICH EACH BRANCH AND BUD IS A PRODUCT OF CONTINGENCY, UNREPEATABLE, UNPREDICTABLE, DEEPENING, AND GROWING WITH THE PASSAGE OF TIME. IN THE SILENCE OF MY PRIVATE CHAMBER, THE ART AND LITERATURE OF MY YOUTH PLAY IN ENDLESS REELS IN MY EVER-RESTLESS MIND.
"I THOUGHT I HAD ERADICATED ***ANY*** CHALLENGE. I WAS CERTAIN I HAD ***ELIMINATED*** THE UNKNOWN.
"UNTIL NOW.
"NOW I MUST TRUST TO ***HOPE*** THAT AN OLD ENEMY HAS NOT RISEN FROM THE DEAD."

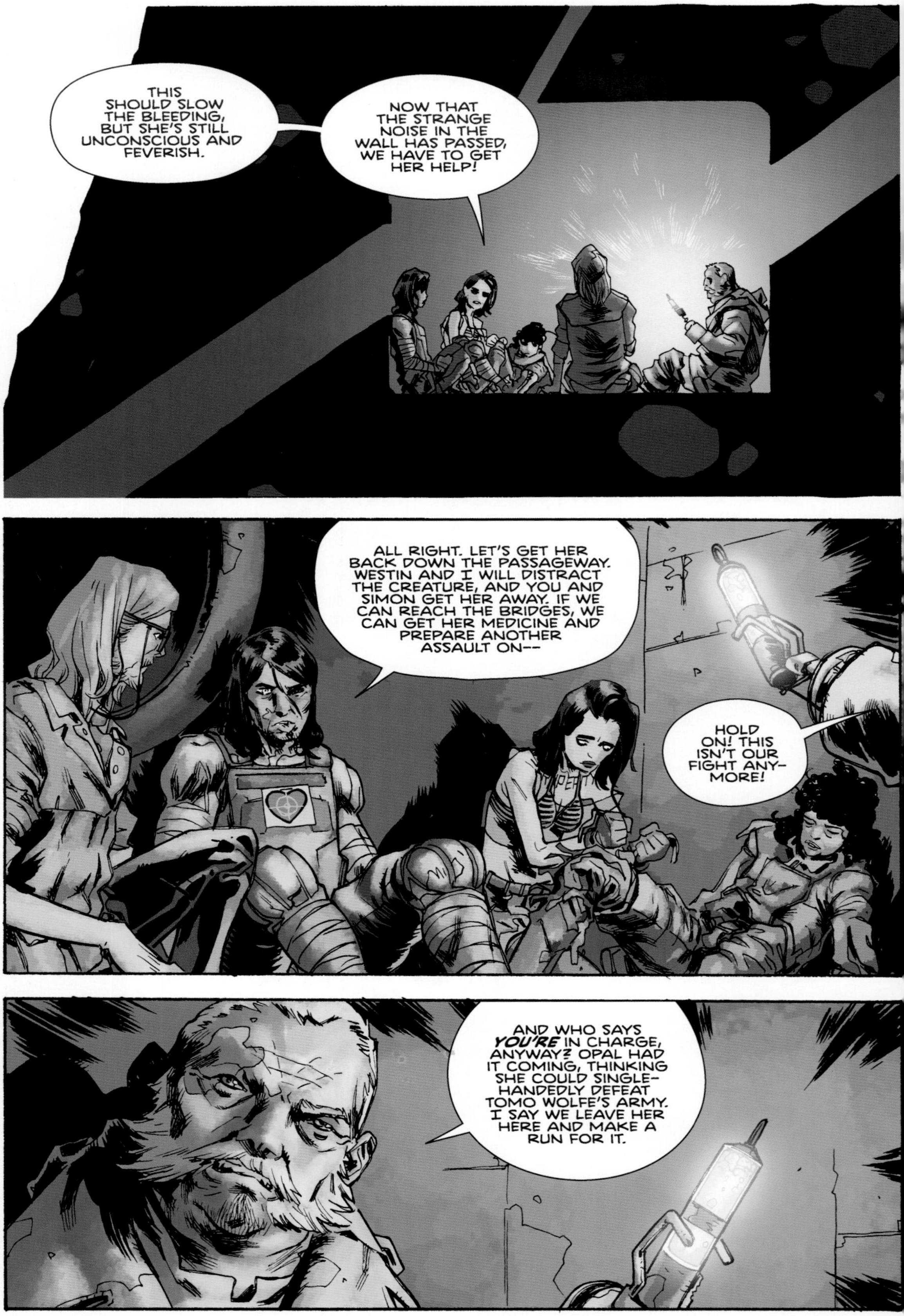
THIS SHOULD SLOW THE BLEEDING, BUT SHE'S STILL UNCONSCIOUS AND FEVERISH.
NOW THAT THE STRANGE NOISE IN THE WALL HAS PASSED, WE HAVE TO GET HER HELP!
ALL RIGHT. LET'S GET HER BACK DOWN THE PASSAGEWAY. WESTIN AND I WILL DISTRACT THE CREATURE, AND YOU AND SIMON GET HER AWAY. IF WE CAN REACH THE BRIDGES, WE CAN GET HER MEDICINE AND PREPARE ANOTHER ASSAULT ON--
HOLD ON! THIS ISN'T OUR FIGHT ANY-MORE!
AND WHO SAYS *YOU'RE* IN CHARGE, ANYWAY? OPAL HAD IT COMING, THINKING SHE COULD SINGLE-HANDEDLY DEFEAT TOMO WOLFE'S ARMY. I SAY WE LEAVE HER HERE AND MAKE A RUN FOR IT.

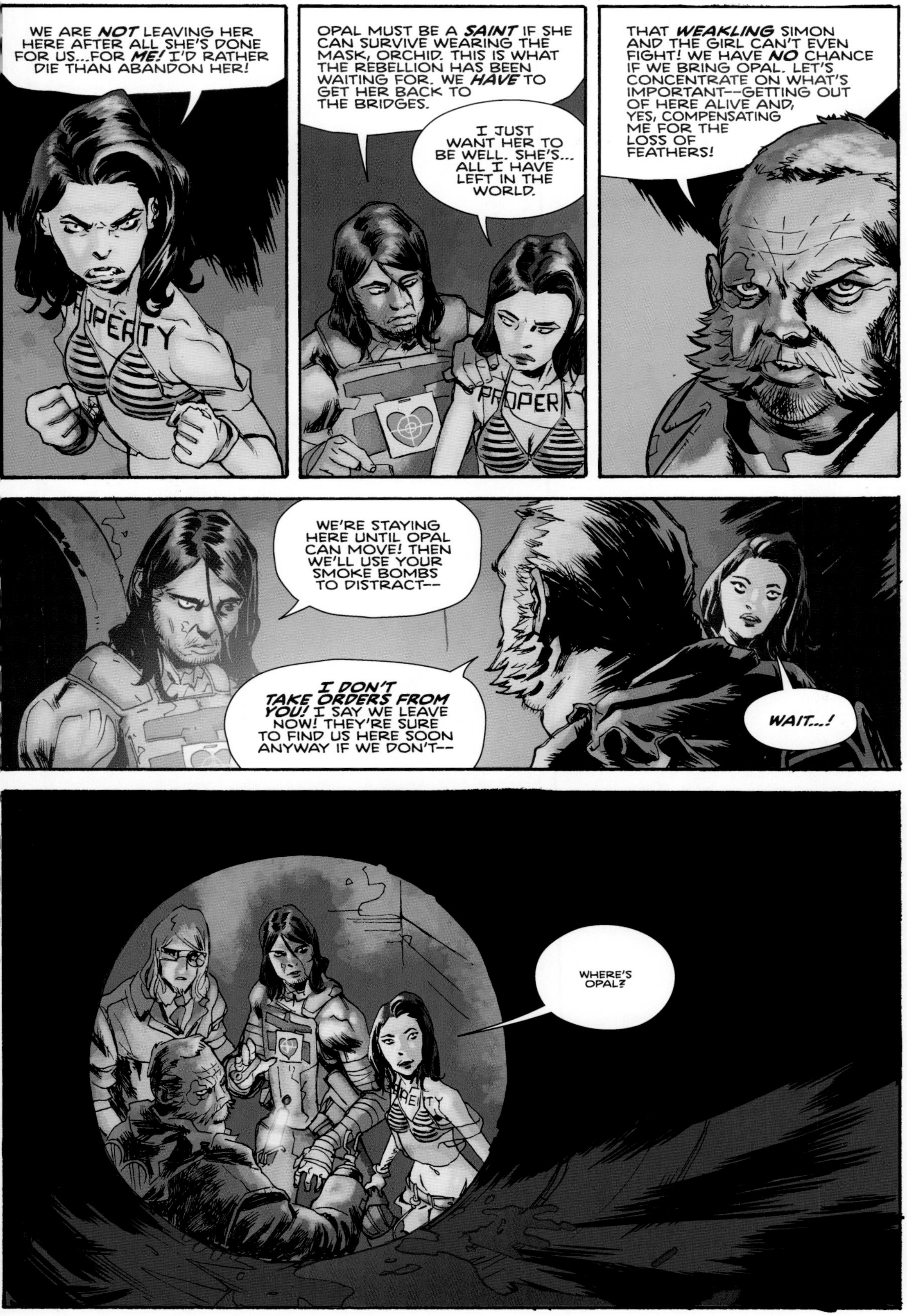
WE ARE NOT LEAVING HER HERE AFTER ALL SHE'S DONE FOR US...FOR ME! I'D RATHER DIE THAN ABANDON HER!
PROPERTY
OPAL MUST BE A SAINT IF SHE CAN SURVIVE WEARING THE MASK, ORCHID. THIS IS WHAT THE REBELLION HAS BEEN WAITING FOR. WE HAVE TO GET HER BACK TO THE BRIDGES.
I JUST WANT HER TO BE WELL. SHE'S... ALL I HAVE LEFT IN THE WORLD.
THAT WEAKLING SIMON AND THE GIRL CAN'T EVEN FIGHT! WE HAVE NO CHANCE IF WE BRING OPAL. LET'S CONCENTRATE ON WHAT'S IMPORTANT--GETTING OUT OF HERE ALIVE AND, YES, COMPENSATING ME FOR THE LOSS OF FEATHERS!
WE'RE STAYING HERE UNTIL OPAL CAN MOVE! THEN WE'LL USE YOUR SMOKE BOMBS TO DISTRACT--
I DON'T TAKE ORDERS FROM YOU! I SAY WE LEAVE NOW! THEY'RE SURE TO FIND US HERE SOON ANYWAY IF WE DON'T--
WAIT...!
WHERE'S OPAL?

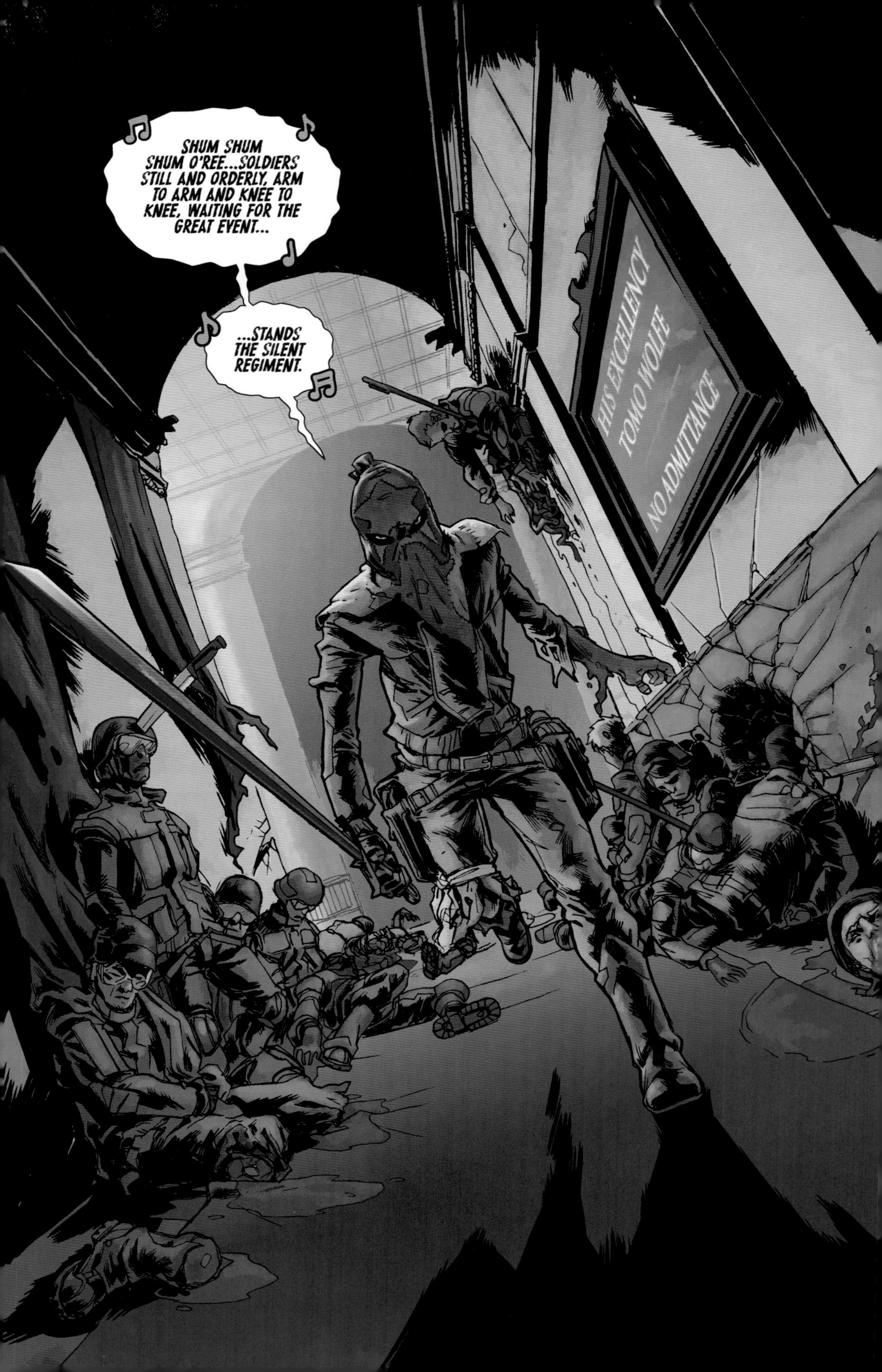
SHUM SHUM SHUM O'REE...SOLDIERS STILL AND ORDERLY, ARM TO ARM AND KNEE TO KNEE, WAITING FOR THE GREAT EVENT...
...STANDS THE SILENT REGIMENT.
HIS EXCELLENCY TOMO WOLFE NO ADMITTANCE

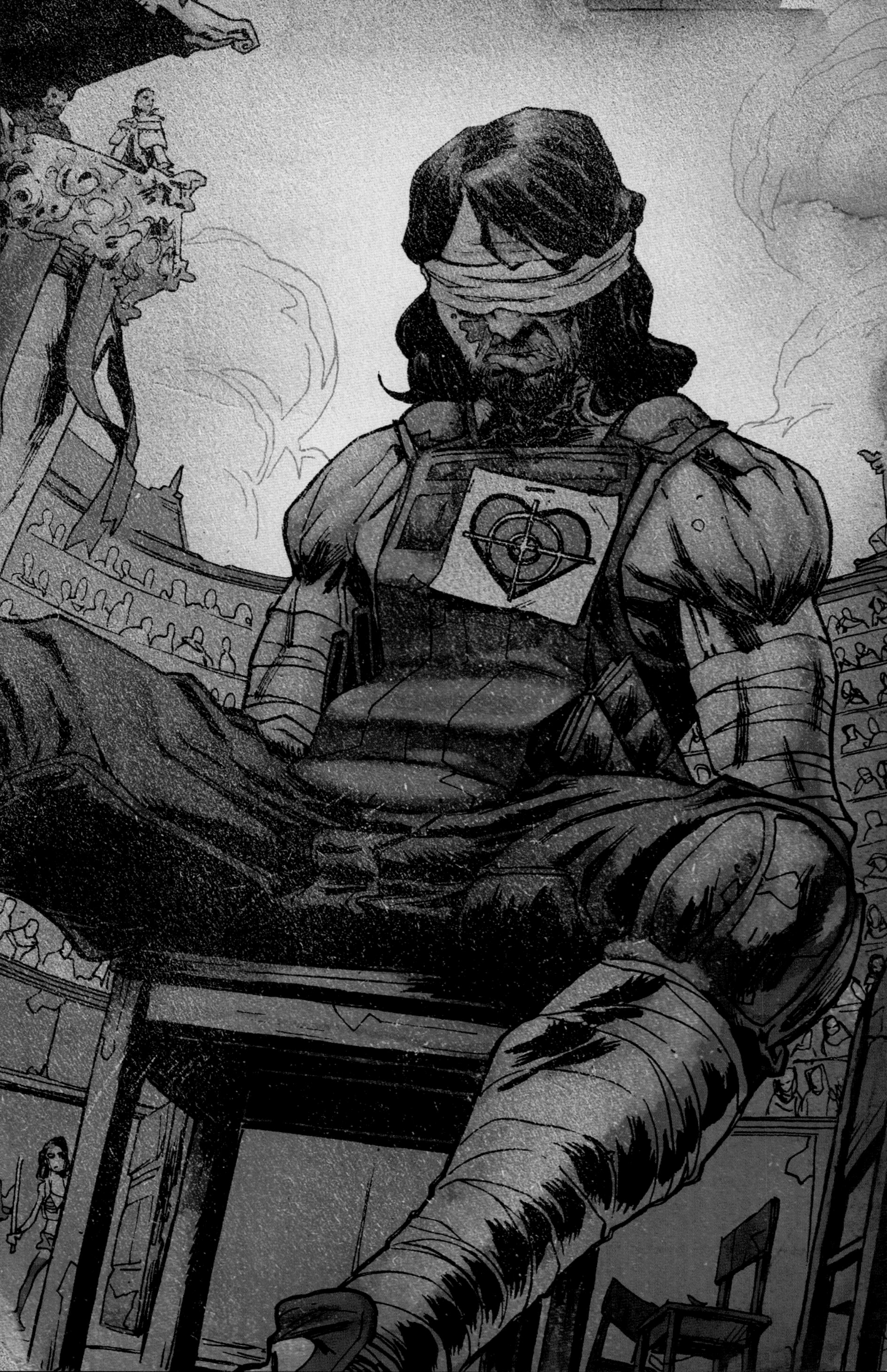

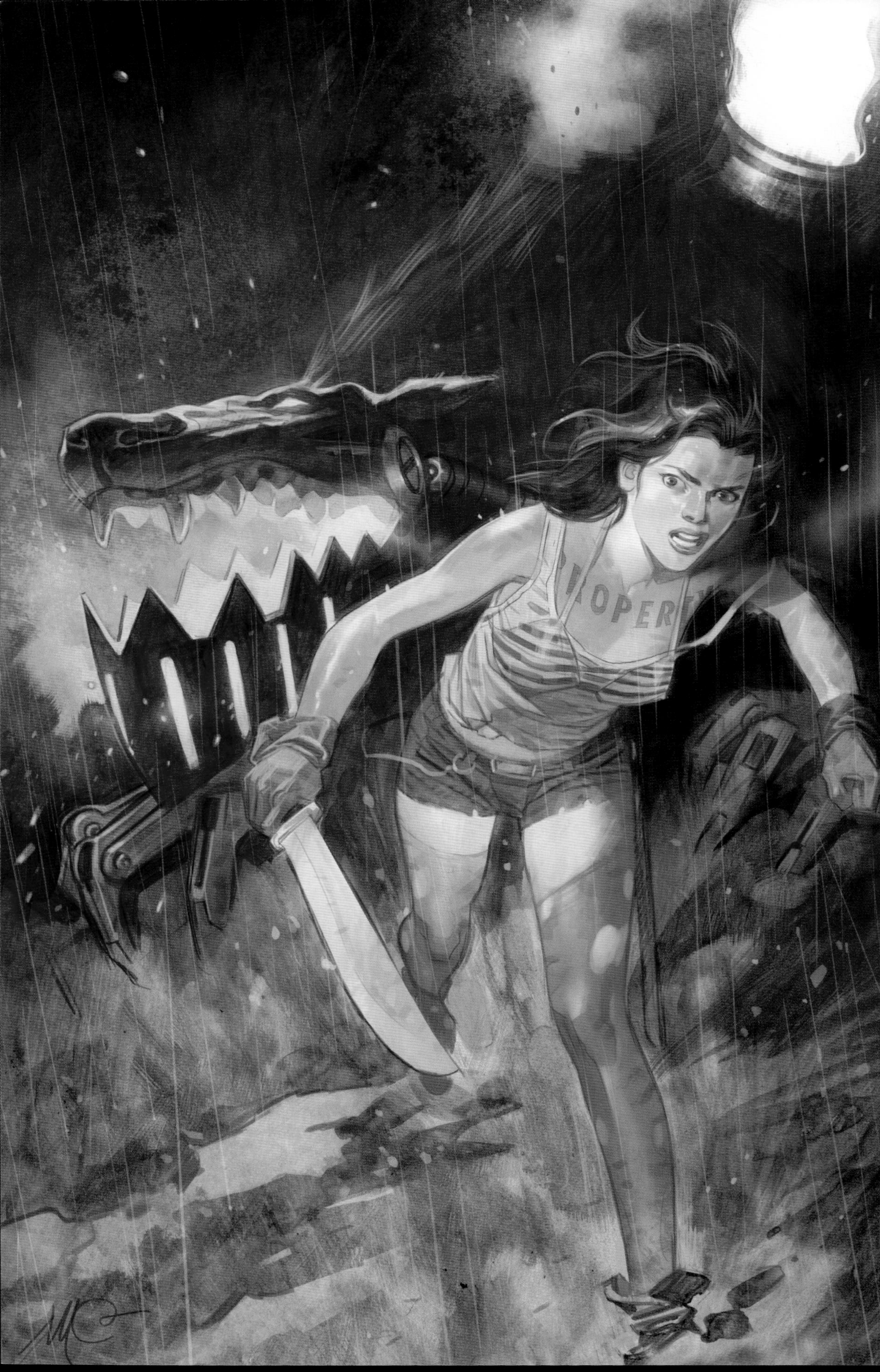

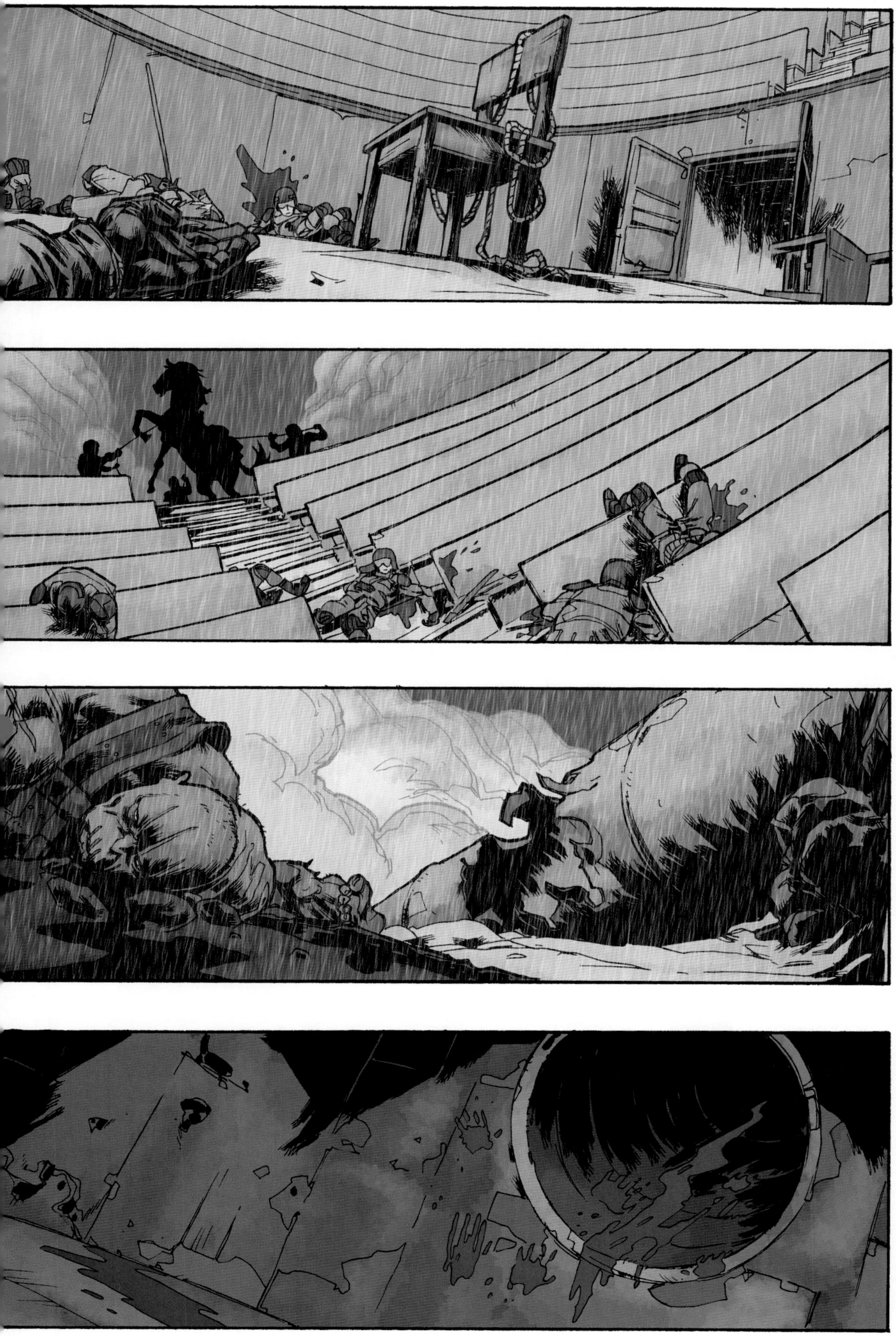

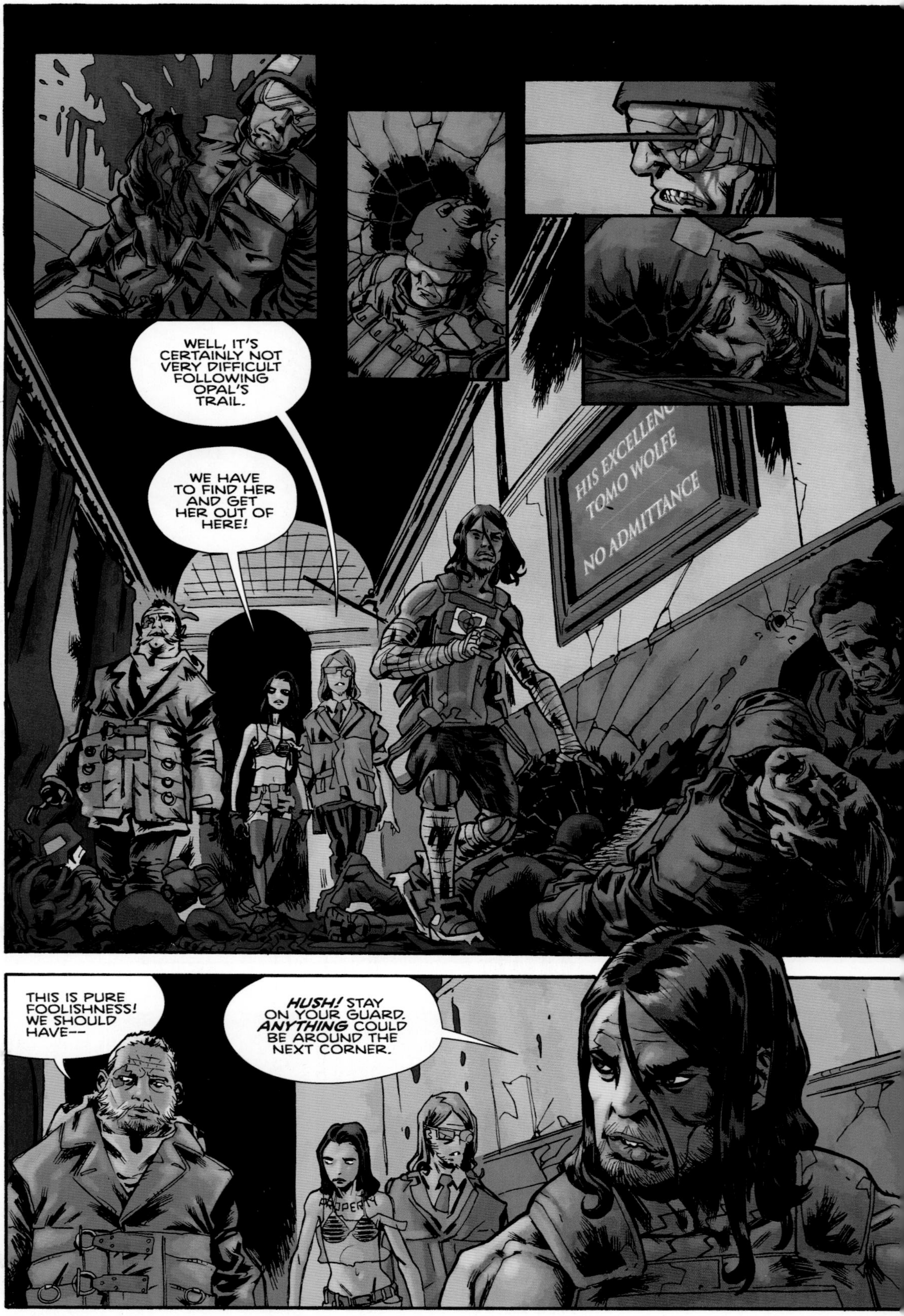
WELL, IT'S CERTAINLY NOT VERY DIFFICULT FOLLOWING OPAL'S TRAIL.
WE HAVE TO FIND HER AND GET HER OUT OF HERE!
HIS EXCELLENC
TOMO WOLFE
NO ADMITTANCE
THIS IS PURE FOOLISHNESS! WE SHOULD HAVE--
HUSH! STAY ON YOUR GUARD. ANYTHING COULD BE AROUND THE NEXT CORNER.
PROPERTY

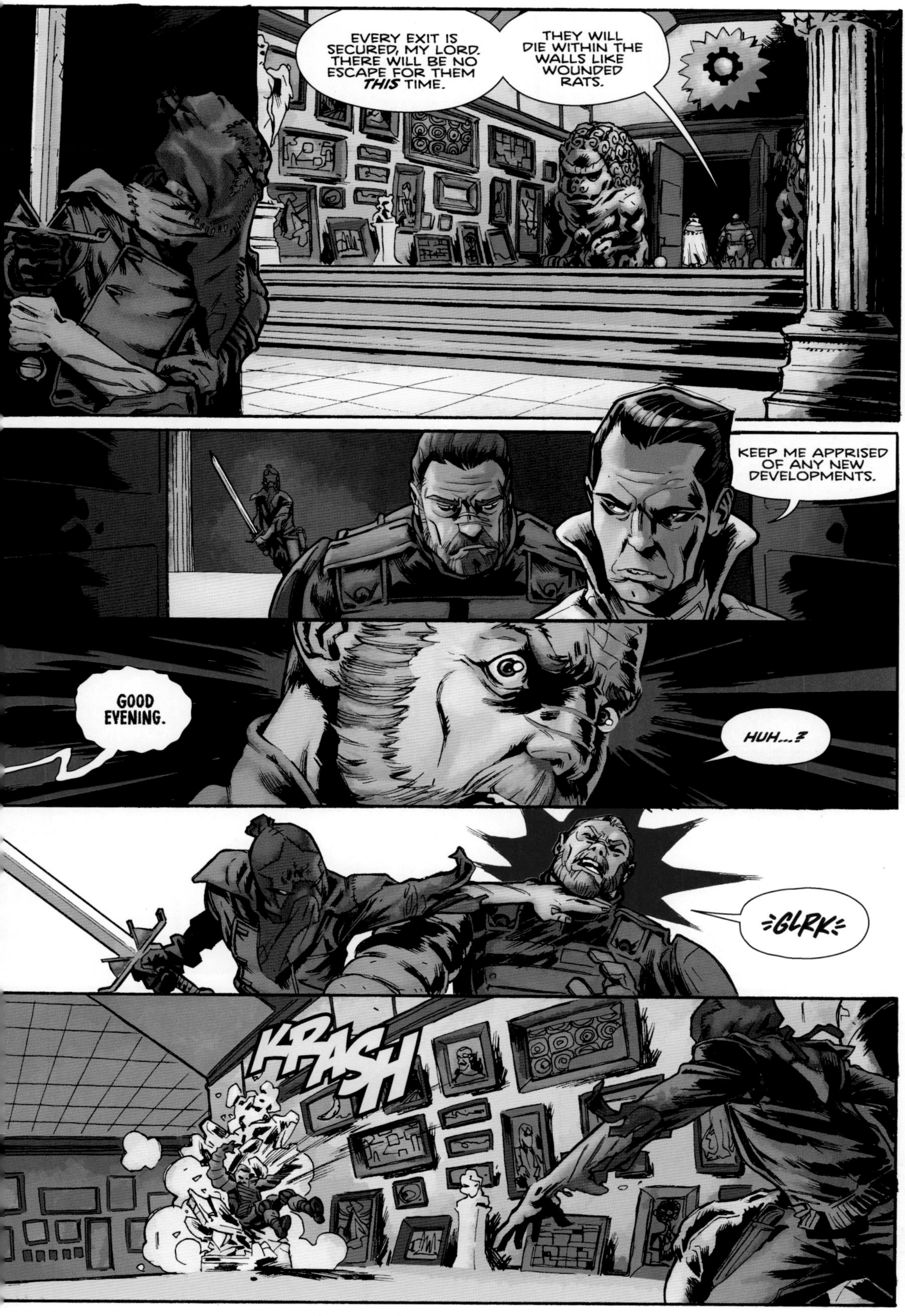
EVERY EXIT IS SECURED, MY LORD. THERE WILL BE NO ESCAPE FOR THEM THIS TIME.
THEY WILL DIE WITHIN THE WALLS LIKE WOUNDED RATS.
KEEP ME APPRISED OF ANY NEW DEVELOPMENTS.
GOOD EVENING.
HUH...?
GLRK
KRASH

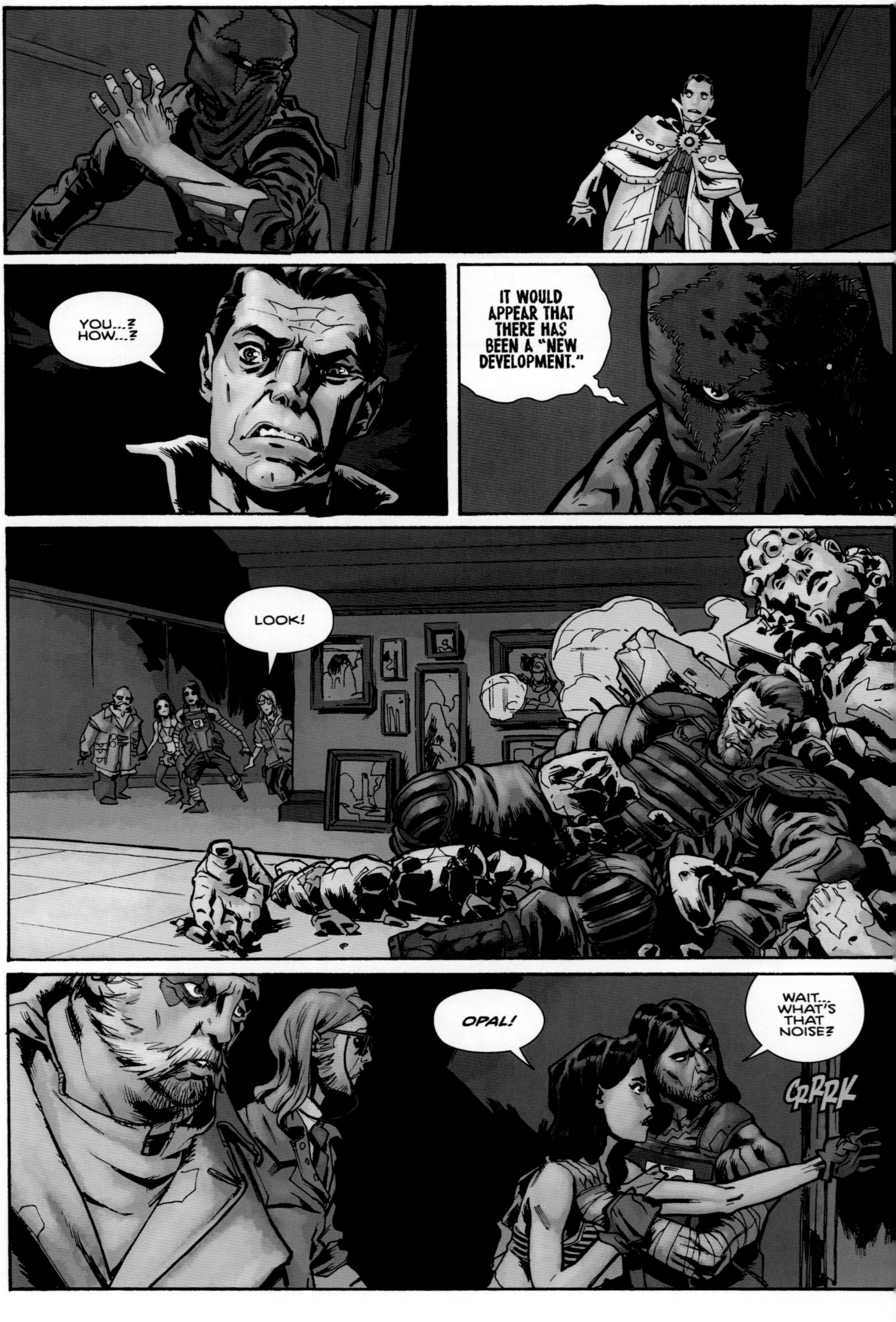

YOU...? HOW...?
IT WOULD APPEAR THAT THERE HAS BEEN A "NEW DEVELOPMENT."
LOOK!
OPAL!
WAIT... WHAT'S THAT NOISE?
CRRRK

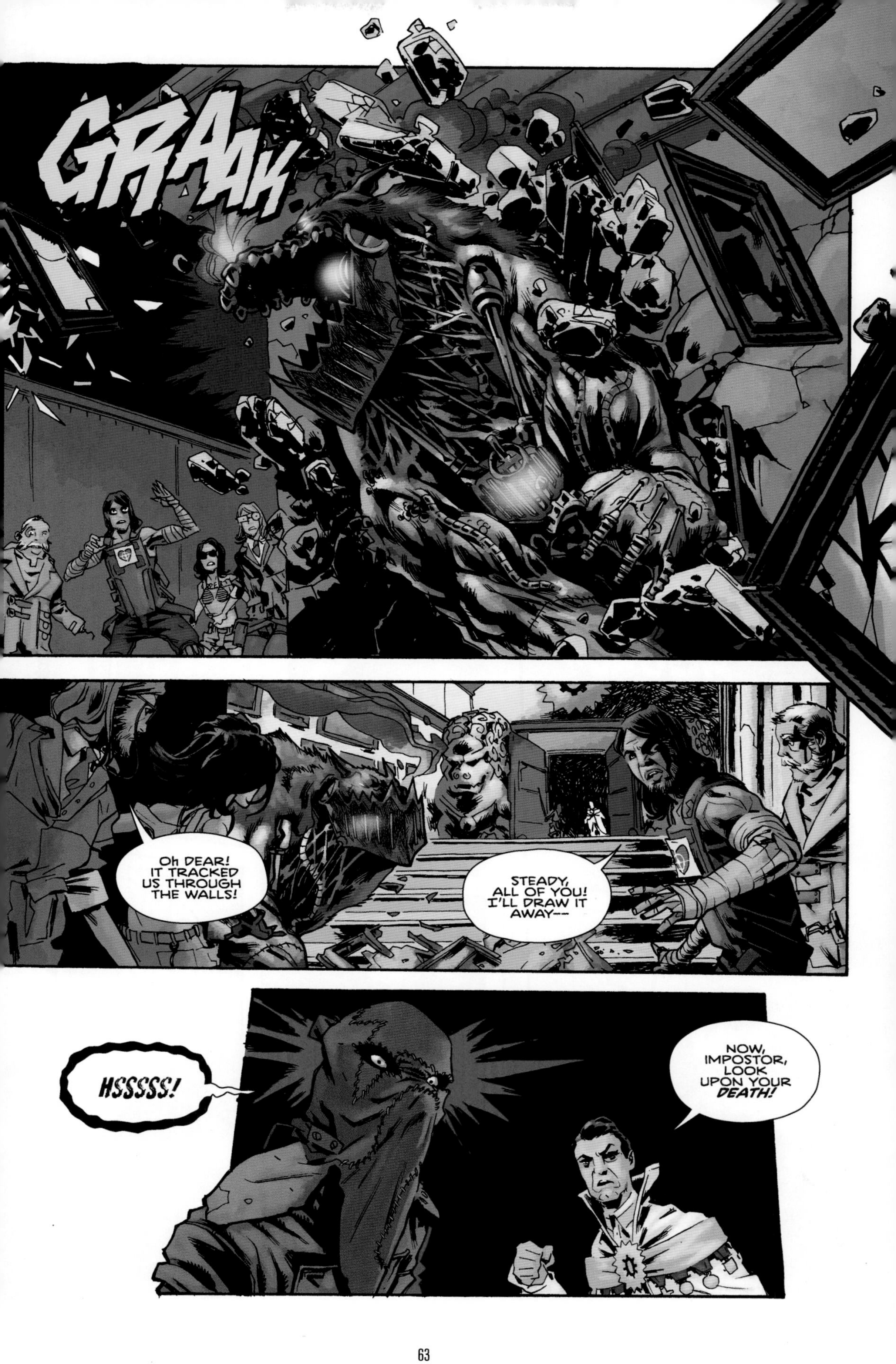
GRAAK
Oh DEAR! IT TRACKED US THROUGH THE WALLS!
STEADY, ALL OF YOU! I'LL DRAW IT AWAY--
HSSSSS!
NOW, IMPOSTOR, LOOK UPON YOUR DEATH!

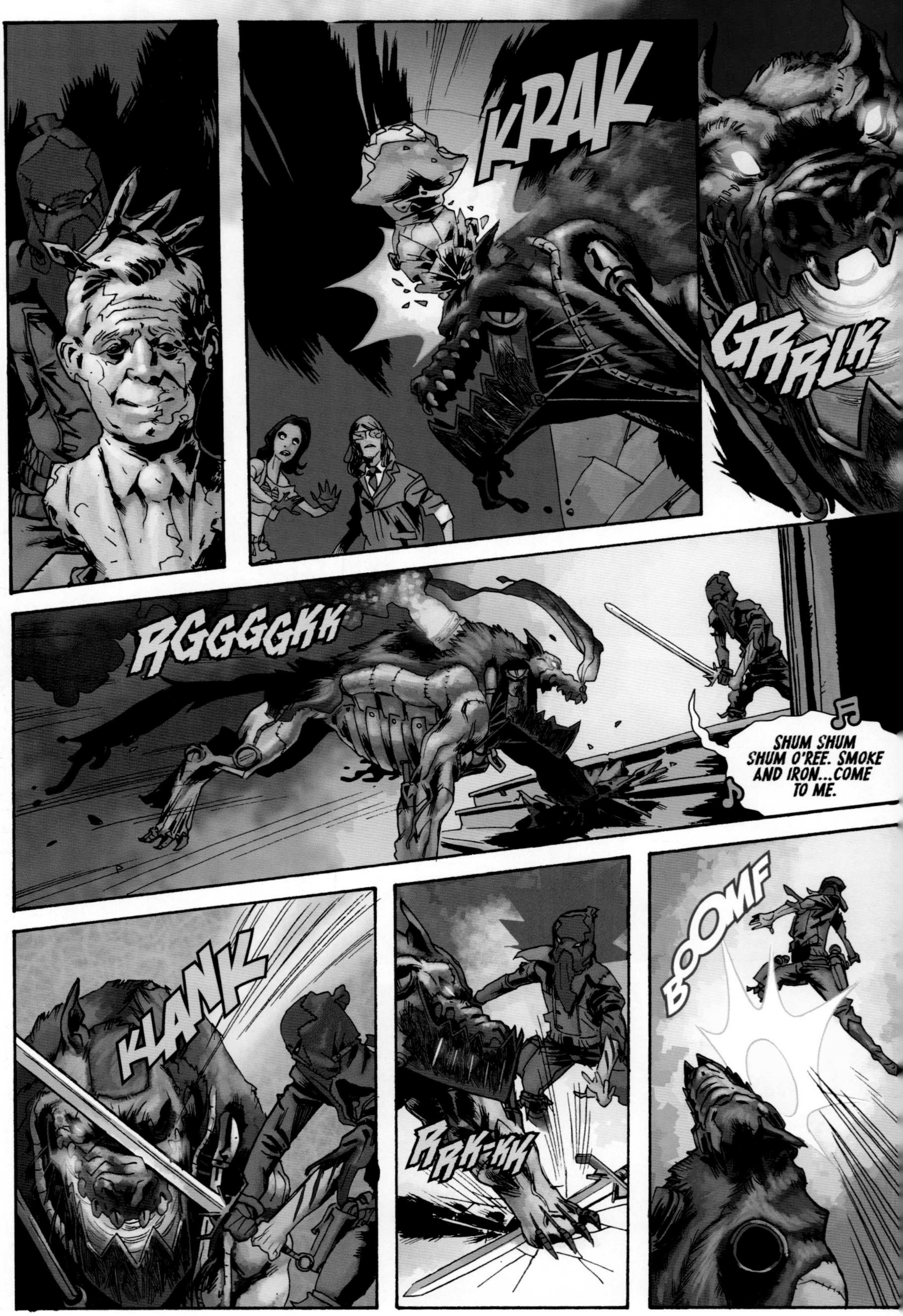
KRAK
GRRLK
RGGGGKK
SHUM SHUM SHUM O'REE. SMOKE AND IRON...COME TO ME.
KLANK
RRK-KK
BOOMF

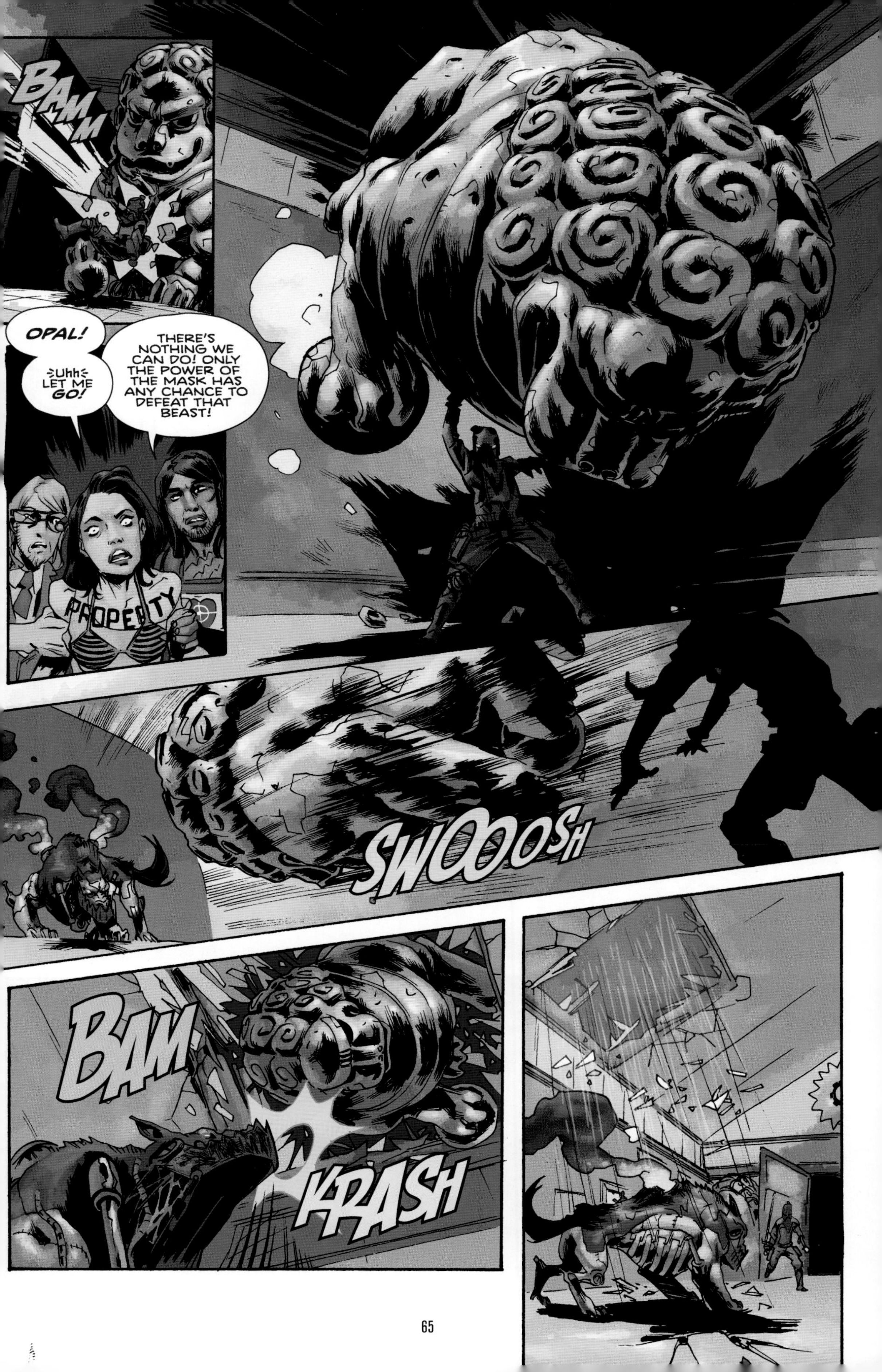
BAMM
OPAL!
Uhh LET ME GO!
THERE'S NOTHING WE CAN DO! ONLY THE POWER OF THE MASK HAS ANY CHANCE TO DEFEAT THAT BEAST!
PROPERTY
SWOOOOSH
BAM
KRASH

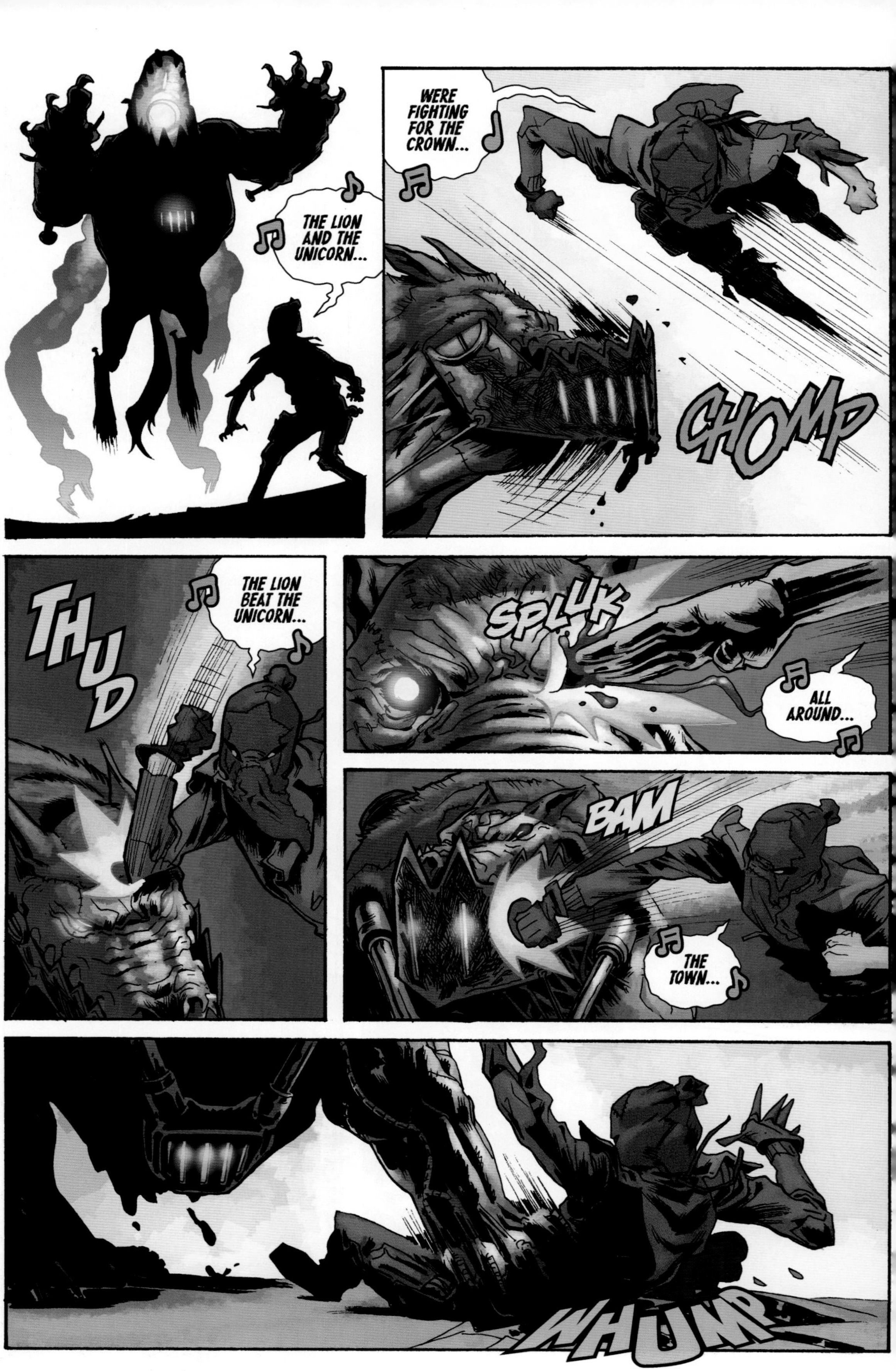
THE LION AND THE UNICORN...
WERE FIGHTING FOR THE CROWN...
CHOMP
THUD
THE LION BEAT THE UNICORN...
SPLUK
ALL AROUND...
BAM
THE TOWN...
WHUMP

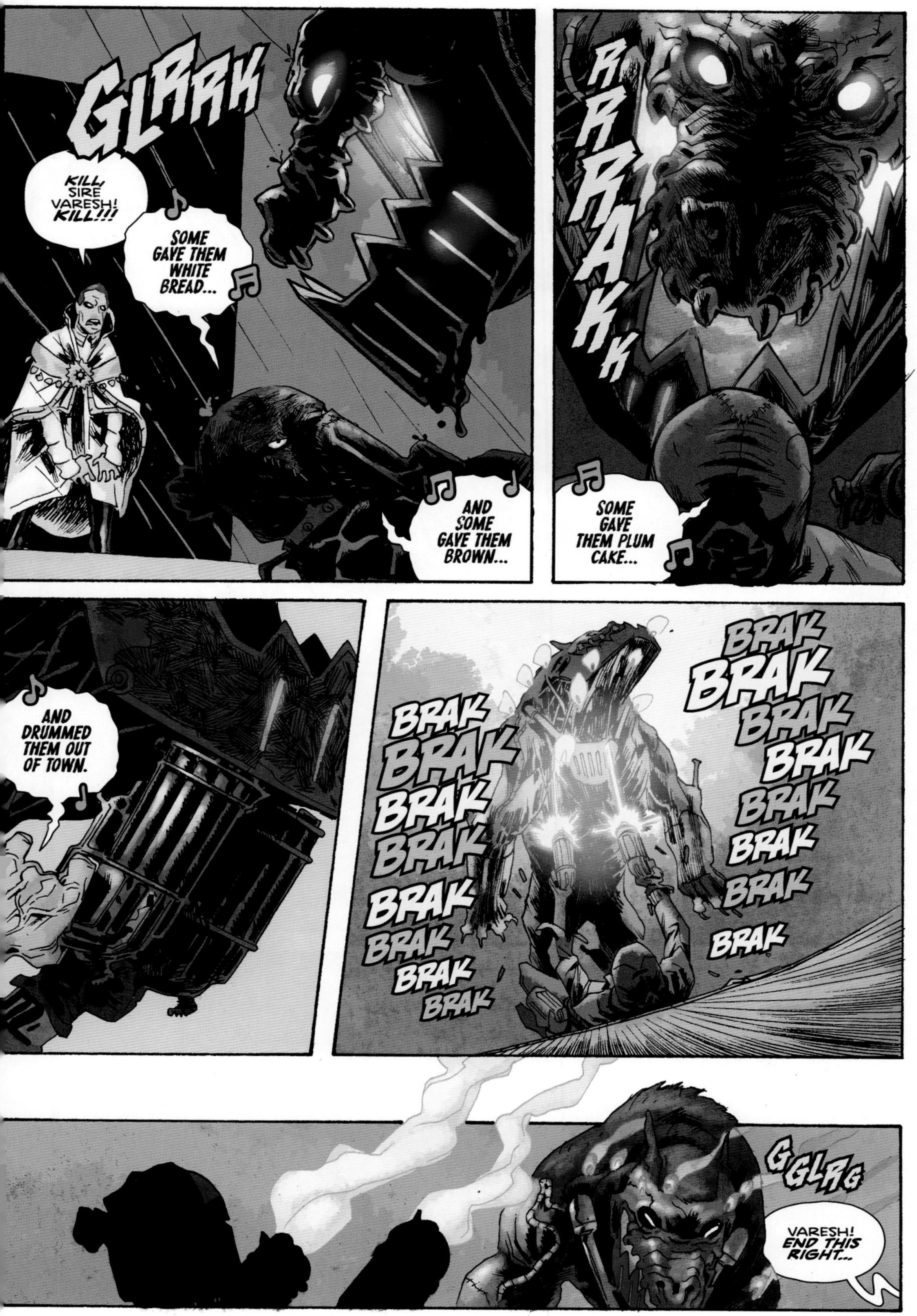
GLRRK
KILL, SIRE VARESH! KILL!!!
SOME GAVE THEM WHITE BREAD...
AND SOME GAVE THEM BROWN...
RRRRAKK
SOME GAVE THEM PLUM CAKE...
AND DRUMMED THEM OUT OF TOWN.
BRAK BRAK BRAK BRAK BRAK BRAK BRAK BRAK
BRAK BRAK BRAK BRAK BRAK BRAK BRAK BRAK
GGLRG
VARESH! END THIS RIGHT...

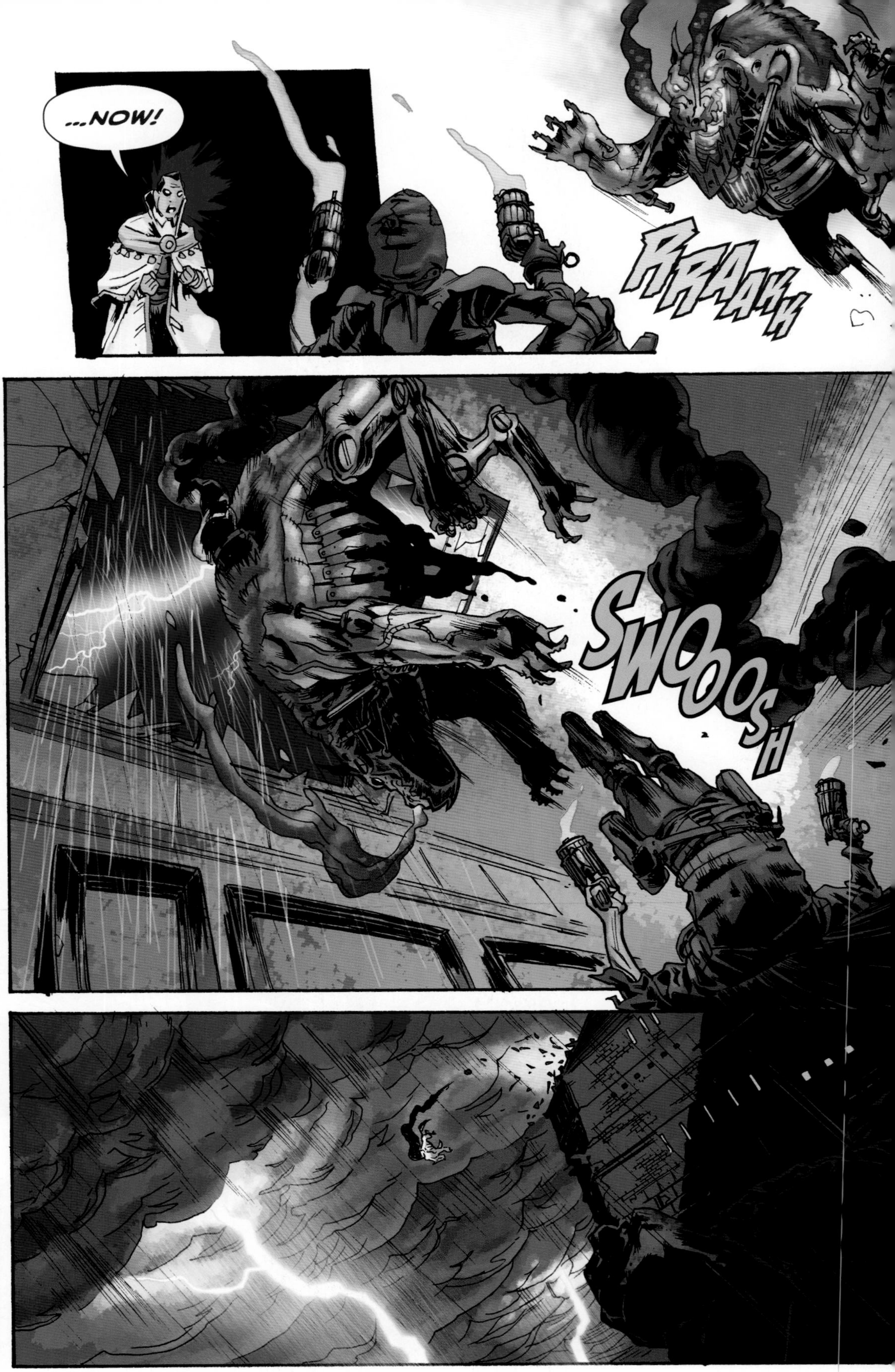
...NOW!
RRAAKK
SWOOOSH

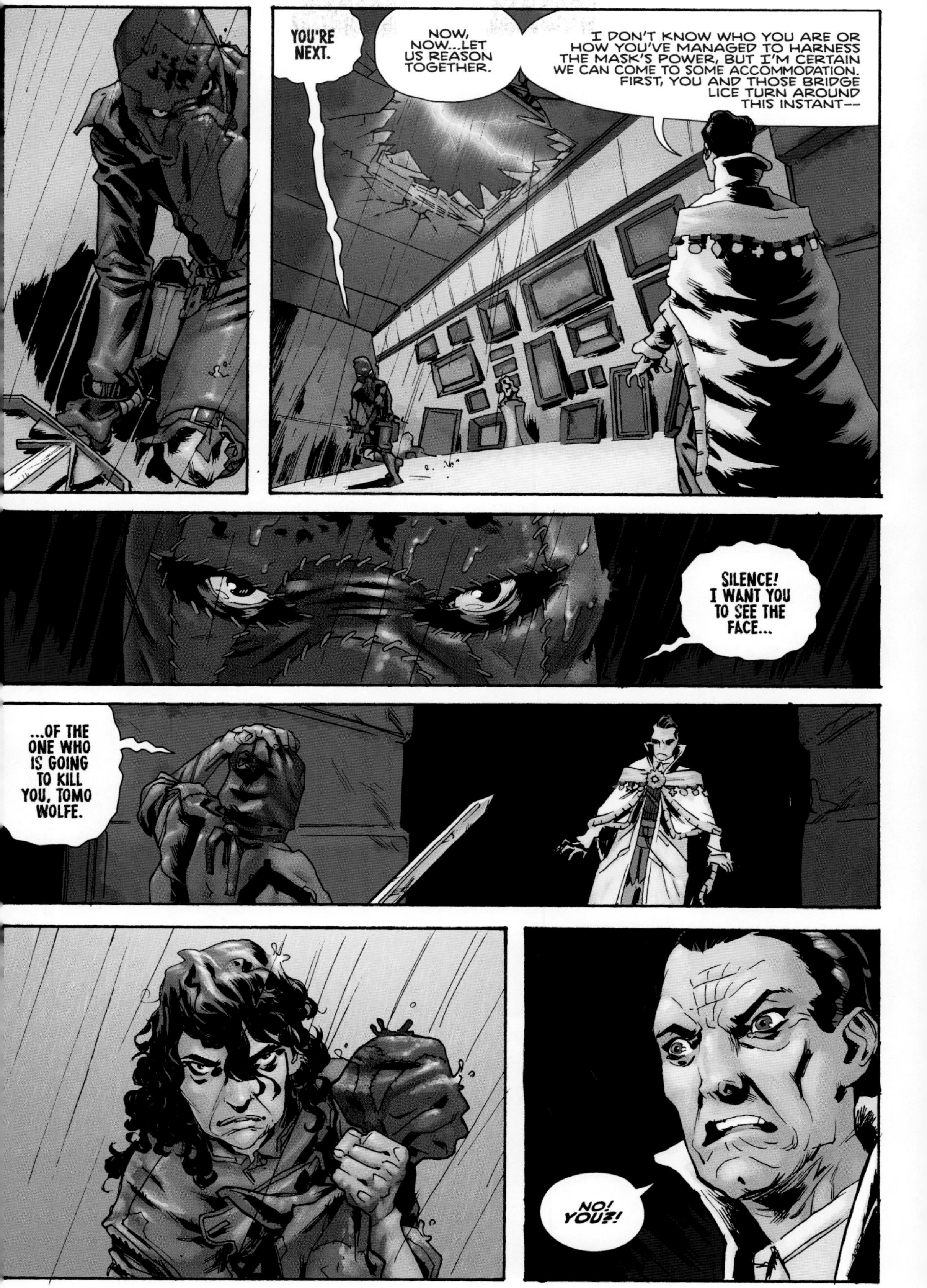
YOU'RE NEXT.
NOW, NOW...LET US REASON TOGETHER.
I DON'T KNOW WHO YOU ARE OR HOW YOU'VE MANAGED TO HARNESS THE MASK'S POWER, BUT I'M CERTAIN WE CAN COME TO SOME ACCOMMODATION. FIRST, YOU AND THOSE BRIDGE LICE TURN AROUND THIS INSTANT--
SILENCE! I WANT YOU TO SEE THE FACE...
...OF THE ONE WHO IS GOING TO KILL YOU, TOMO WOLFE.
NO! YOU?!

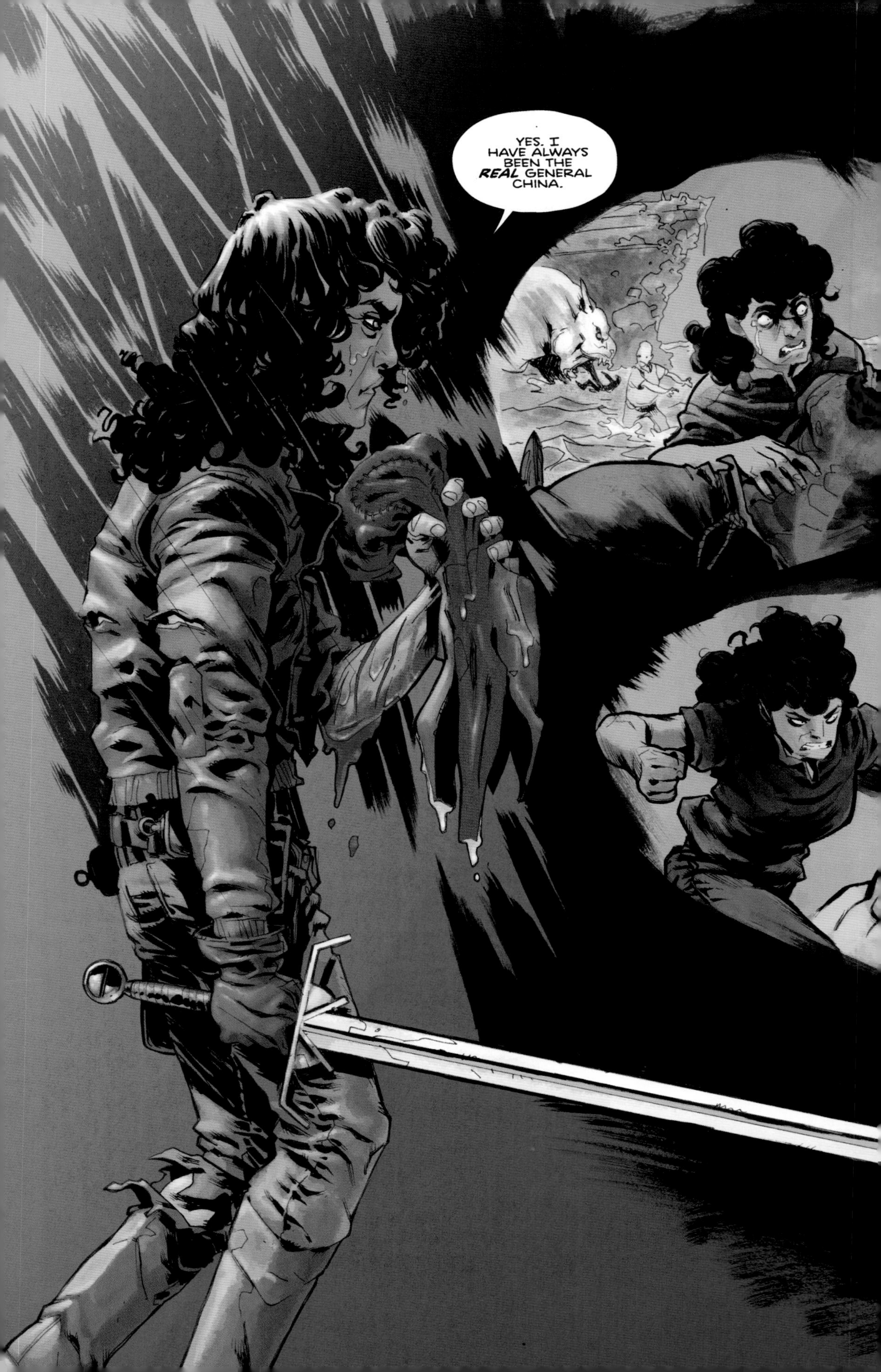
YES. I HAVE ALWAYS BEEN THE REAL GENERAL CHINA.

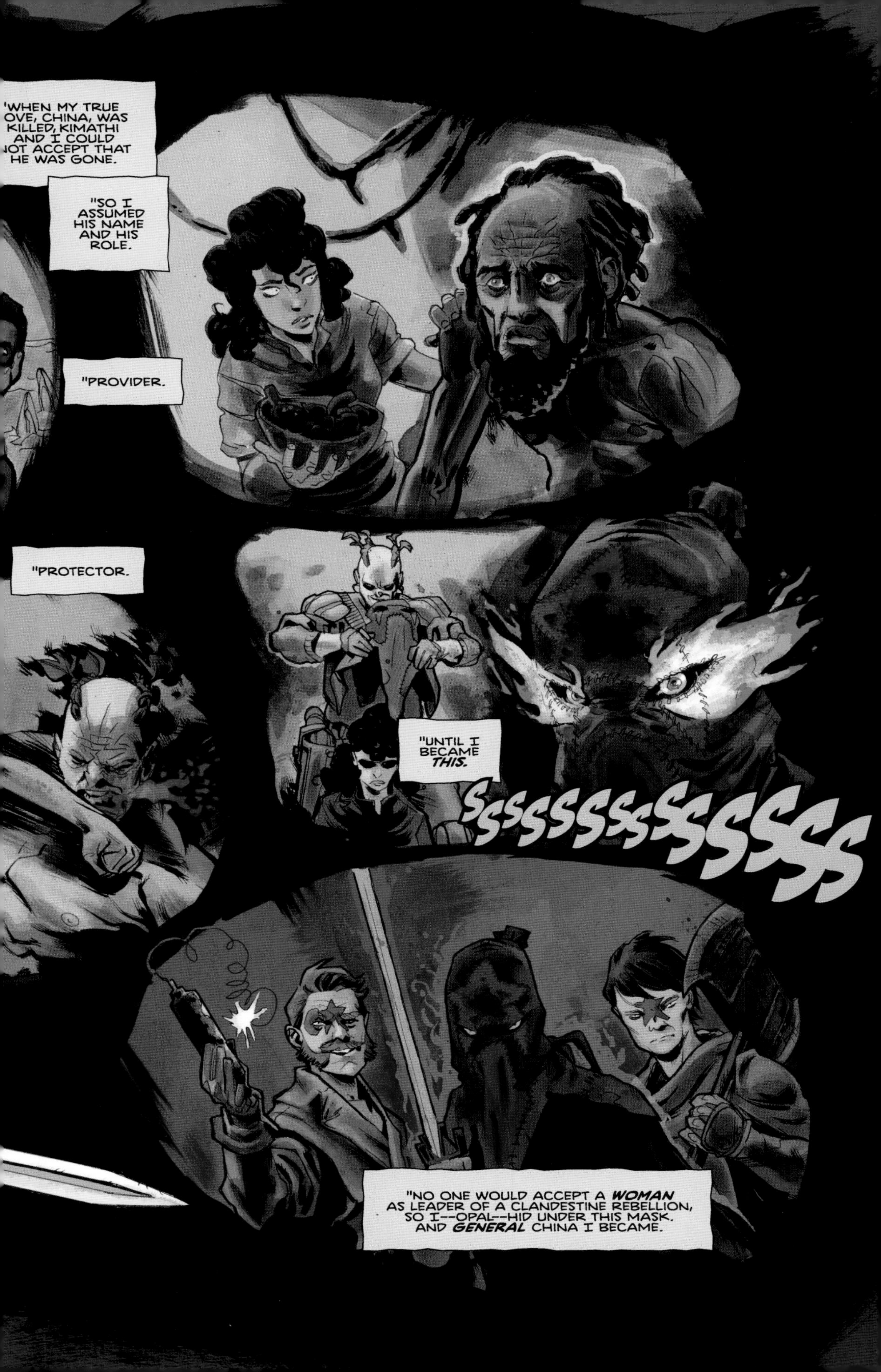
"WHEN MY TRUE LOVE, CHINA, WAS KILLED, KIMATHI AND I COULD NOT ACCEPT THAT HE WAS GONE.
"SO I ASSUMED HIS NAME AND HIS ROLE.
"PROVIDER.
"PROTECTOR.
"UNTIL I BECAME THIS.
SSSSSSSSSSSSS
"NO ONE WOULD ACCEPT A WOMAN AS LEADER OF A CLANDESTINE REBELLION, SO I--OPAL--HID UNDER THIS MASK. AND GENERAL CHINA I BECAME.

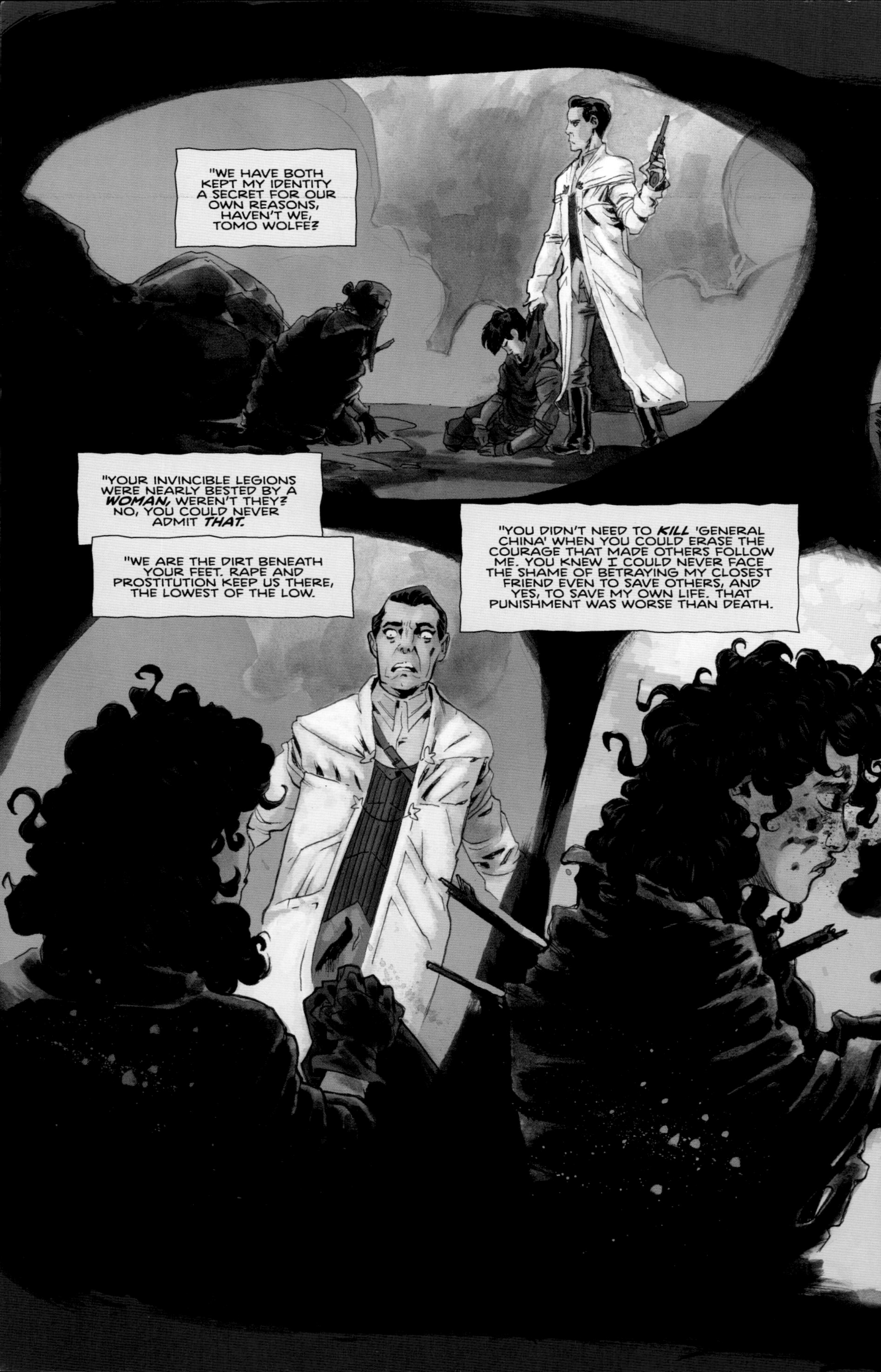
"WE HAVE BOTH KEPT MY IDENTITY A SECRET FOR OUR OWN REASONS, HAVEN'T WE, TOMO WOLFE?
"YOUR INVINCIBLE LEGIONS WERE NEARLY BESTED BY A WOMAN, WEREN'T THEY? NO, YOU COULD NEVER ADMIT THAT.
"WE ARE THE DIRT BENEATH YOUR FEET. RAPE AND PROSTITUTION KEEP US THERE, THE LOWEST OF THE LOW.
"YOU DIDN'T NEED TO KILL 'GENERAL CHINA' WHEN YOU COULD ERASE THE COURAGE THAT MADE OTHERS FOLLOW ME. YOU KNEW I COULD NEVER FACE THE SHAME OF BETRAYING MY CLOSEST FRIEND EVEN TO SAVE OTHERS, AND YES, TO SAVE MY OWN LIFE. THAT PUNISHMENT WAS WORSE THAN DEATH.

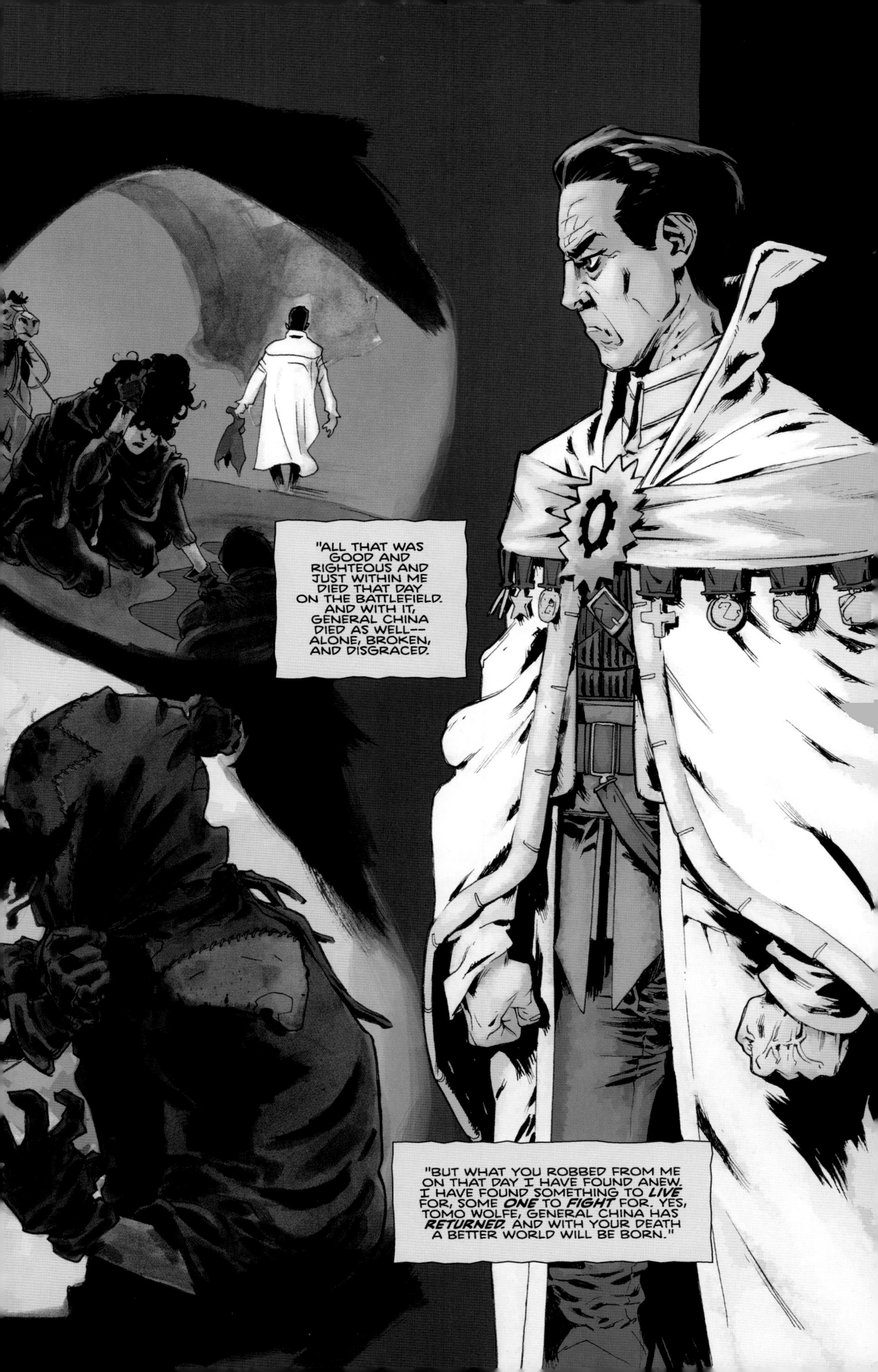
"ALL THAT WAS GOOD AND RIGHTEOUS AND JUST WITHIN ME DIED THAT DAY ON THE BATTLEFIELD. AND WITH IT, GENERAL CHINA DIED AS WELL-- ALONE, BROKEN, AND DISGRACED.
"BUT WHAT YOU ROBBED FROM ME ON THAT DAY I HAVE FOUND ANEW. I HAVE FOUND SOMETHING TO LIVE FOR, SOME ONE TO FIGHT FOR. YES, TOMO WOLFE, GENERAL CHINA HAS RETURNED. AND WITH YOUR DEATH A BETTER WORLD WILL BE BORN."

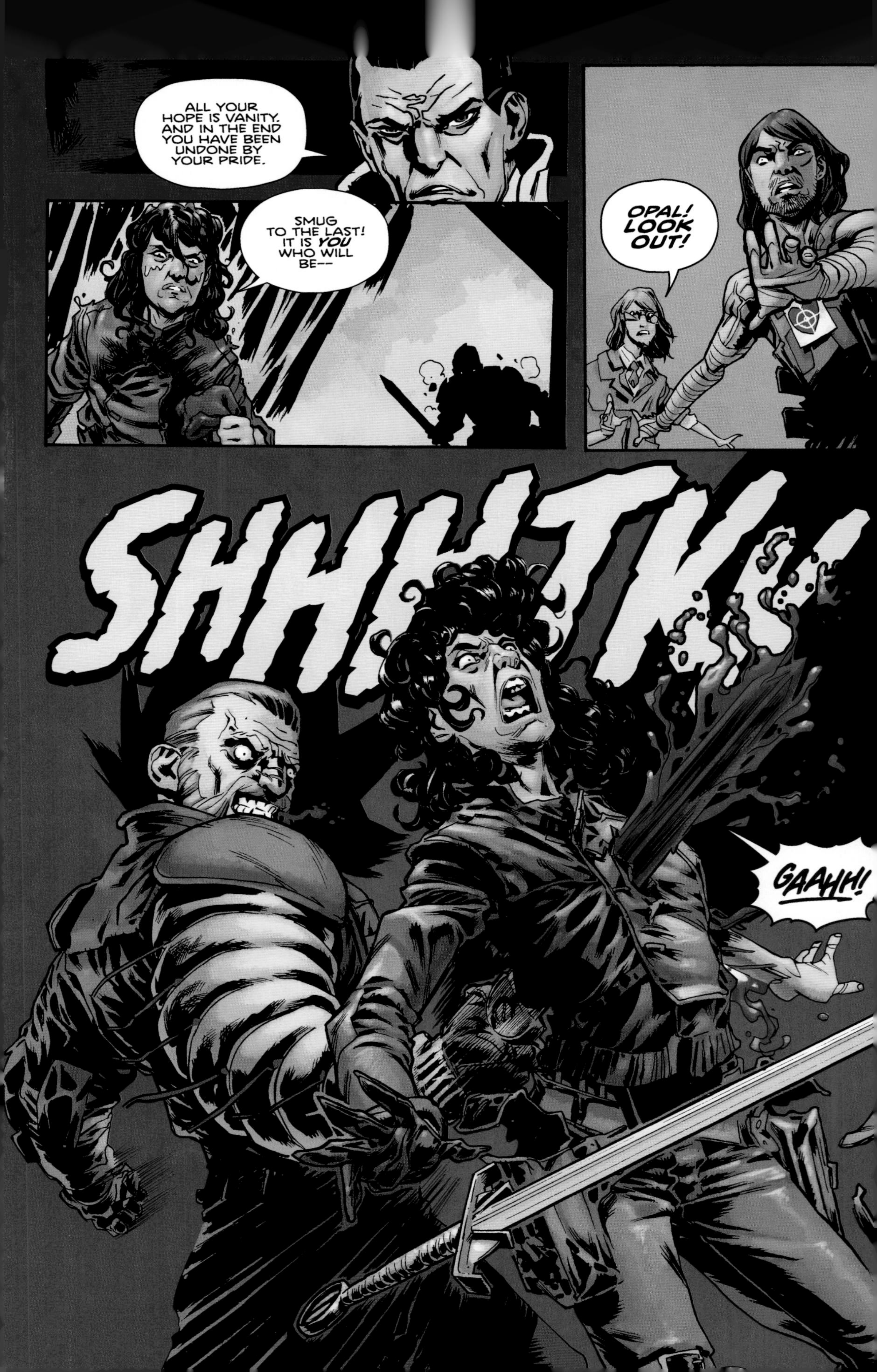
ALL YOUR HOPE IS VANITY. AND IN THE END YOU HAVE BEEN UNDONE BY YOUR PRIDE.
SMUG TO THE LAST! IT IS *YOU* WHO WILL BE--
OPAL! LOOK OUT!
GAAHH!

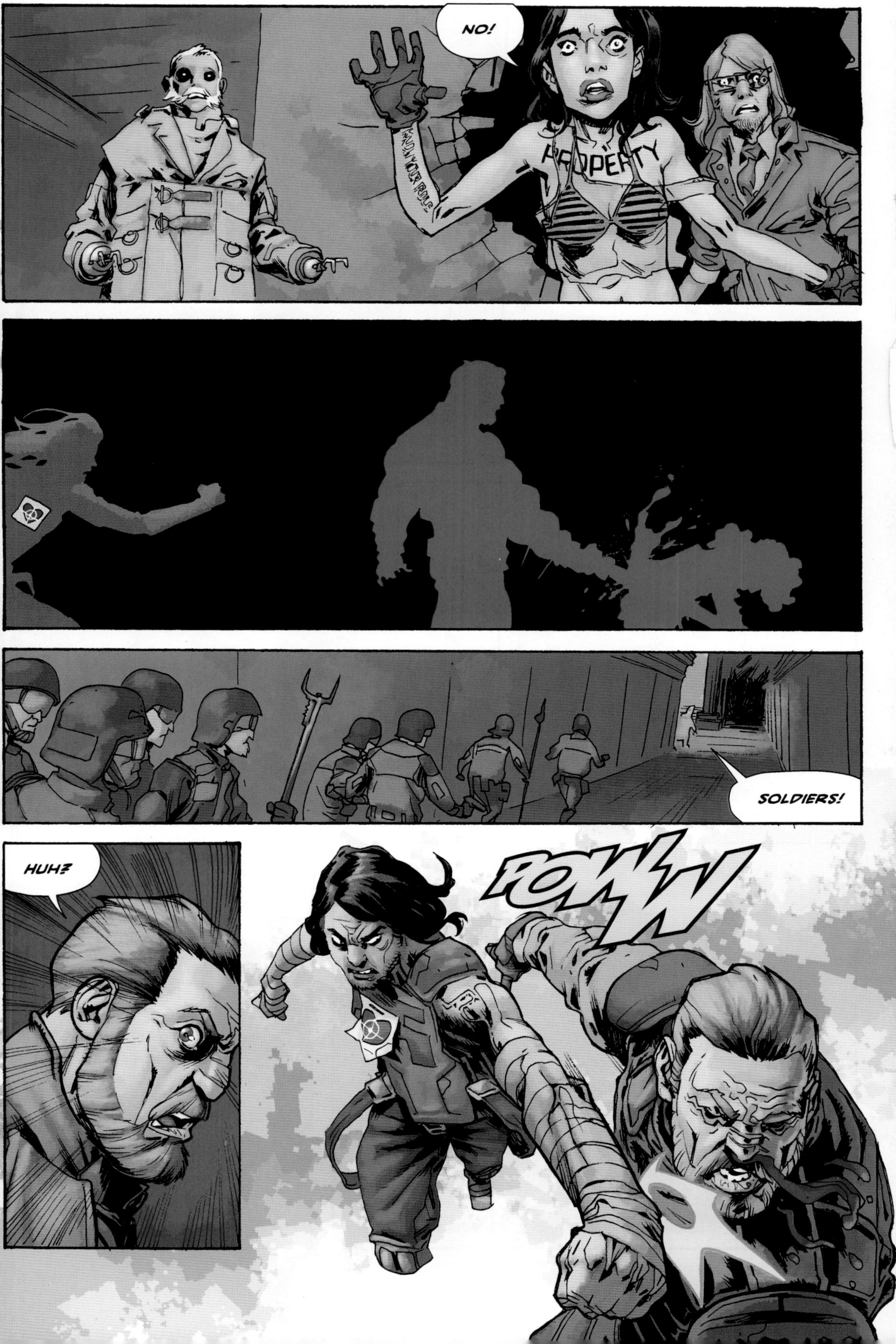
NO!
PROPERTY
SOLDIERS!
HUH?
POWW

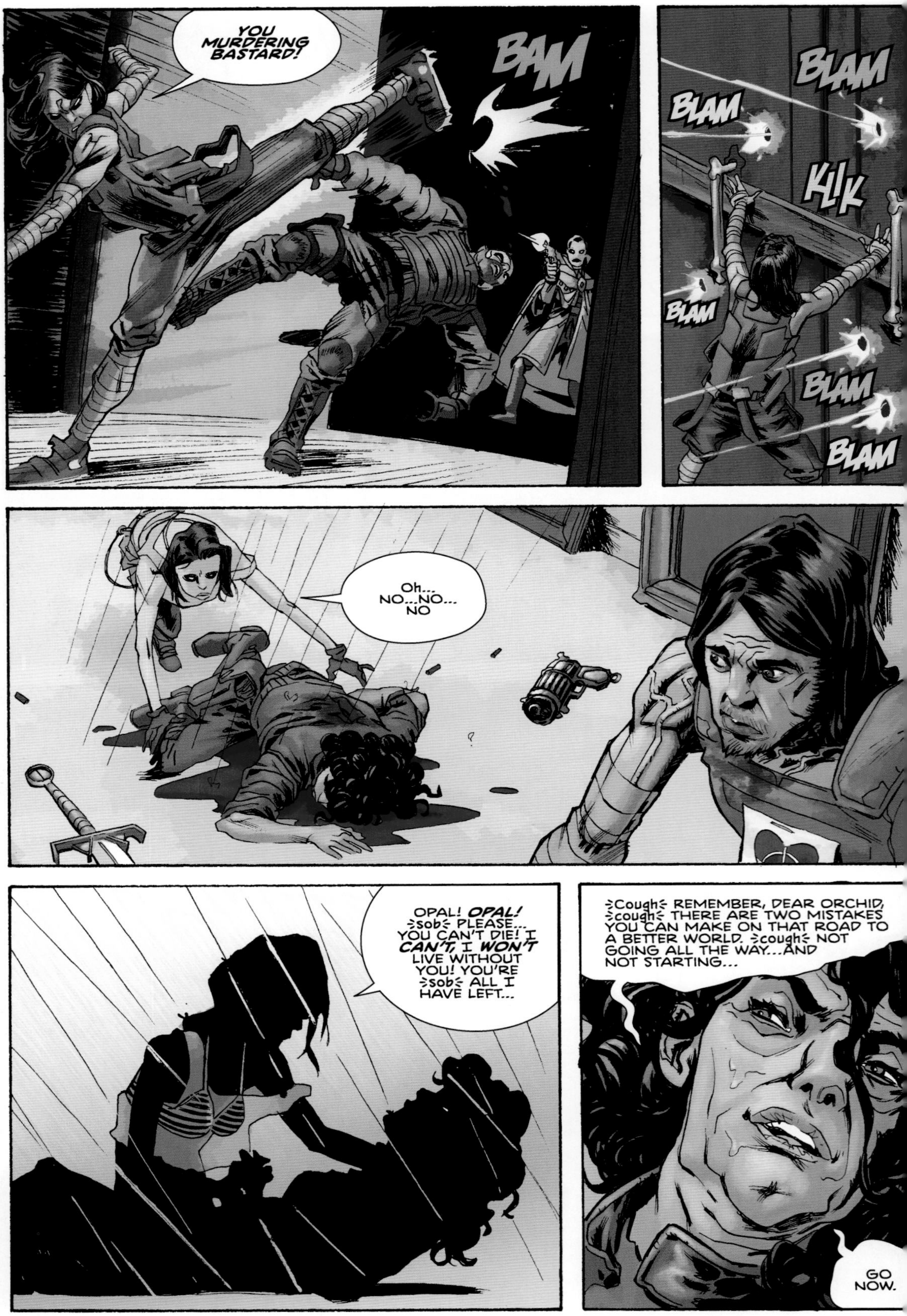
YOU MURDERING BASTARD!
BAM
BLAM
BLAM
KLIK
BLAM
BLAM
BLAM
Oh... NO...NO... NO
OPAL! OPAL! ⋛sob⋚ PLEASE... YOU CAN'T DIE! I CAN'T, I WON'T LIVE WITHOUT YOU! YOU'RE ⋛sob⋚ ALL I HAVE LEFT...
⋛Cough⋚ REMEMBER, DEAR ORCHID, ⋛cough⋚ THERE ARE TWO MISTAKES YOU CAN MAKE ON THAT ROAD TO A BETTER WORLD. ⋛cough⋚ NOT GOING ALL THE WAY...AND NOT STARTING...
GO NOW.

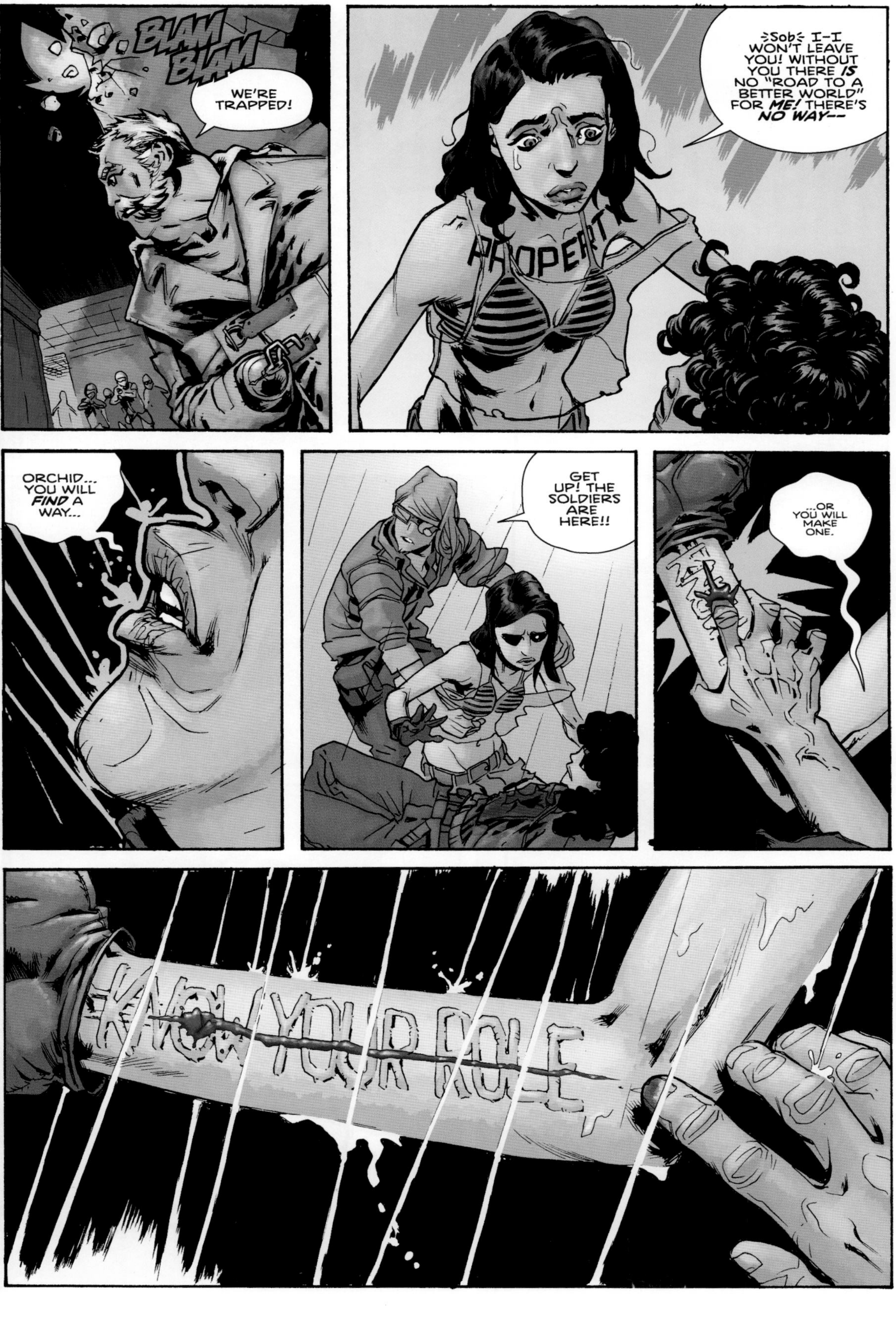
BLAM BLAM
WE'RE TRAPPED!
Sob I-I WON'T LEAVE YOU! WITHOUT YOU THERE IS NO "ROAD TO A BETTER WORLD" FOR ME! THERE'S NO WAY--
PROPERTY
ORCHID... YOU WILL FIND A WAY...
GET UP! THE SOLDIERS ARE HERE!!
...OR YOU WILL MAKE ONE.
KNOW YOUR ROLE

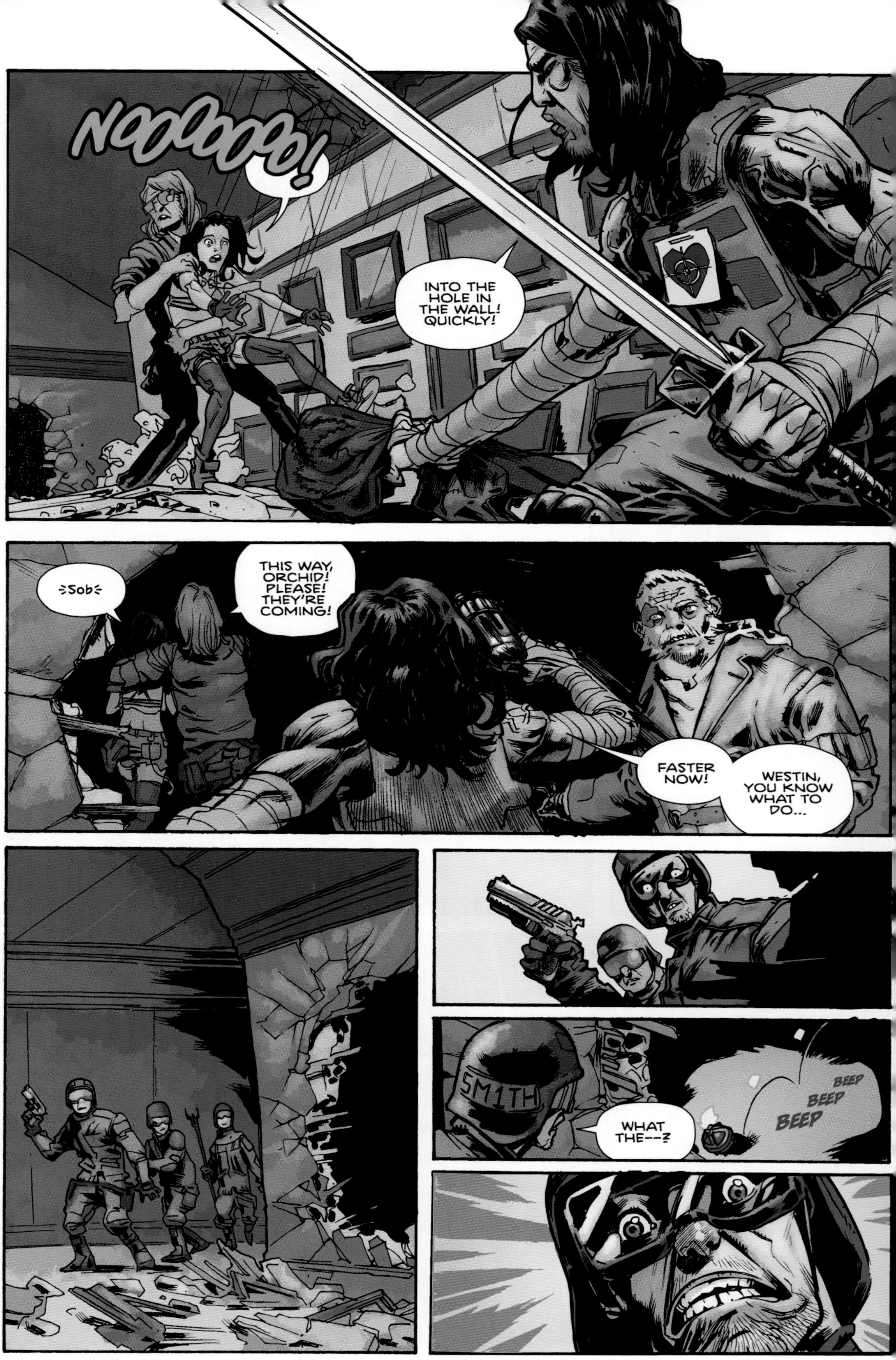
NOOOOOOO!
INTO THE HOLE IN THE WALL! QUICKLY!
⪢Sob⪡
THIS WAY, ORCHID! PLEASE! THEY'RE COMING!
FASTER NOW!
WESTIN, YOU KNOW WHAT TO DO...
SM1TH
BEEP
BEEP
BEEP
WHAT THE--?

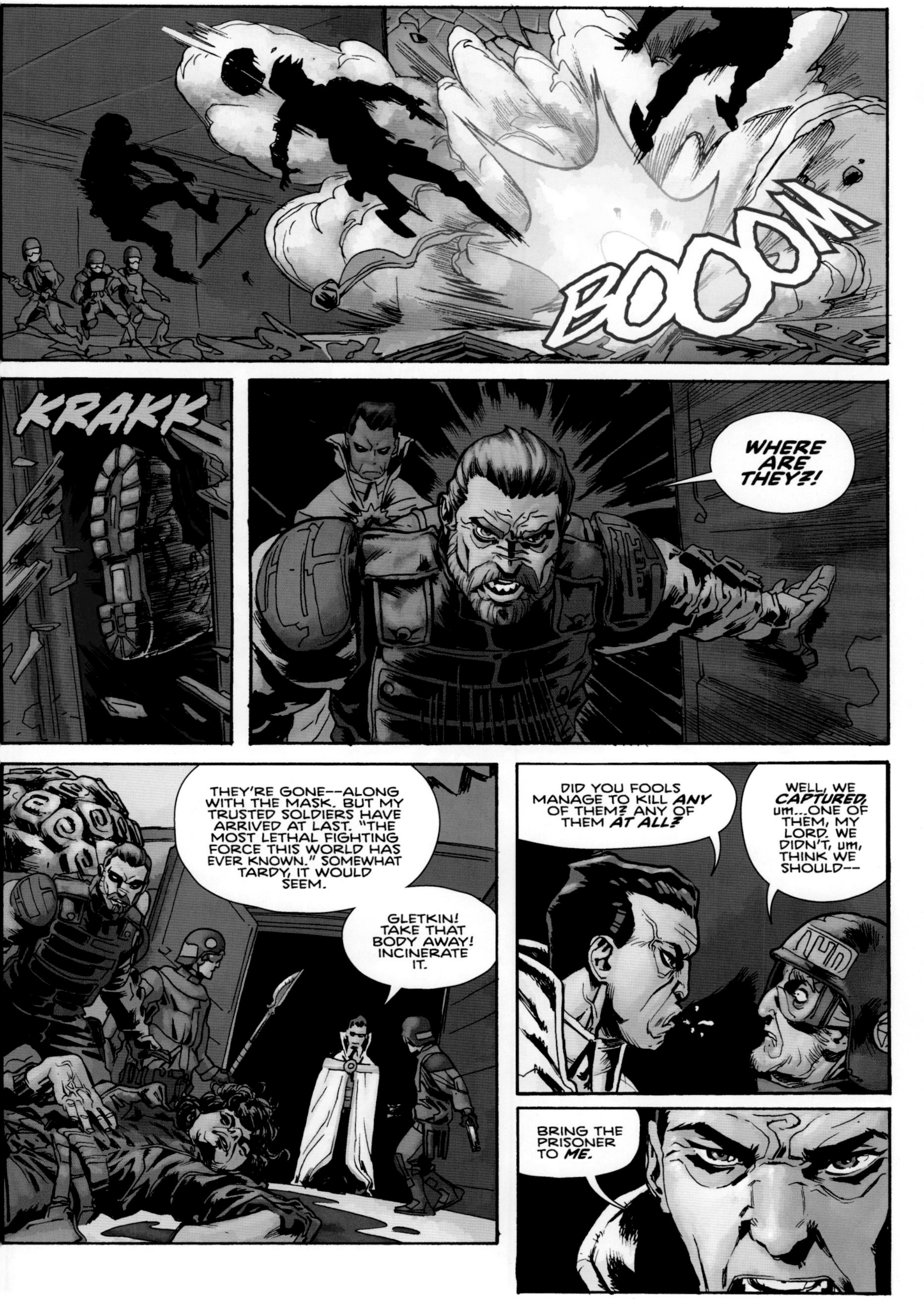
BOOOM
KRAKK
WHERE ARE THEY?!
THEY'RE GONE--ALONG WITH THE MASK. BUT MY TRUSTED SOLDIERS HAVE ARRIVED AT LAST. "THE MOST LETHAL FIGHTING FORCE THIS WORLD HAS EVER KNOWN." SOMEWHAT TARDY, IT WOULD SEEM.
GLETKIN! TAKE THAT BODY AWAY! INCINERATE IT.
DID YOU FOOLS MANAGE TO KILL *ANY* OF THEM? ANY OF THEM *AT ALL?*
WELL, WE *CAPTURED*, UM...ONE OF THEM, MY LORD. WE DIDN'T, UM, THINK WE SHOULD--
BRING THE PRISONER TO *ME.*

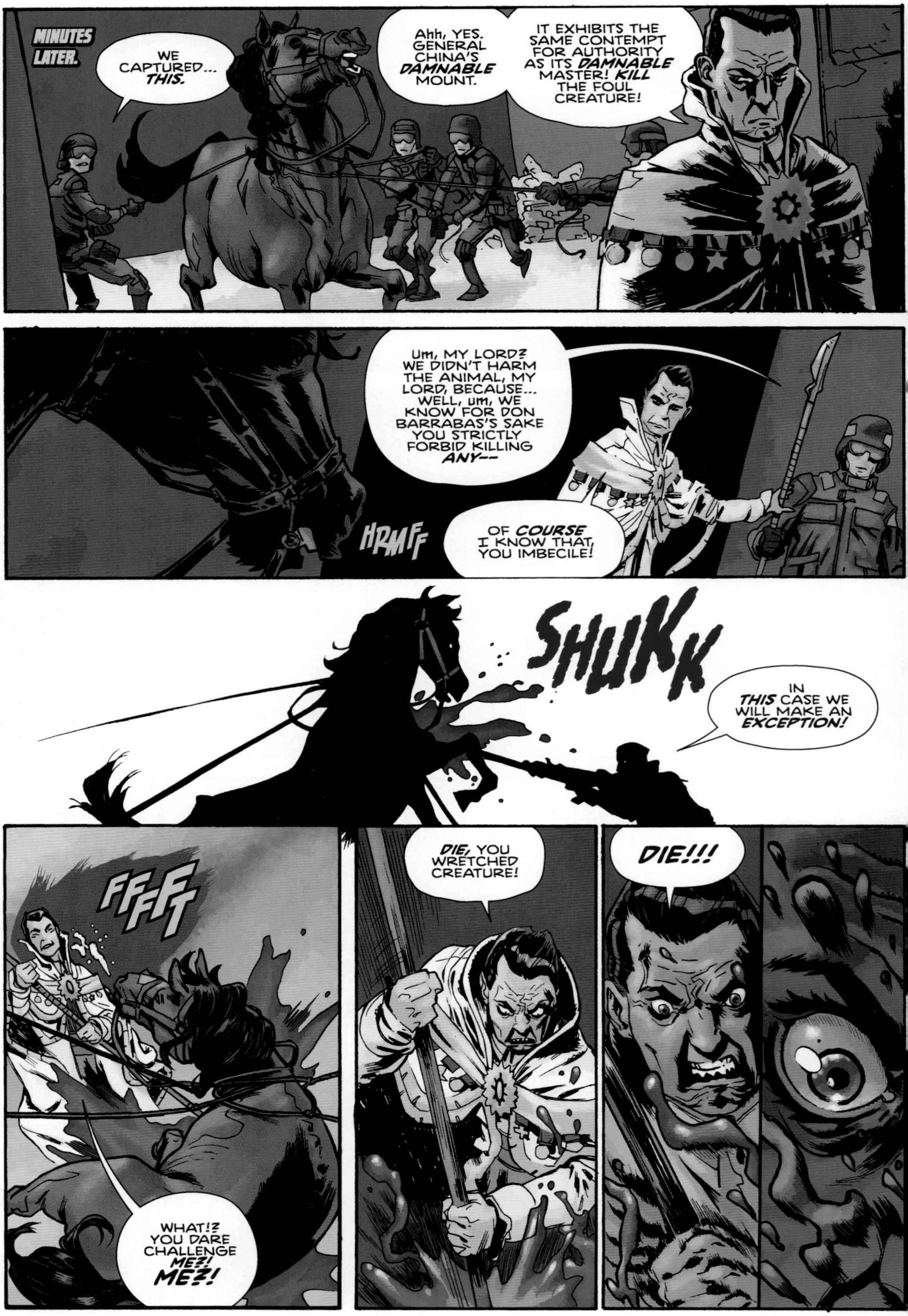
MINUTES LATER.
WE CAPTURED... THIS.
Ahh, YES. GENERAL CHINA'S DAMNABLE MOUNT.
IT EXHIBITS THE SAME CONTEMPT FOR AUTHORITY AS ITS DAMNABLE MASTER! KILL THE FOUL CREATURE!
Um, MY LORD? WE DIDN'T HARM THE ANIMAL, MY LORD, BECAUSE... WELL, um, WE KNOW FOR DON BARRABAS'S SAKE YOU STRICTLY FORBID KILLING ANY--
HRMFF
OF COURSE I KNOW THAT, YOU IMBECILE!
SHUKK
IN THIS CASE WE WILL MAKE AN EXCEPTION!
FFFFT
WHAT!? YOU DARE CHALLENGE ME?! ME?!
DIE, YOU WRETCHED CREATURE!
DIE!!!

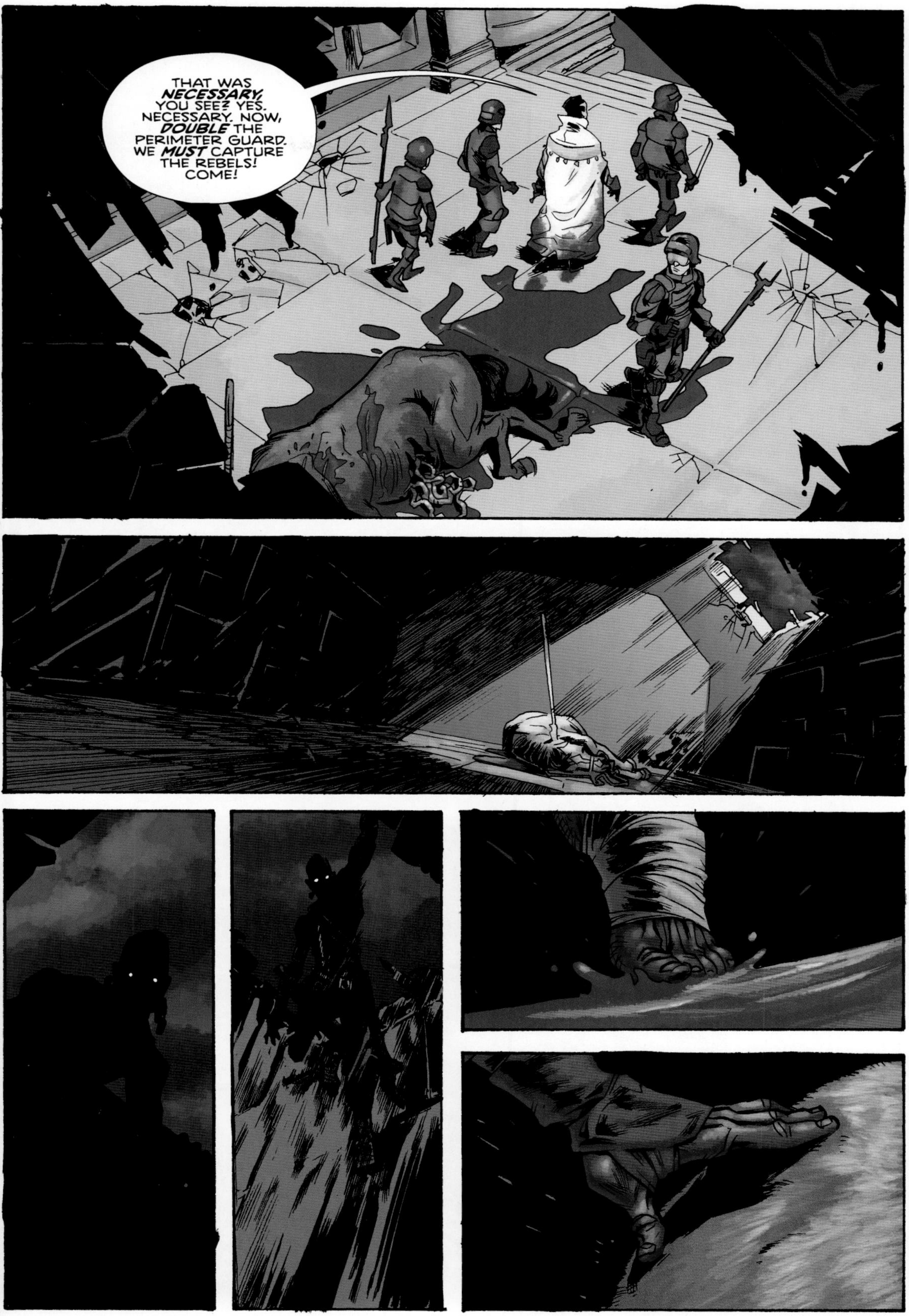
THAT WAS NECESSARY, YOU SEE? YES. NECESSARY. NOW, DOUBLE THE PERIMETER GUARD. WE MUST CAPTURE THE REBELS! COME!

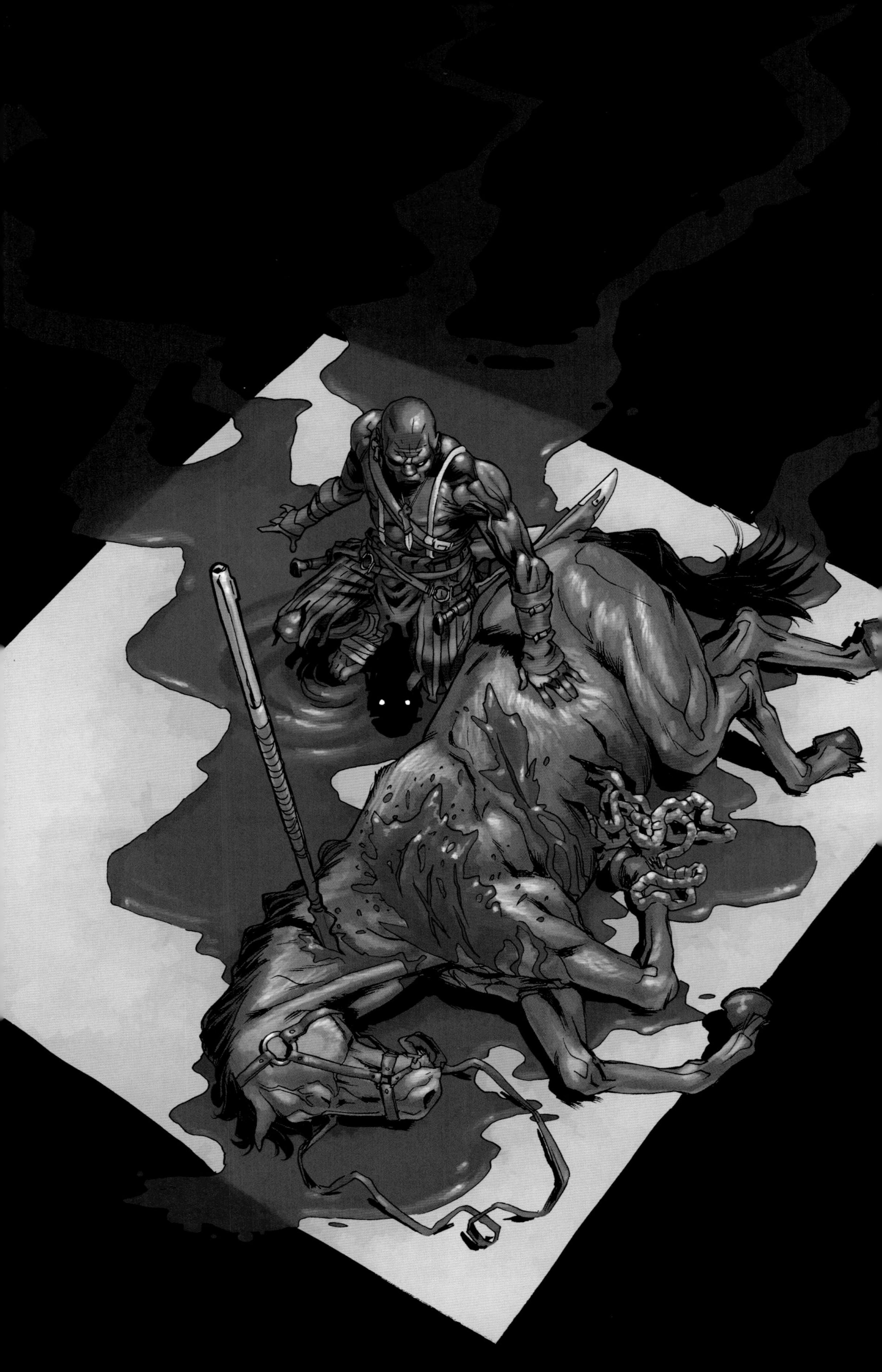

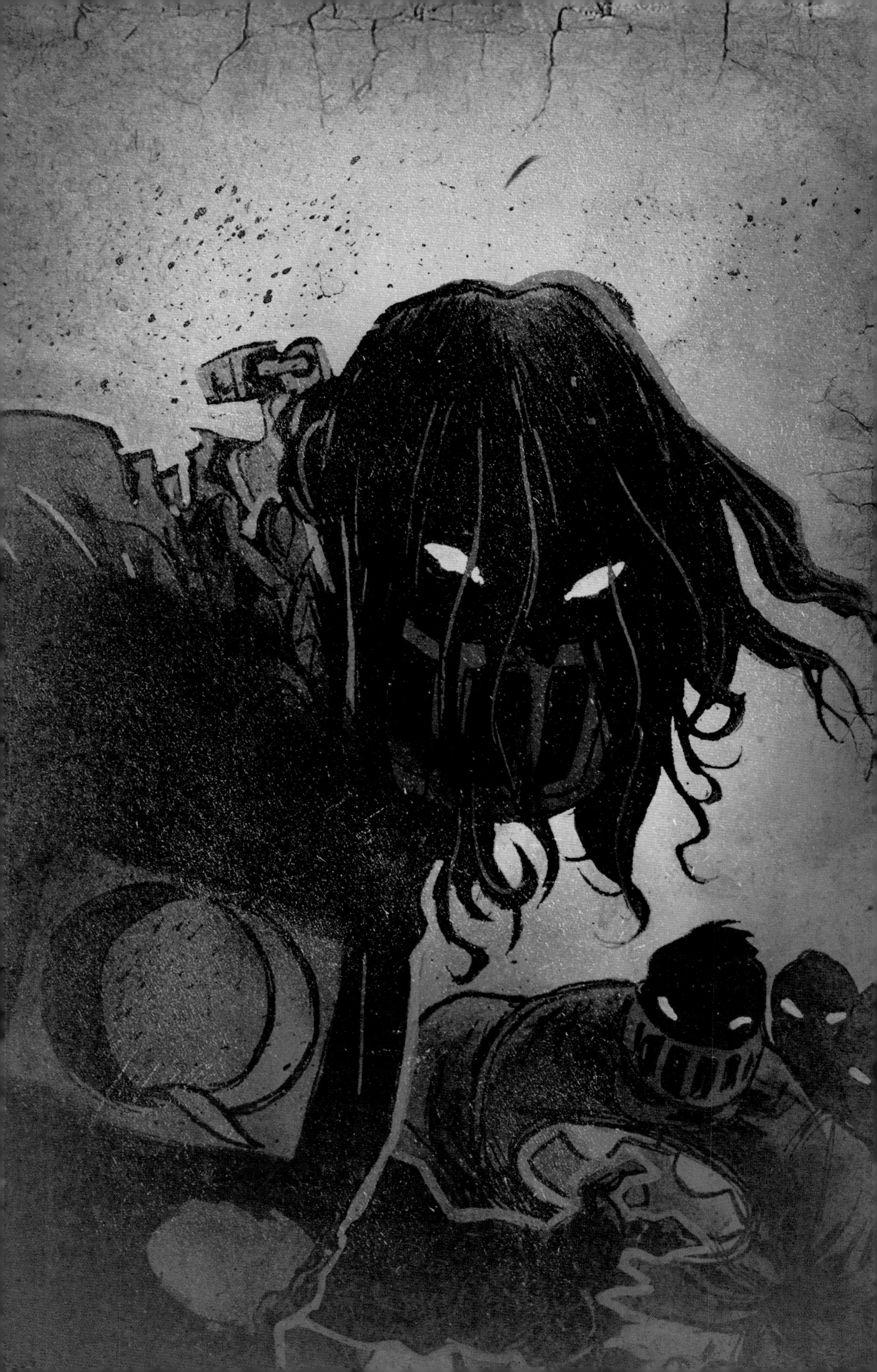

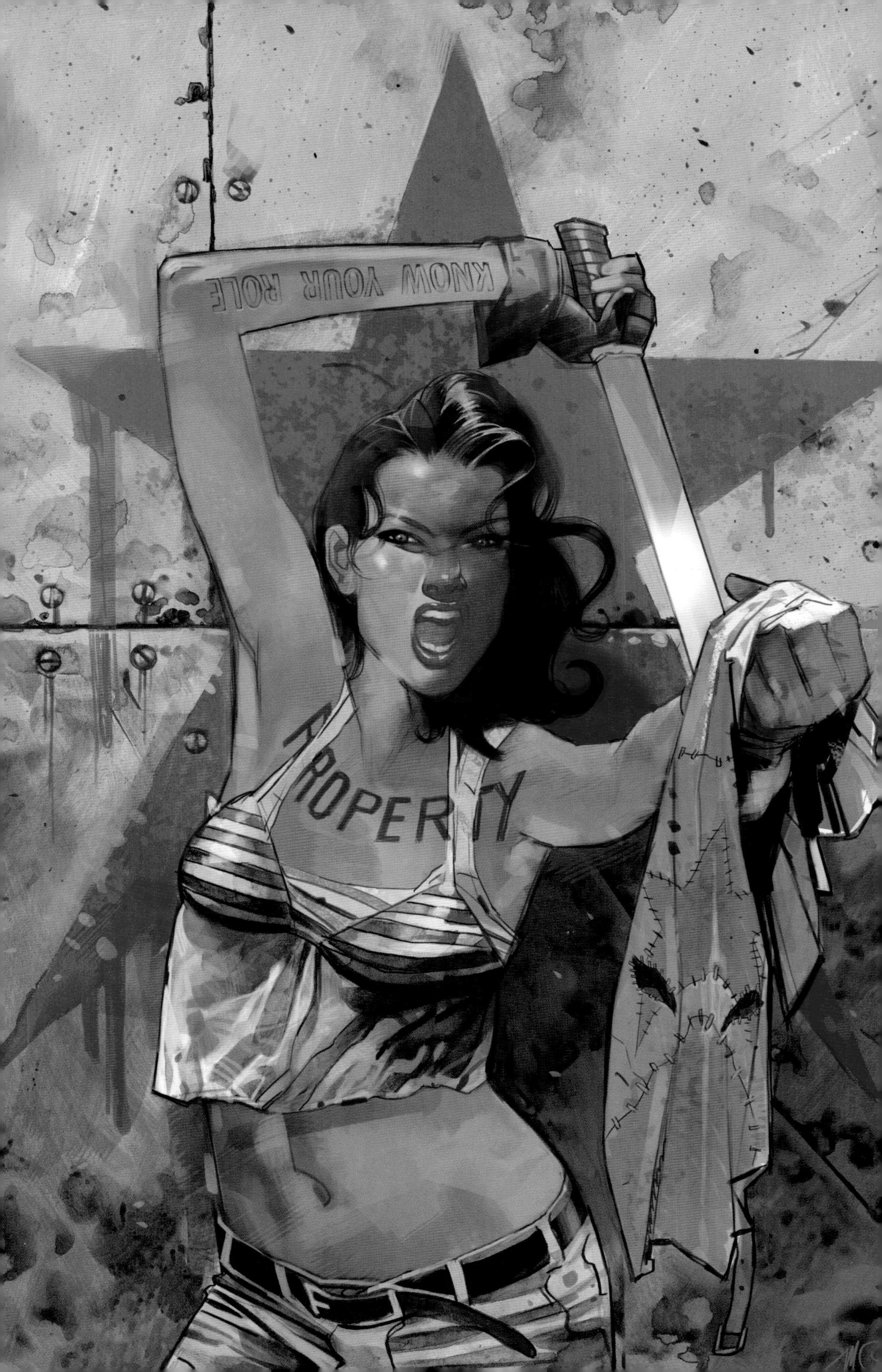
KNOW YOUR ROLE
PROPERTY

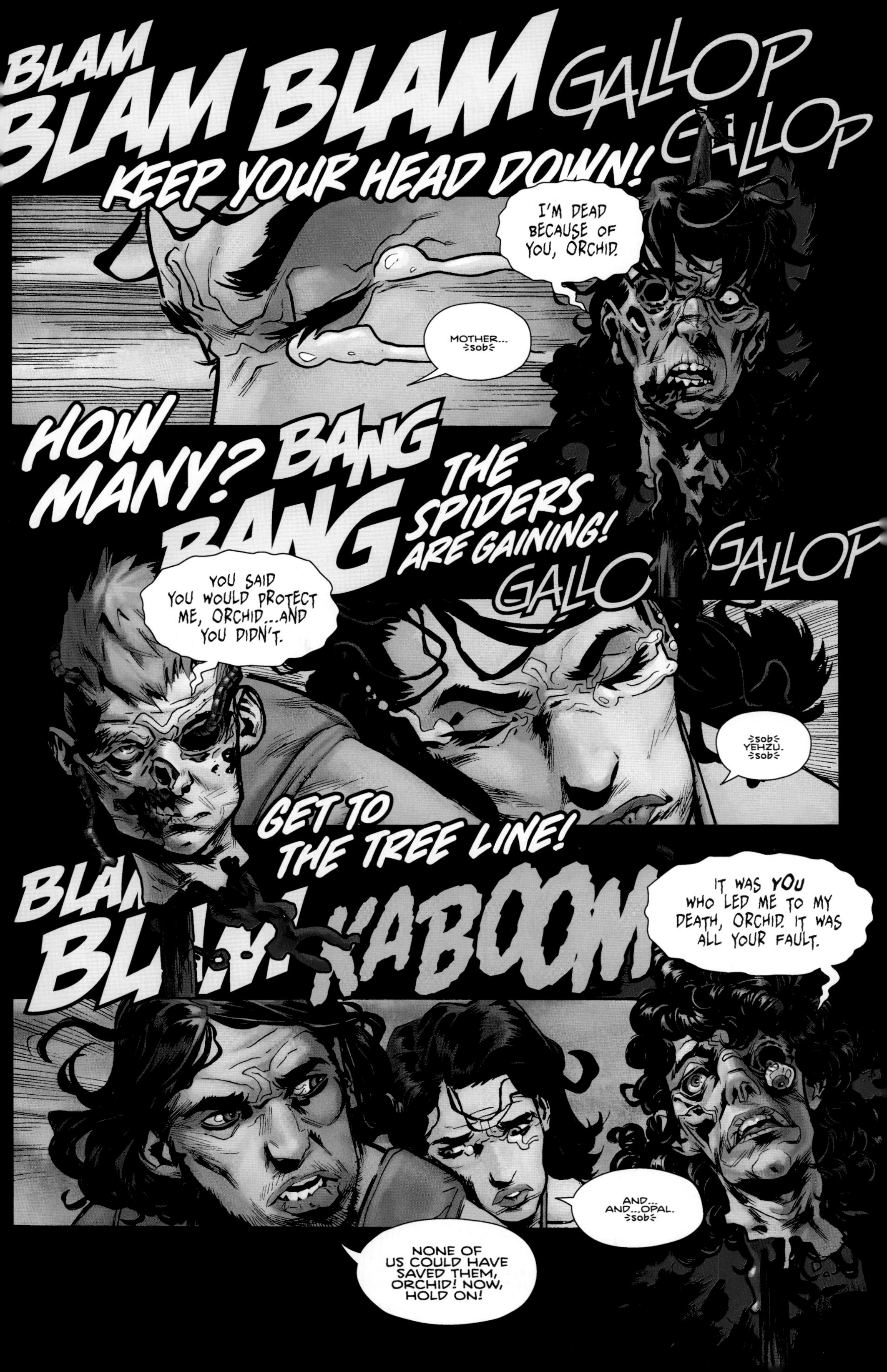
BLAM
BLAM BLAM
GALLOP
GALLOP
KEEP YOUR HEAD DOWN!
I'M DEAD BECAUSE OF YOU, ORCHID.
MOTHER... sob
HOW MANY?
BANG
BANG
THE SPIDERS ARE GAINING!
GALLOP
GALLOP
YOU SAID YOU WOULD PROTECT ME, ORCHID...AND YOU DIDN'T.
sob YEHZU. sob
GET TO THE TREE LINE!
KABOOM
IT WAS YOU WHO LED ME TO MY DEATH, ORCHID. IT WAS ALL YOUR FAULT.
AND... AND...OPAL. sob
NONE OF US COULD HAVE SAVED THEM, ORCHID! NOW, HOLD ON!

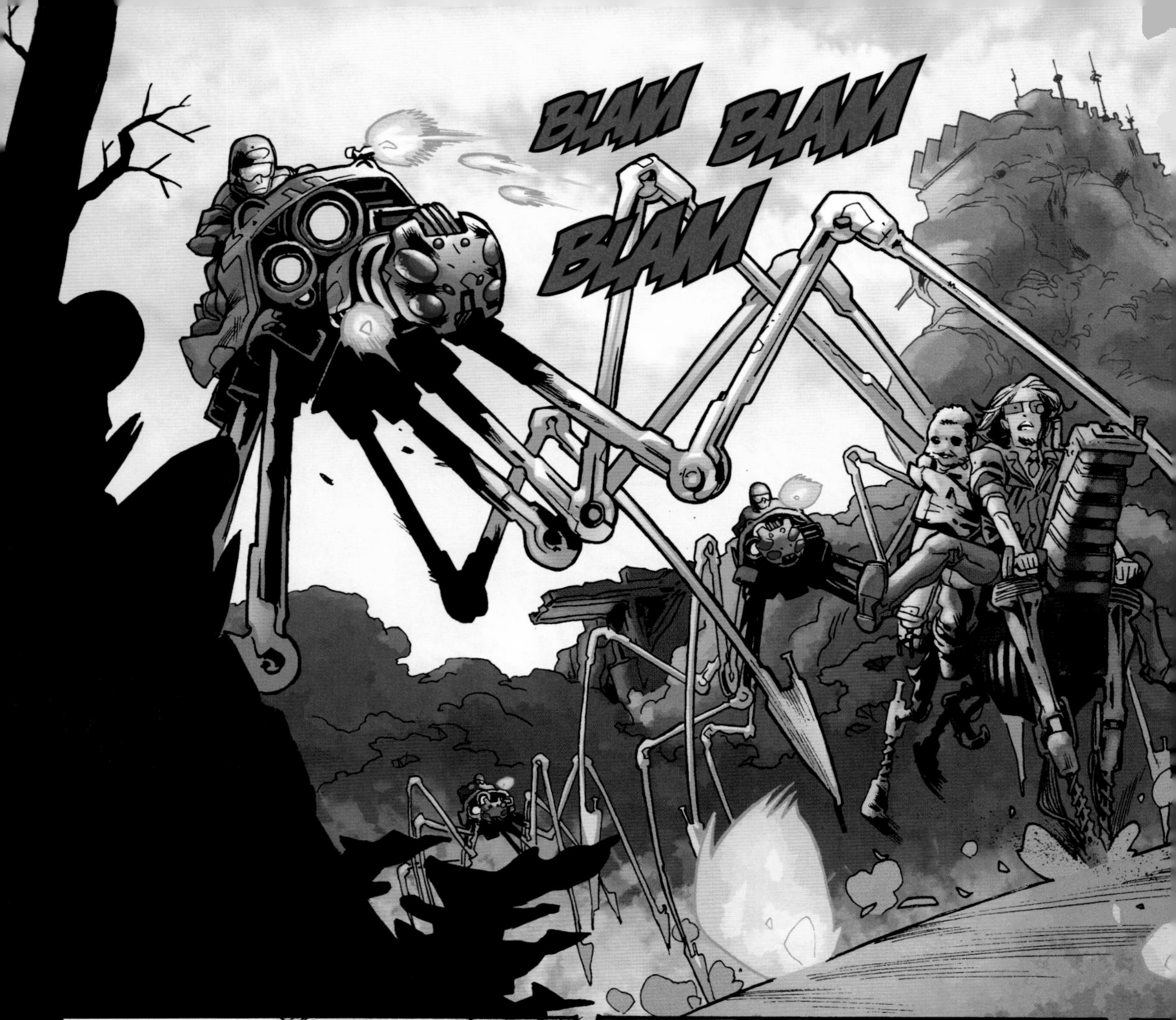
BLAM BLAM
BLAM

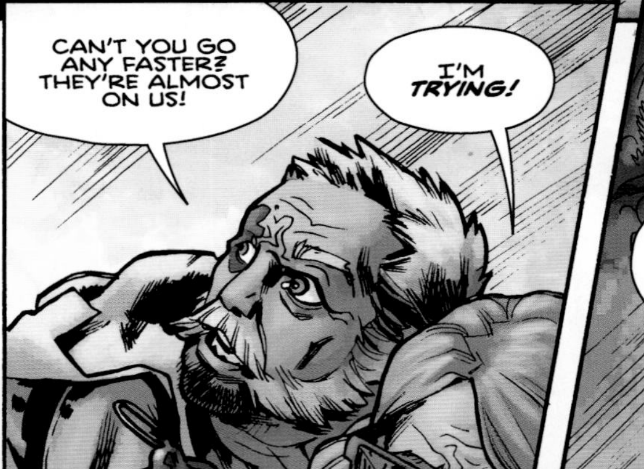
CAN'T YOU GO ANY FASTER? THEY'RE ALMOST ON US!
I'M *TRYING!*

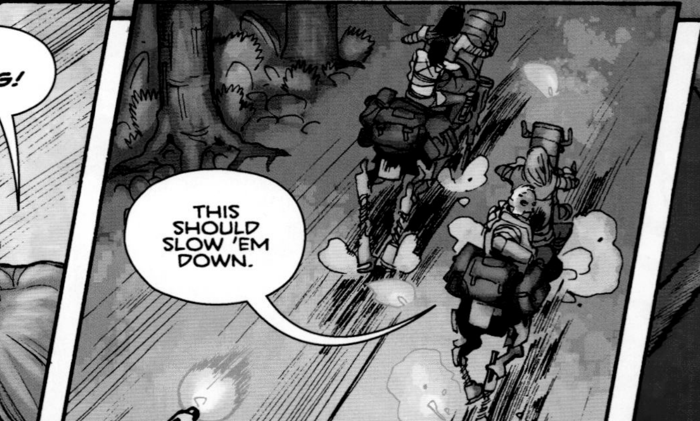
THIS SHOULD SLOW 'EM DOWN.

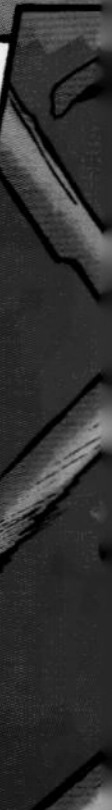

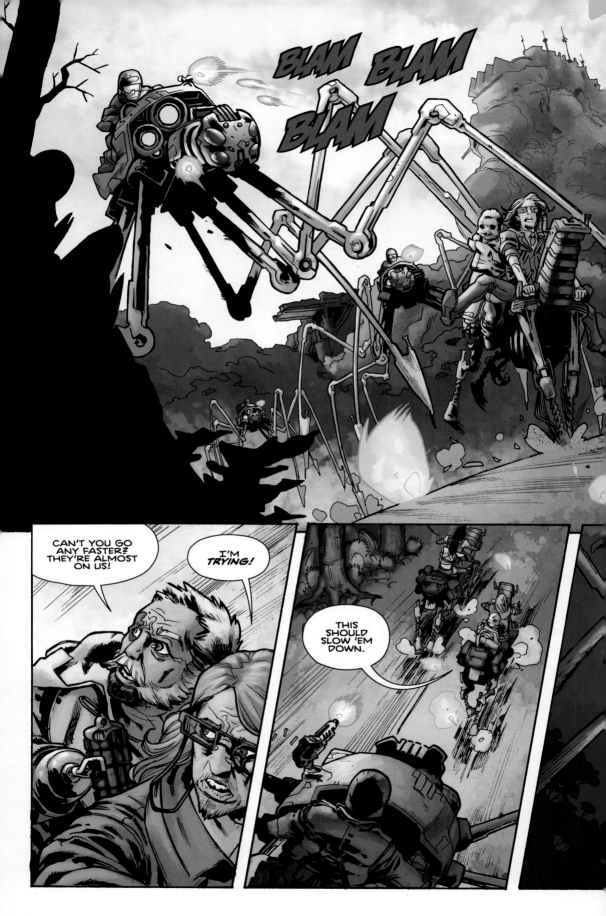

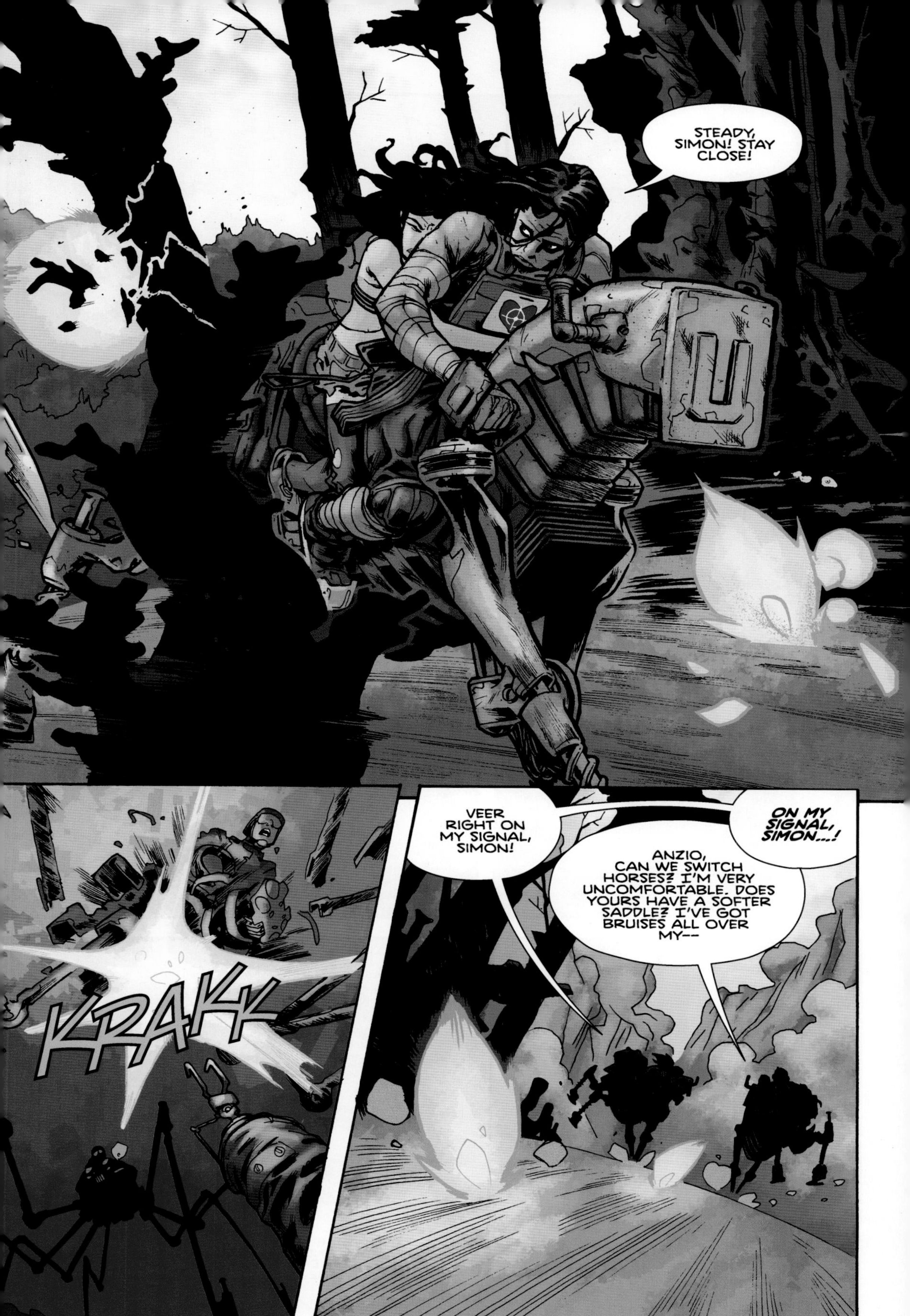
STEADY, SIMON! STAY CLOSE!
KRAKK
VEER RIGHT ON MY SIGNAL, SIMON!
ANZIO, CAN WE SWITCH HORSES? I'M VERY UNCOMFORTABLE. DOES YOURS HAVE A SOFTER SADDLE? I'VE GOT BRUISES ALL OVER MY--
ON MY SIGNAL, SIMON...!

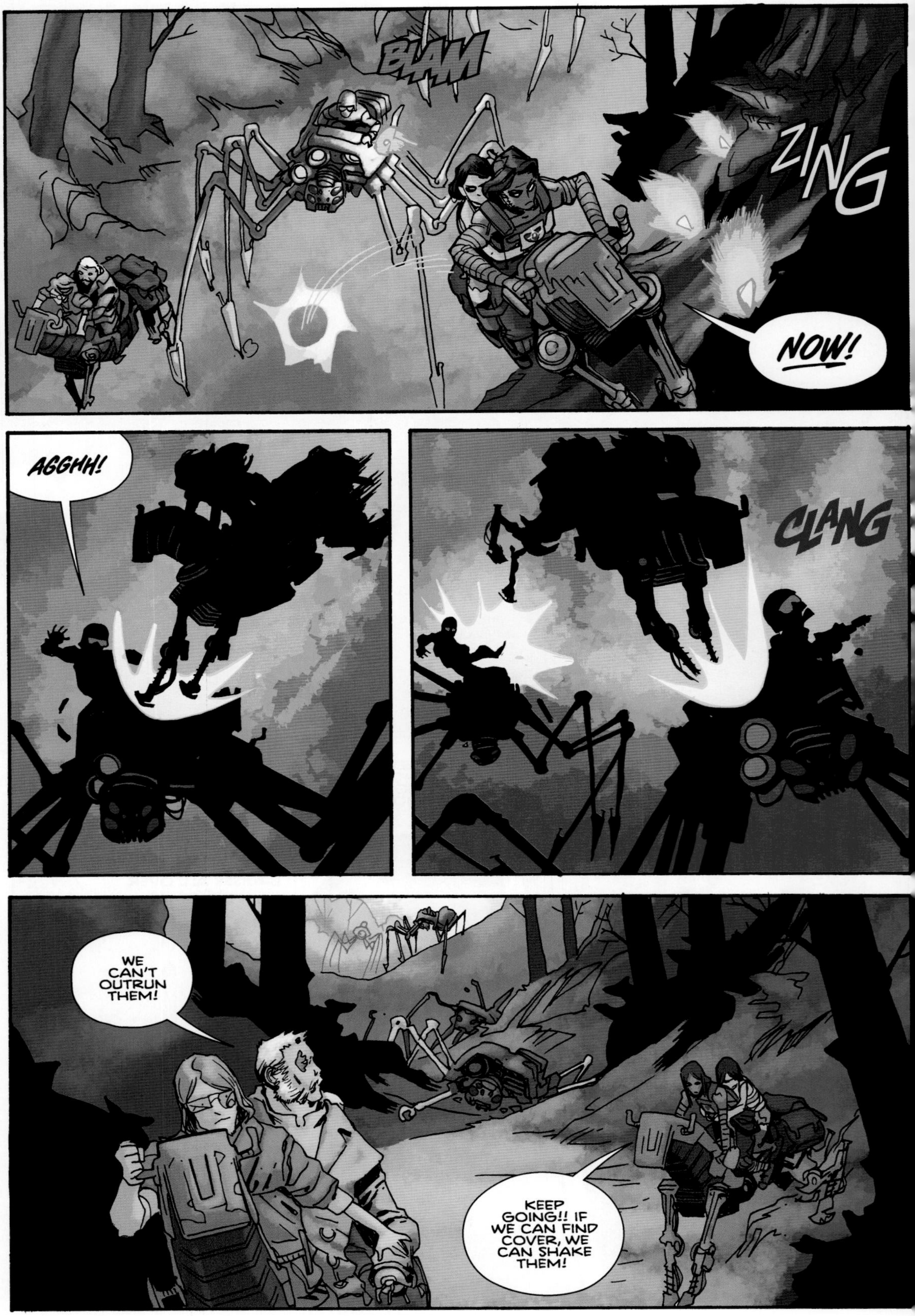
BLAM
ZING
NOW!
AGGHH!
CLANG
WE CAN'T OUTRUN THEM!
KEEP GOING!! IF WE CAN FIND COVER, WE CAN SHAKE THEM!

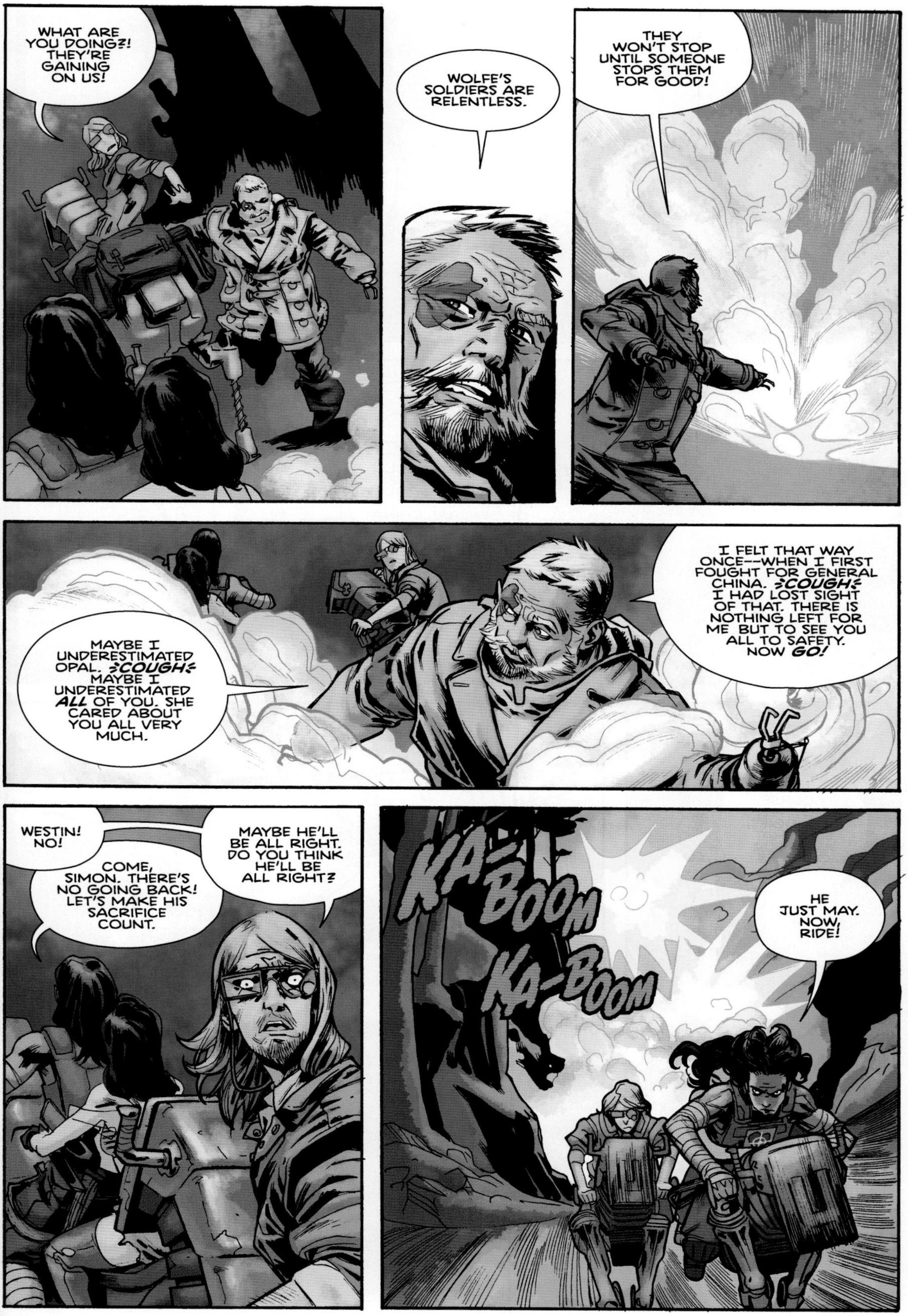

WHAT ARE YOU DOING?! THEY'RE GAINING ON US!
WOLFE'S SOLDIERS ARE RELENTLESS.
THEY WON'T STOP UNTIL SOMEONE STOPS THEM FOR GOOD!
MAYBE I UNDERESTIMATED OPAL. *COUGH* MAYBE I UNDERESTIMATED ALL OF YOU. SHE CARED ABOUT YOU ALL VERY MUCH.
I FELT THAT WAY ONCE--WHEN I FIRST FOUGHT FOR GENERAL CHINA. *COUGH* I HAD LOST SIGHT OF THAT. THERE IS NOTHING LEFT FOR ME BUT TO SEE YOU ALL TO SAFETY. NOW GO!
WESTIN! NO!
COME, SIMON. THERE'S NO GOING BACK! LET'S MAKE HIS SACRIFICE COUNT.
MAYBE HE'LL BE ALL RIGHT. DO YOU THINK HE'LL BE ALL RIGHT?
KA-BOOM
KA-BOOM
HE JUST MAY. NOW, RIDE!

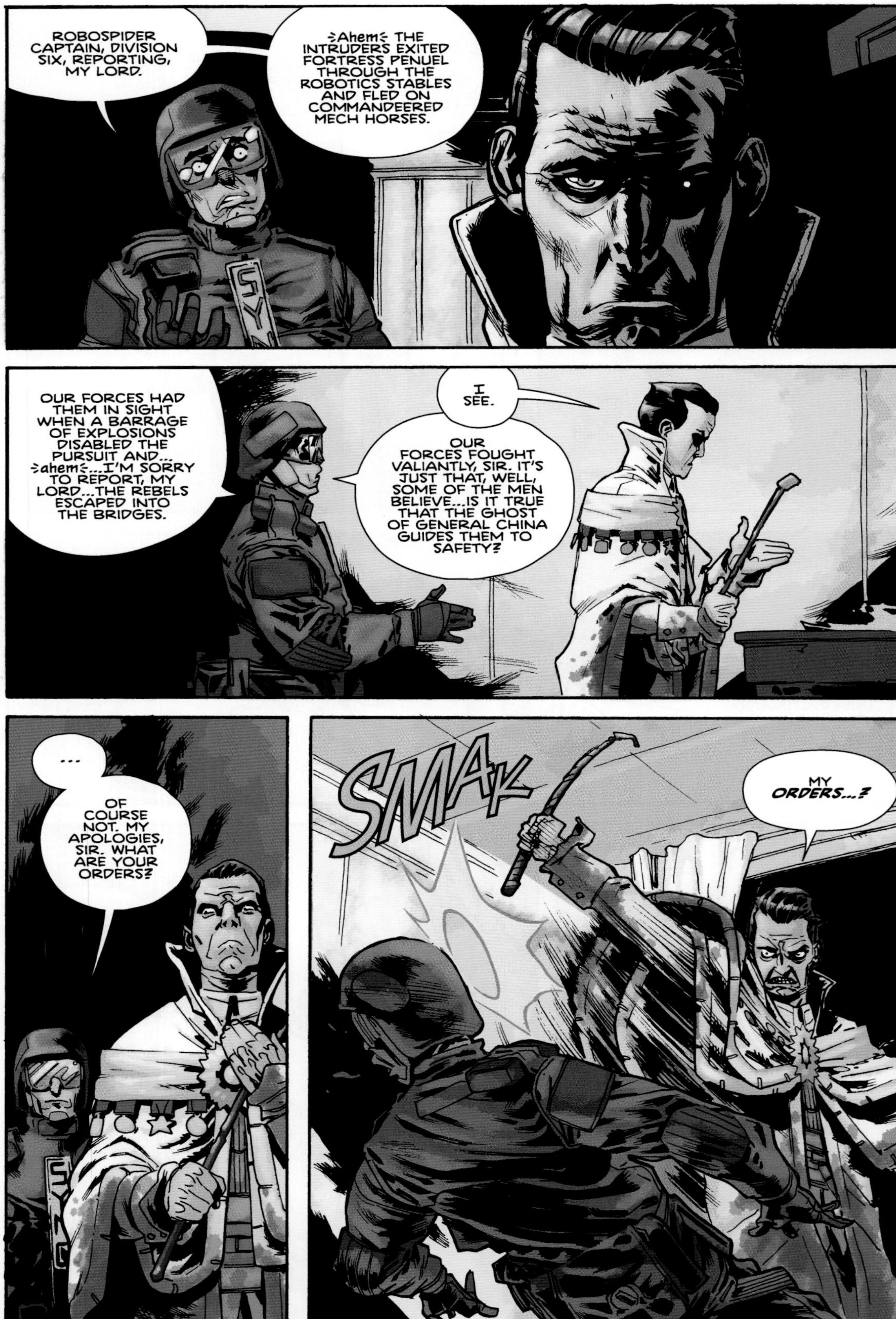
ROBOSPIDER CAPTAIN, DIVISION SIX, REPORTING, MY LORD.
≥Ahem≤ THE INTRUDERS EXITED FORTRESS PENUEL THROUGH THE ROBOTICS STABLES AND FLED ON COMMANDEERED MECH HORSES.
OUR FORCES HAD THEM IN SIGHT WHEN A BARRAGE OF EXPLOSIONS DISABLED THE PURSUIT AND... ≥ahem≤...I'M SORRY TO REPORT, MY LORD...THE REBELS ESCAPED INTO THE BRIDGES.
I SEE.
OUR FORCES FOUGHT VALIANTLY, SIR. IT'S JUST THAT, WELL, SOME OF THE MEN BELIEVE...IS IT TRUE THAT THE GHOST OF GENERAL CHINA GUIDES THEM TO SAFETY?
...
OF COURSE NOT. MY APOLOGIES, SIR. WHAT ARE YOUR ORDERS?
SMAK
MY ORDERS...?

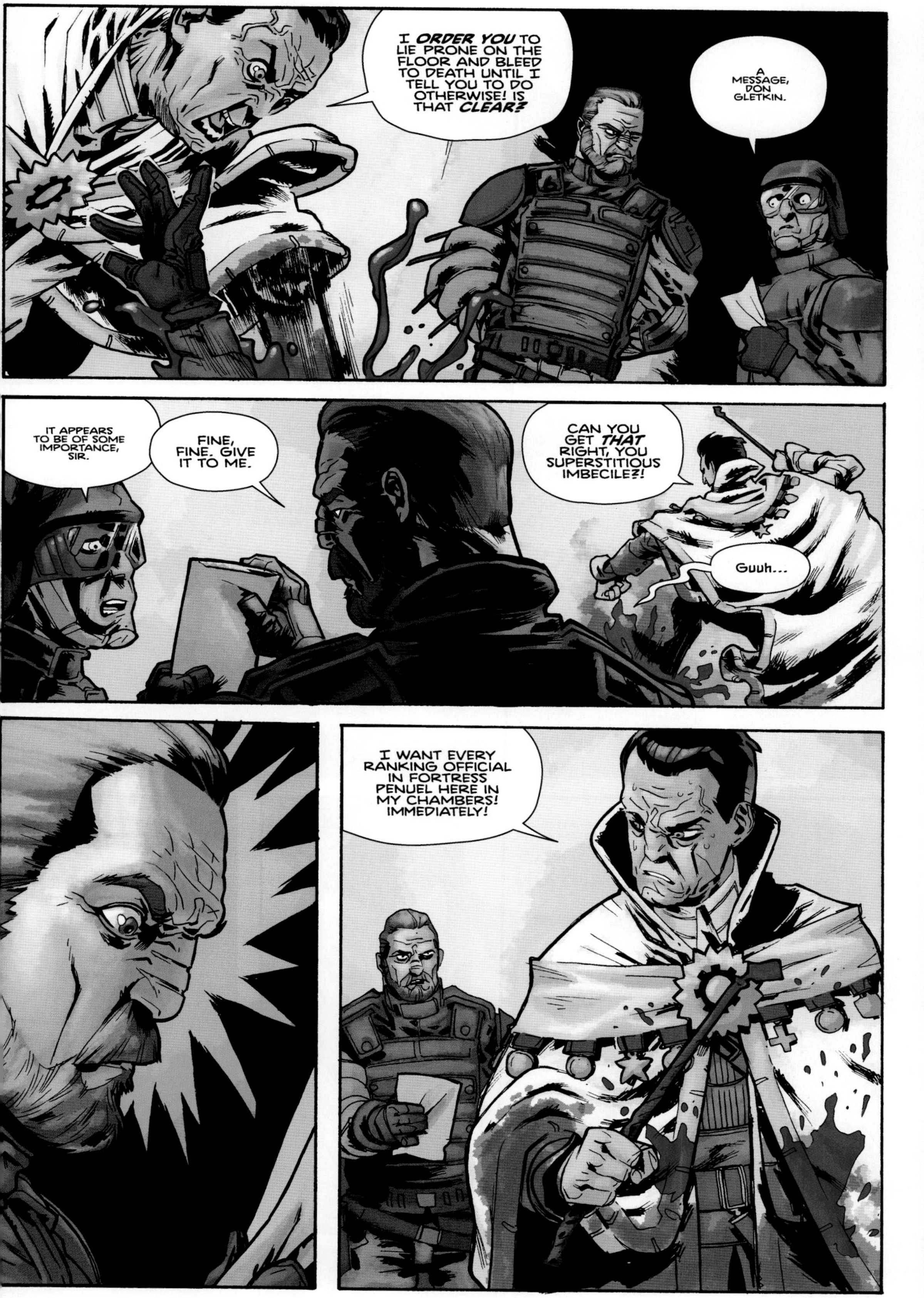
I ORDER YOU TO LIE PRONE ON THE FLOOR AND BLEED TO DEATH UNTIL I TELL YOU TO DO OTHERWISE! IS THAT CLEAR?
A MESSAGE, DON GLETKIN.
IT APPEARS TO BE OF SOME IMPORTANCE, SIR.
FINE, FINE. GIVE IT TO ME.
CAN YOU GET THAT RIGHT, YOU SUPERSTITIOUS IMBECILE?!
Guuh...
I WANT EVERY RANKING OFFICIAL IN FORTRESS PENUEL HERE IN MY CHAMBERS! IMMEDIATELY!

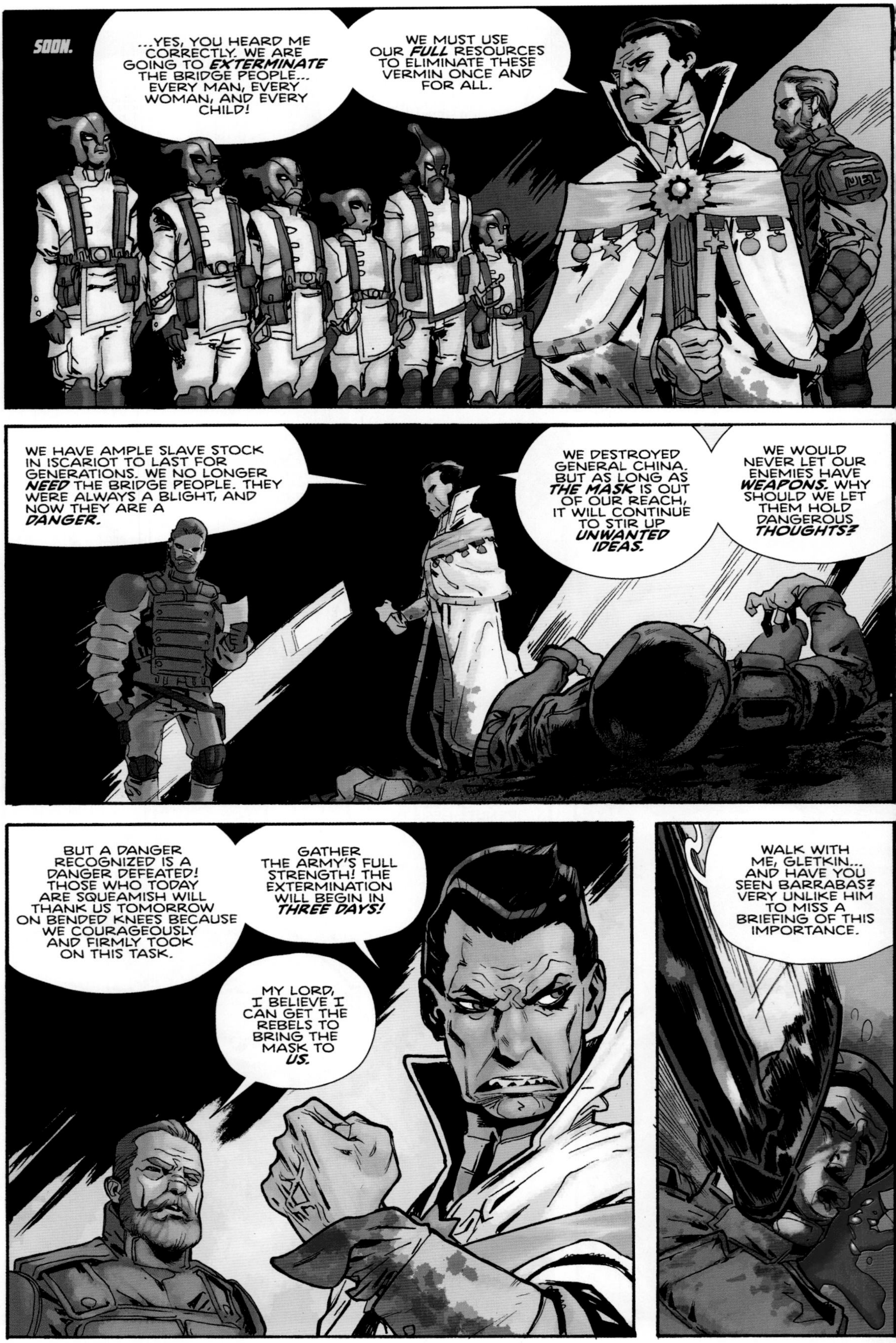
SOON.
...YES, YOU HEARD ME CORRECTLY. WE ARE GOING TO EXTERMINATE THE BRIDGE PEOPLE... EVERY MAN, EVERY WOMAN, AND EVERY CHILD!
WE MUST USE OUR FULL RESOURCES TO ELIMINATE THESE VERMIN ONCE AND FOR ALL.
WE HAVE AMPLE SLAVE STOCK IN ISCARIOT TO LAST FOR GENERATIONS. WE NO LONGER NEED THE BRIDGE PEOPLE. THEY WERE ALWAYS A BLIGHT, AND NOW THEY ARE A DANGER.
WE DESTROYED GENERAL CHINA. BUT AS LONG AS THE MASK IS OUT OF OUR REACH, IT WILL CONTINUE TO STIR UP UNWANTED IDEAS.
WE WOULD NEVER LET OUR ENEMIES HAVE WEAPONS. WHY SHOULD WE LET THEM HOLD DANGEROUS THOUGHTS?
BUT A DANGER RECOGNIZED IS A DANGER DEFEATED! THOSE WHO TODAY ARE SQUEAMISH WILL THANK US TOMORROW ON BENDED KNEES BECAUSE WE COURAGEOUSLY AND FIRMLY TOOK ON THIS TASK.
GATHER THE ARMY'S FULL STRENGTH! THE EXTERMINATION WILL BEGIN IN THREE DAYS!
MY LORD, I BELIEVE I CAN GET THE REBELS TO BRING THE MASK TO US.
WALK WITH ME, GLETKIN... AND HAVE YOU SEEN BARRABAS? VERY UNLIKE HIM TO MISS A BRIEFING OF THIS IMPORTANCE.

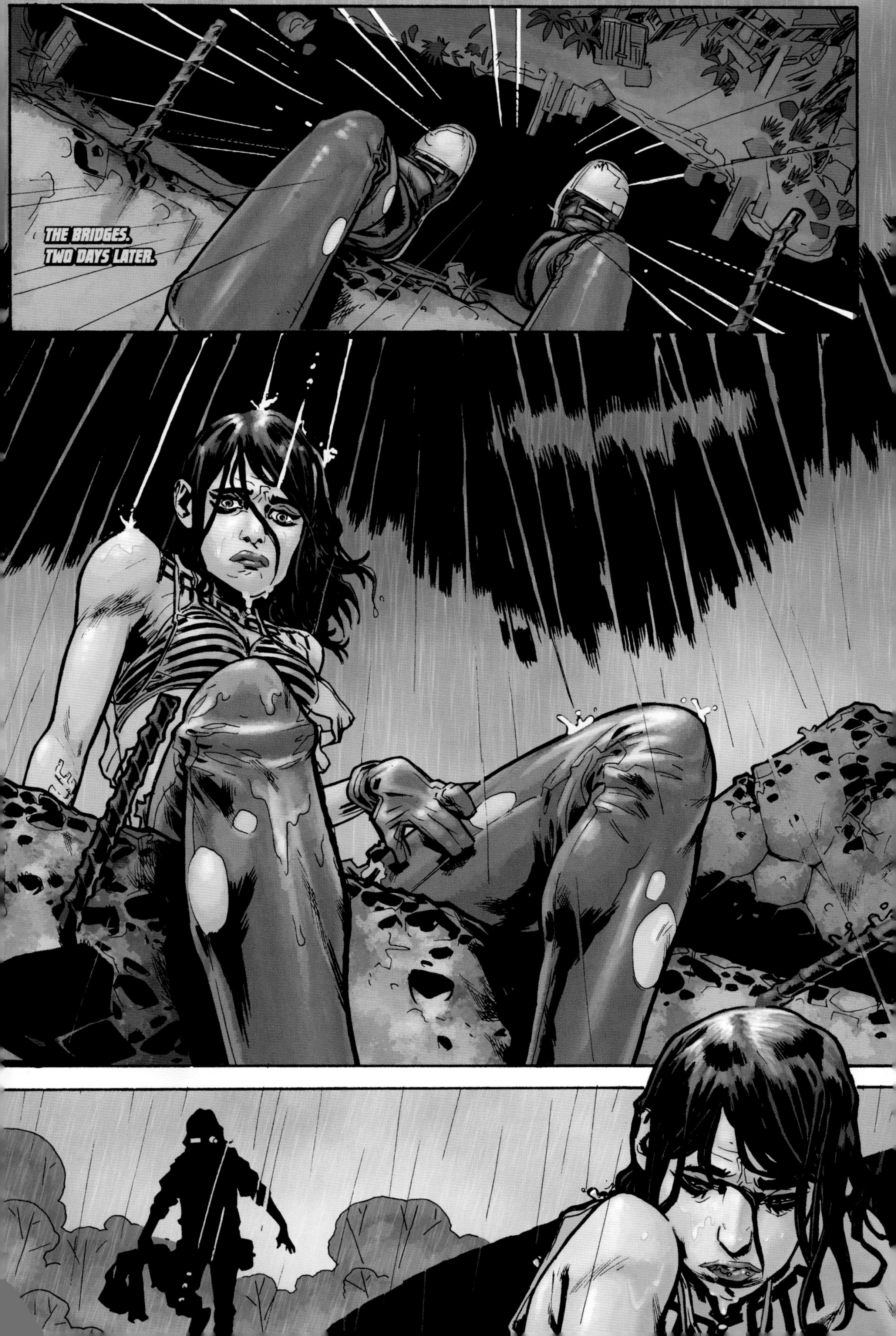
THE BRIDGES.
TWO DAYS LATER.

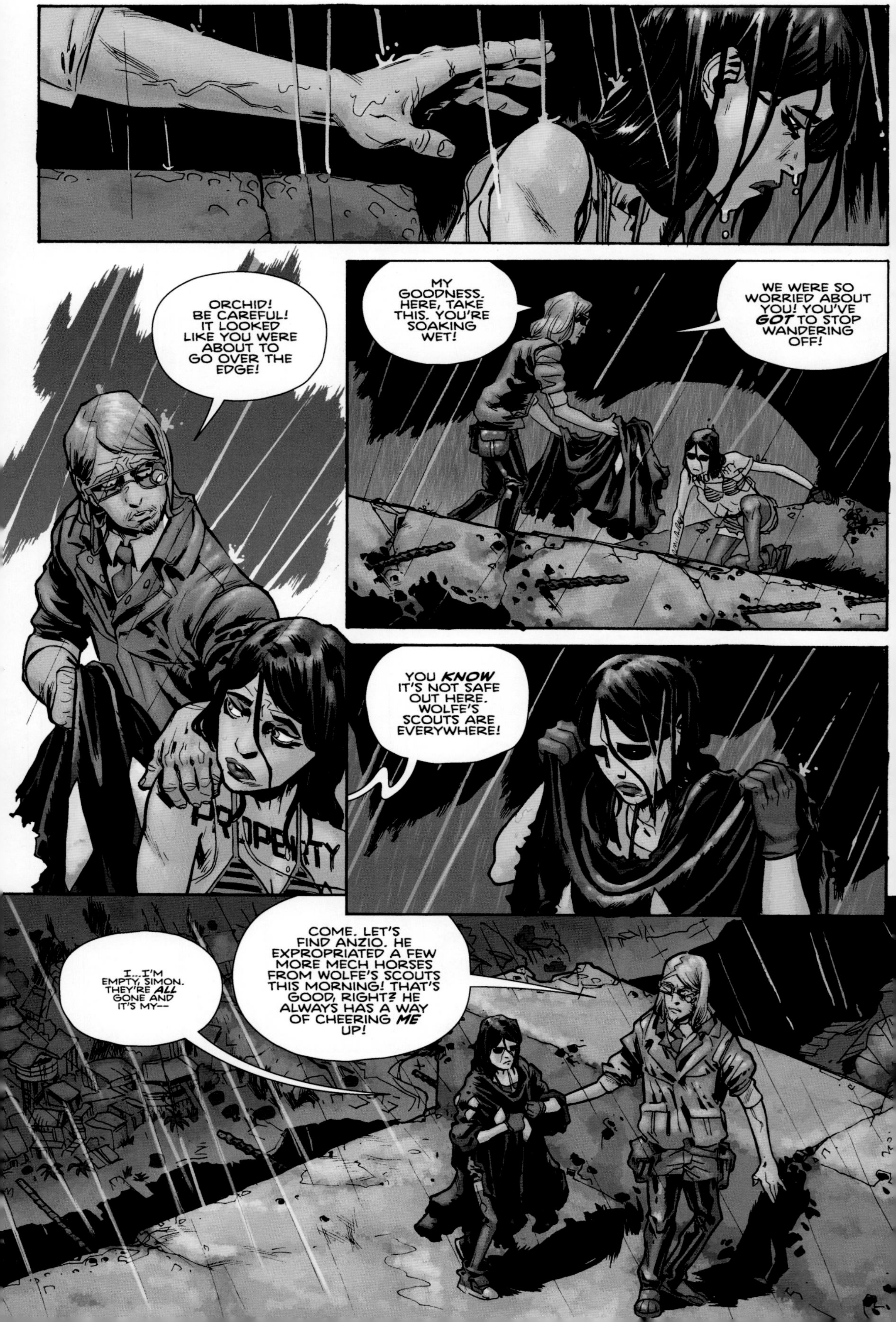
ORCHID! BE CAREFUL! IT LOOKED LIKE YOU WERE ABOUT TO GO OVER THE EDGE!
MY GOODNESS. HERE, TAKE THIS. YOU'RE SOAKING WET!
WE WERE SO WORRIED ABOUT YOU! YOU'VE GOT TO STOP WANDERING OFF!
YOU KNOW IT'S NOT SAFE OUT HERE. WOLFE'S SCOUTS ARE EVERYWHERE!
COME. LET'S FIND ANZIO. HE EXPROPRIATED A FEW MORE MECH HORSES FROM WOLFE'S SCOUTS THIS MORNING! THAT'S GOOD, RIGHT? HE ALWAYS HAS A WAY OF CHEERING ME UP!
I...I'M EMPTY, SIMON. THEY'RE ALL GONE AND IT'S MY--
PROPERTY

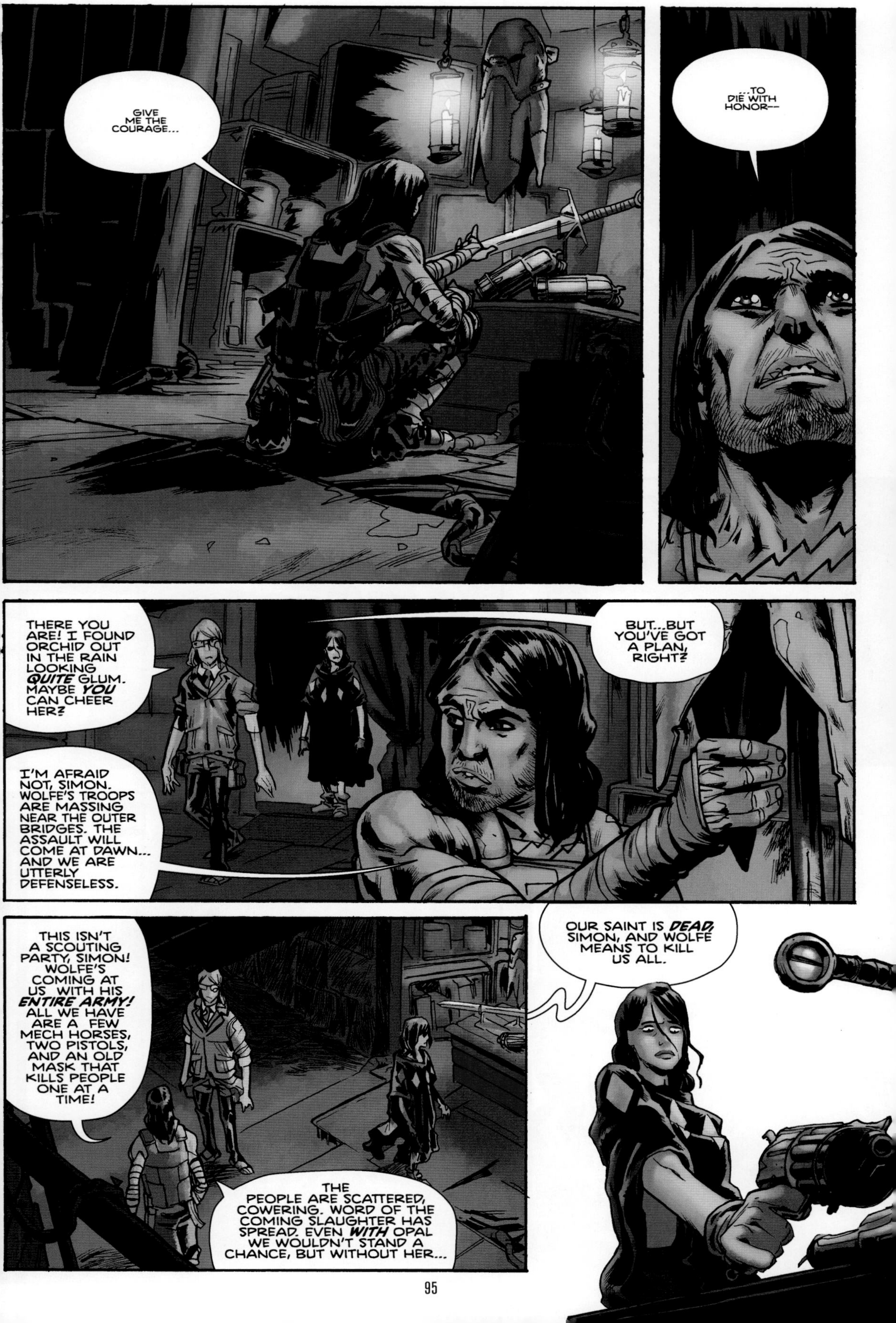
GIVE ME THE COURAGE...
...TO DIE WITH HONOR--
THERE YOU ARE! I FOUND ORCHID OUT IN THE RAIN LOOKING QUITE GLUM. MAYBE YOU CAN CHEER HER?
BUT...BUT YOU'VE GOT A PLAN, RIGHT?
I'M AFRAID NOT, SIMON. WOLFE'S TROOPS ARE MASSING NEAR THE OUTER BRIDGES. THE ASSAULT WILL COME AT DAWN... AND WE ARE UTTERLY DEFENSELESS.
THIS ISN'T A SCOUTING PARTY, SIMON! WOLFE'S COMING AT US WITH HIS ENTIRE ARMY! ALL WE HAVE ARE A FEW MECH HORSES, TWO PISTOLS, AND AN OLD MASK THAT KILLS PEOPLE ONE AT A TIME!
OUR SAINT IS DEAD, SIMON, AND WOLFE MEANS TO KILL US ALL.
THE PEOPLE ARE SCATTERED, COWERING. WORD OF THE COMING SLAUGHTER HAS SPREAD. EVEN WITH OPAL WE WOULDN'T STAND A CHANCE, BUT WITHOUT HER...

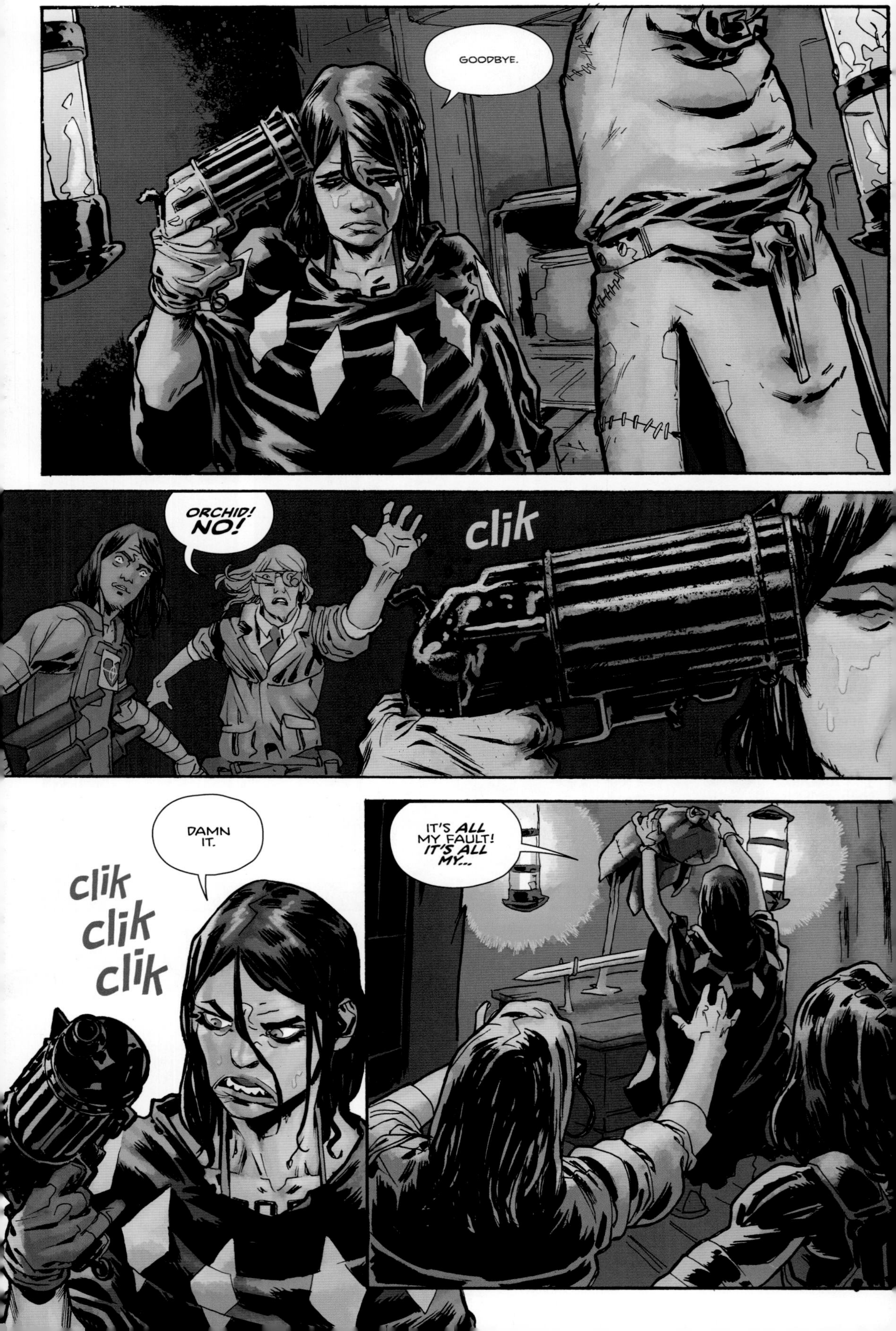
GOODBYE.
ORCHID! NO!
clik
DAMN IT.
clik
clik
clik
IT'S ALL MY FAULT! IT'S ALL MY...

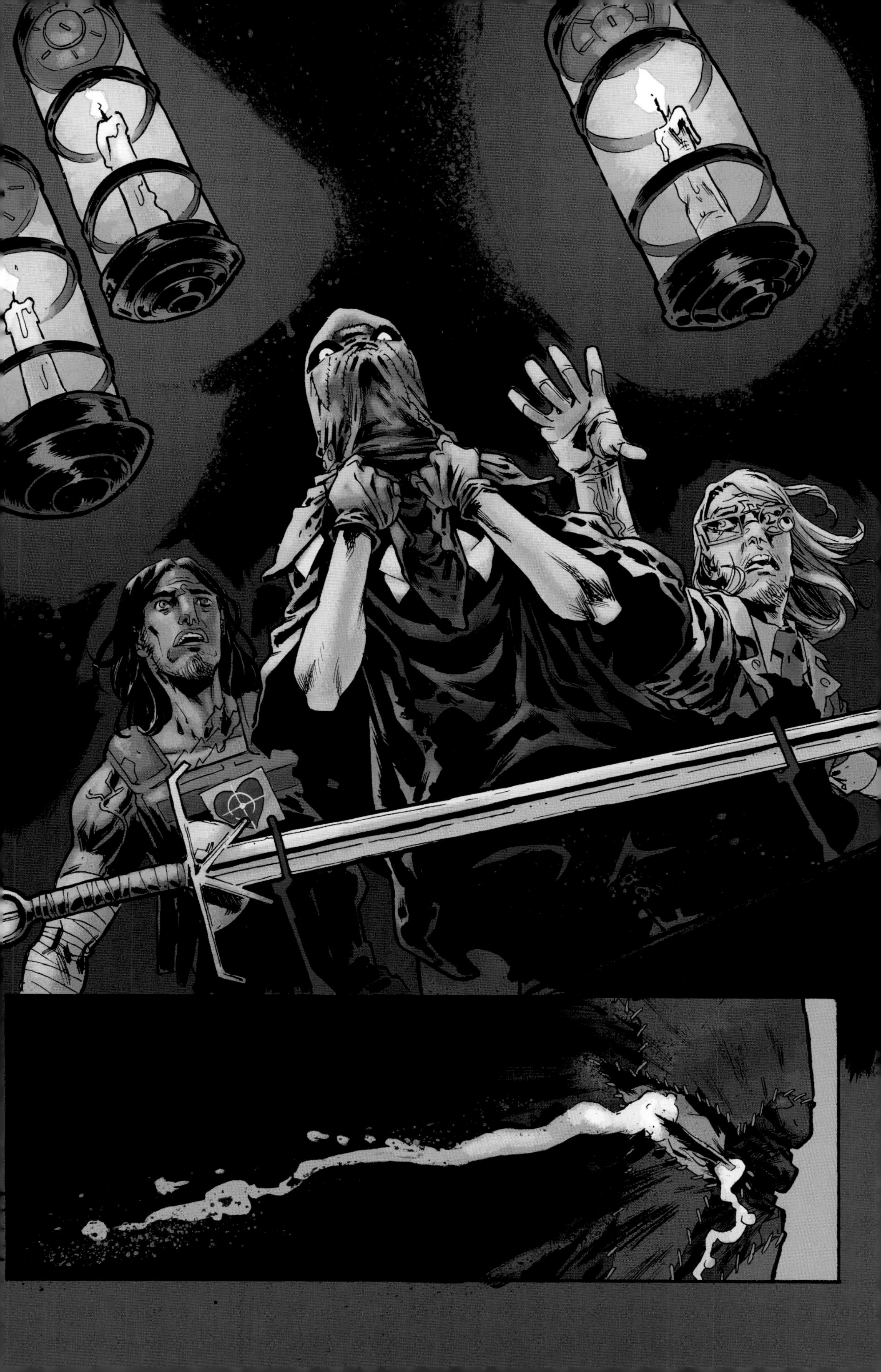

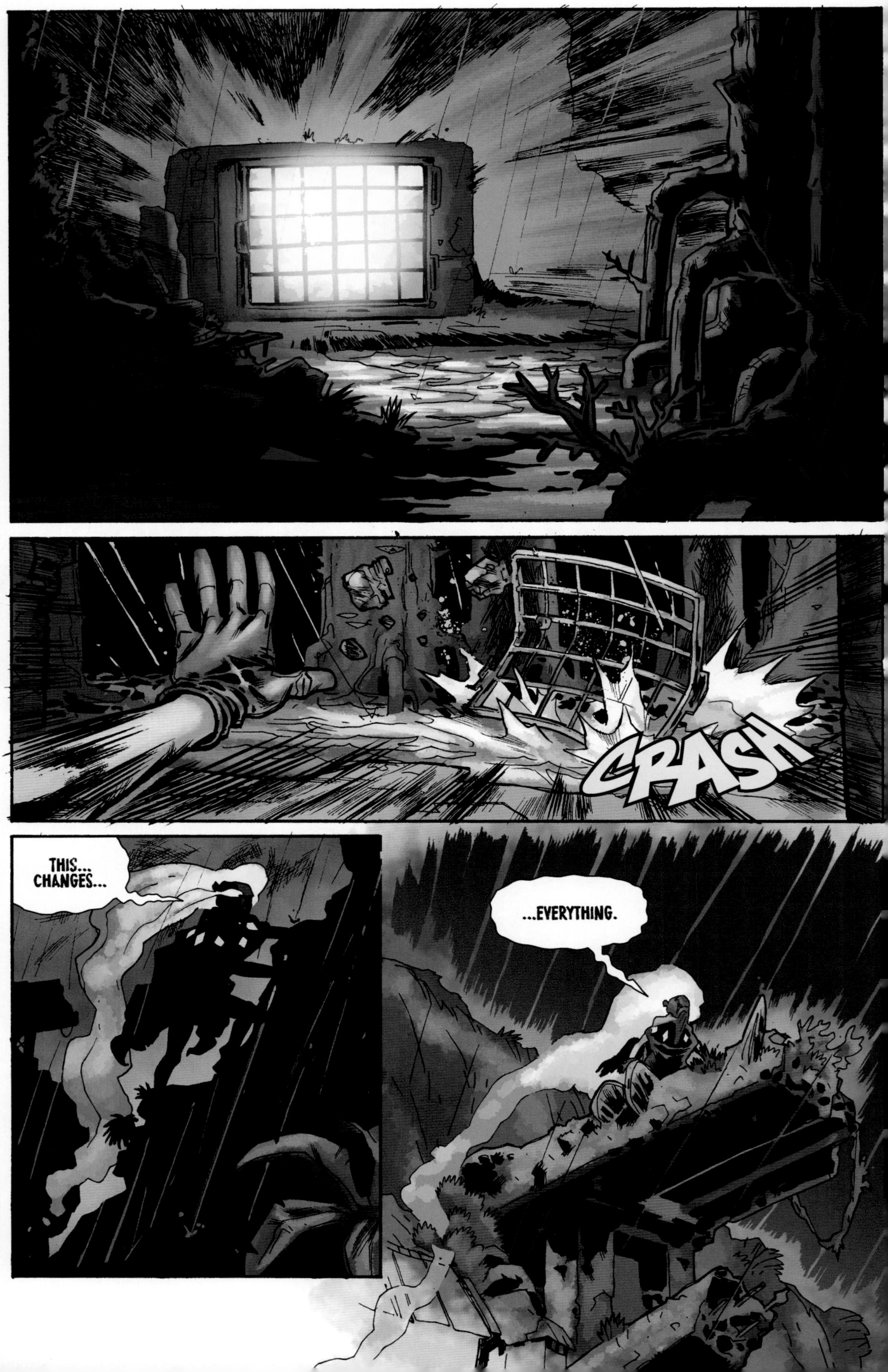
CRASH
THIS... CHANGES...
...EVERYTHING.

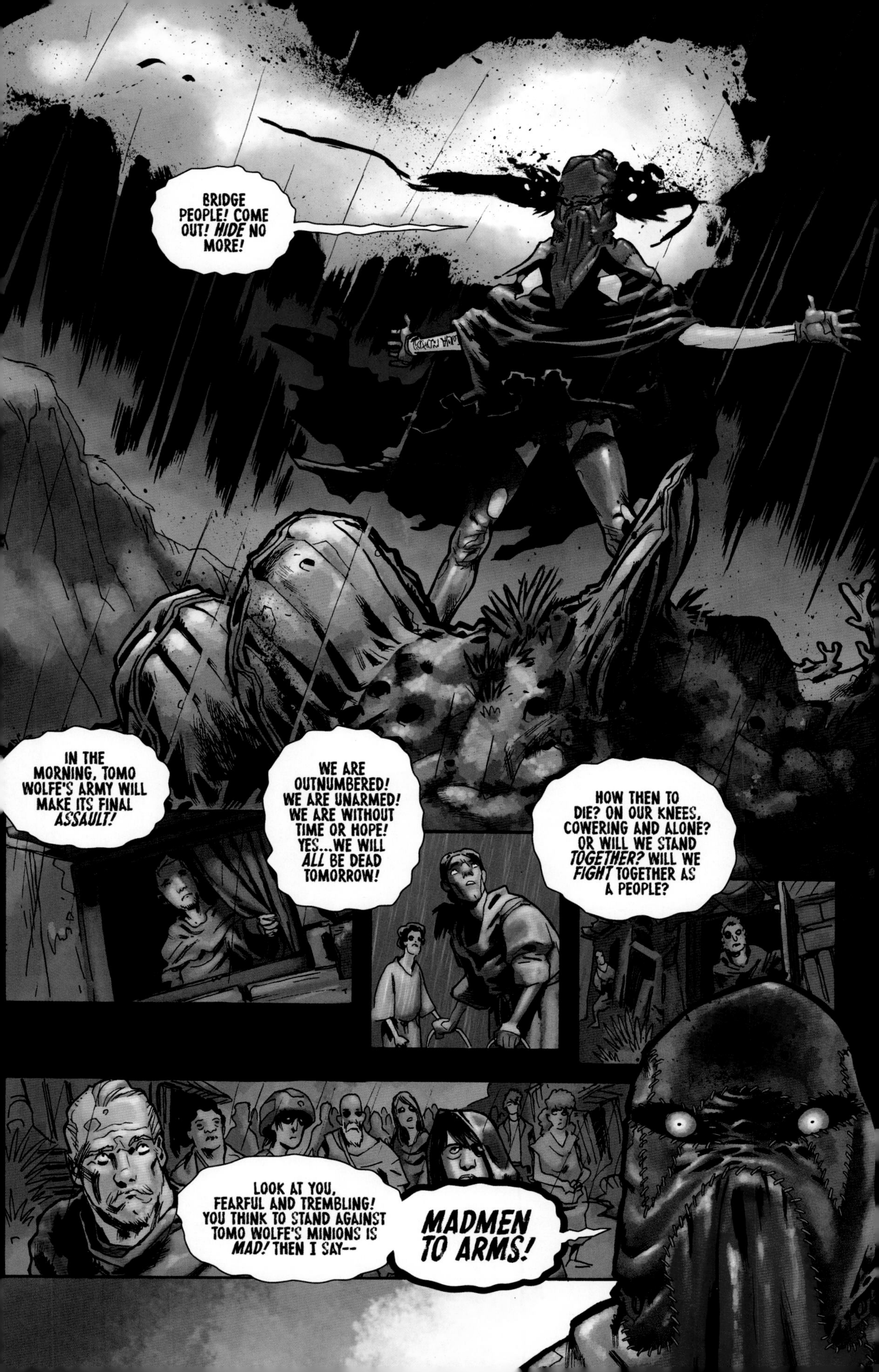
BRIDGE PEOPLE! COME OUT! *HIDE* NO MORE!
IN THE MORNING, TOMO WOLFE'S ARMY WILL MAKE ITS FINAL *ASSAULT!*
WE ARE OUTNUMBERED! WE ARE UNARMED! WE ARE WITHOUT TIME OR HOPE! YES...WE WILL *ALL* BE DEAD TOMORROW!
HOW THEN TO DIE? ON OUR KNEES, COWERING AND ALONE? OR WILL WE STAND *TOGETHER?* WILL WE *FIGHT* TOGETHER AS A PEOPLE?
LOOK AT YOU, FEARFUL AND TREMBLING! YOU THINK TO STAND AGAINST TOMO WOLFE'S MINIONS IS *MAD!* THEN I SAY--
MADMEN TO ARMS!

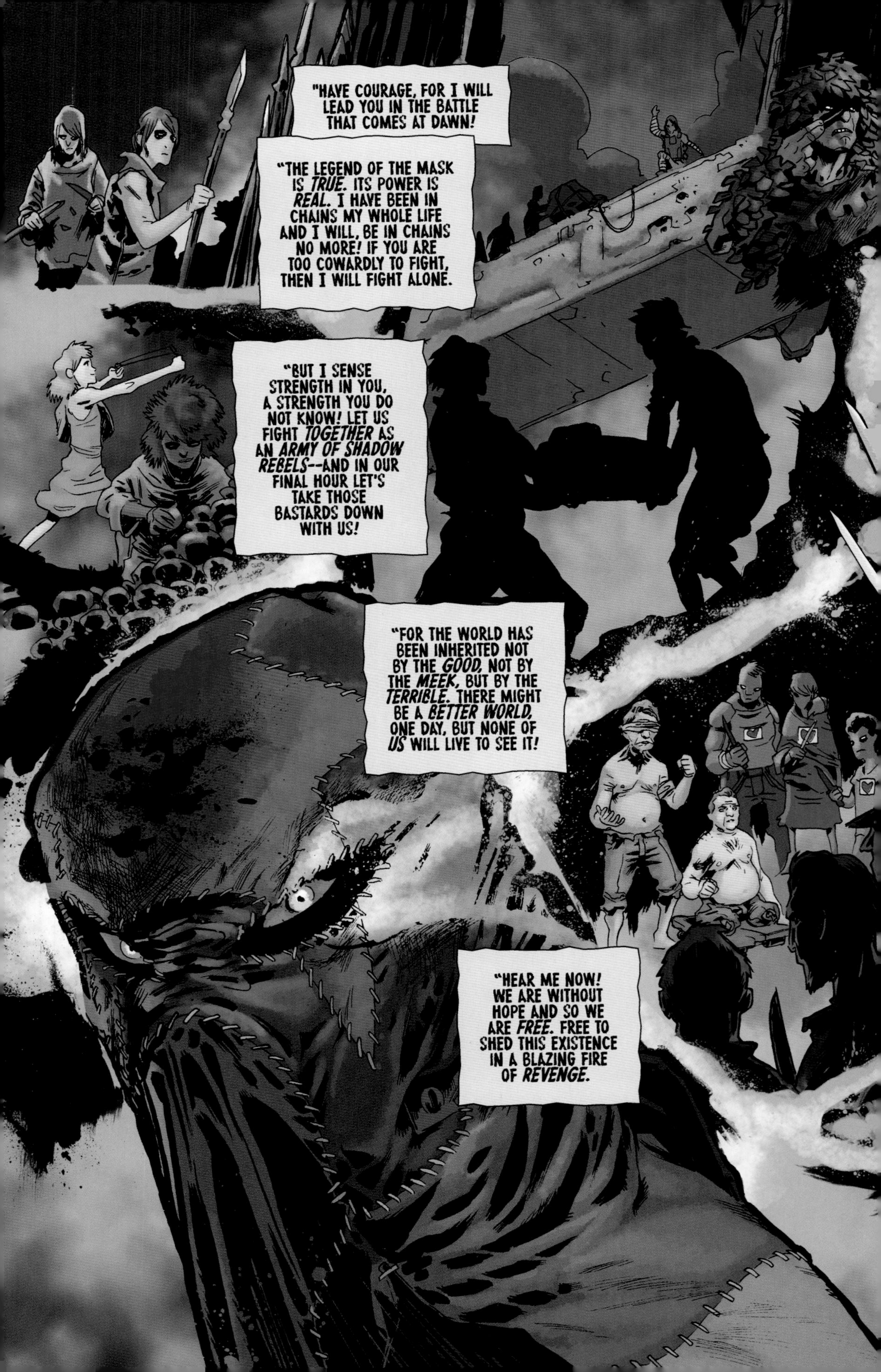
"HAVE COURAGE, FOR I WILL LEAD YOU IN THE BATTLE THAT COMES AT DAWN!
"THE LEGEND OF THE MASK IS *TRUE*. ITS POWER IS *REAL*. I HAVE BEEN IN CHAINS MY WHOLE LIFE AND I WILL, BE IN CHAINS NO MORE! IF YOU ARE TOO COWARDLY TO FIGHT, THEN I WILL FIGHT ALONE.
"BUT I SENSE STRENGTH IN YOU, A STRENGTH YOU DO NOT KNOW! LET US FIGHT *TOGETHER* AS AN *ARMY OF SHADOW REBELS*--AND IN OUR FINAL HOUR LET'S TAKE THOSE BASTARDS DOWN WITH US!
"FOR THE WORLD HAS BEEN INHERITED NOT BY THE *GOOD*, NOT BY THE *MEEK*, BUT BY THE *TERRIBLE*. THERE MIGHT BE A *BETTER WORLD*, ONE DAY, BUT NONE OF *US* WILL LIVE TO SEE IT!
"HEAR ME NOW! WE ARE WITHOUT HOPE AND SO WE ARE *FREE*. FREE TO SHED THIS EXISTENCE IN A BLAZING FIRE OF *REVENGE*.

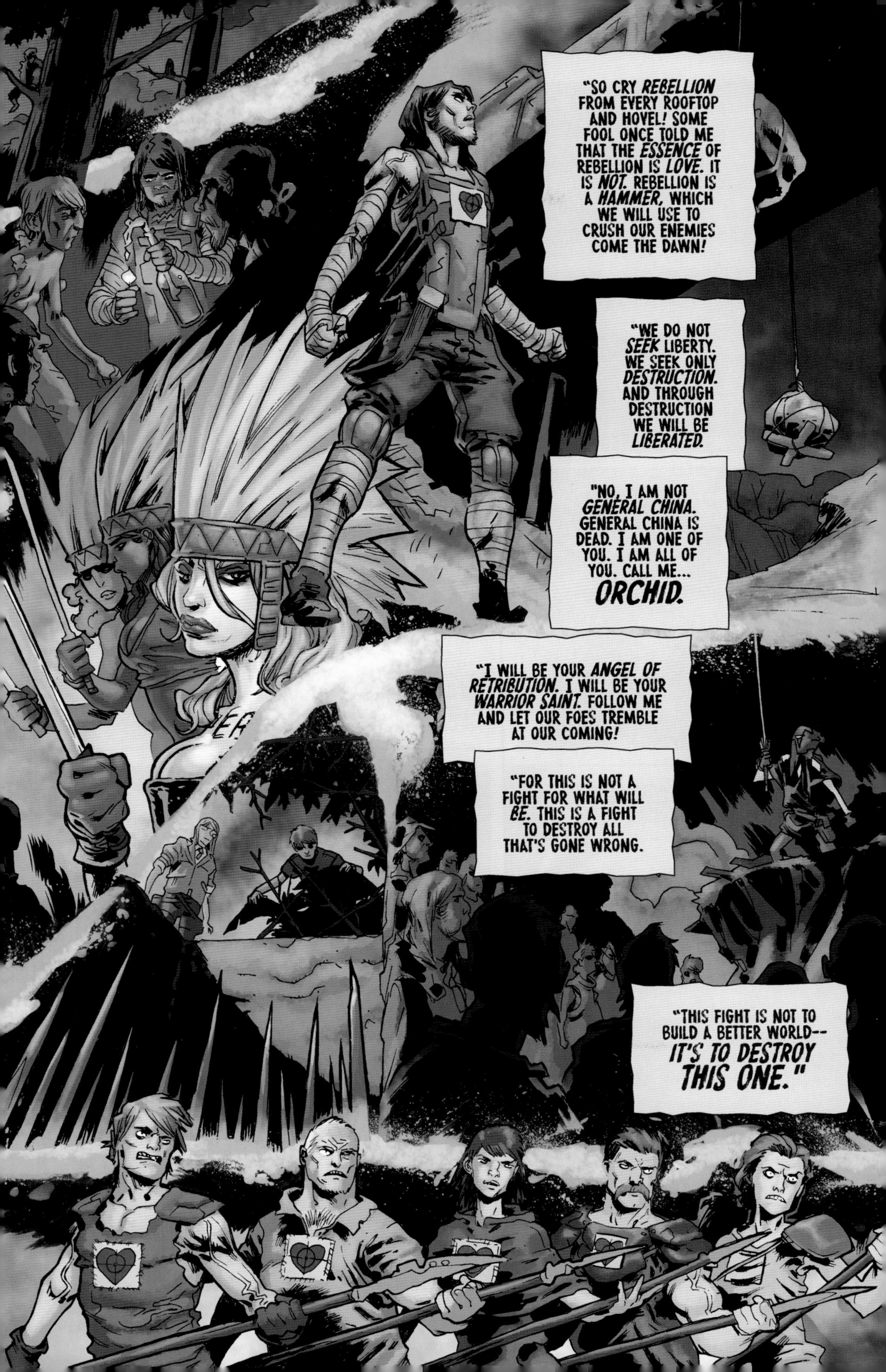
"SO CRY REBELLION FROM EVERY ROOFTOP AND HOVEL! SOME FOOL ONCE TOLD ME THAT THE ESSENCE OF REBELLION IS LOVE. IT IS NOT. REBELLION IS A HAMMER, WHICH WE WILL USE TO CRUSH OUR ENEMIES COME THE DAWN!
"WE DO NOT SEEK LIBERTY. WE SEEK ONLY DESTRUCTION. AND THROUGH DESTRUCTION WE WILL BE LIBERATED.
"NO, I AM NOT GENERAL CHINA. GENERAL CHINA IS DEAD. I AM ONE OF YOU. I AM ALL OF YOU. CALL ME... ORCHID.
"I WILL BE YOUR ANGEL OF RETRIBUTION. I WILL BE YOUR WARRIOR SAINT. FOLLOW ME AND LET OUR FOES TREMBLE AT OUR COMING!
"FOR THIS IS NOT A FIGHT FOR WHAT WILL BE. THIS IS A FIGHT TO DESTROY ALL THAT'S GONE WRONG.
"THIS FIGHT IS NOT TO BUILD A BETTER WORLD-- IT'S TO DESTROY THIS ONE."

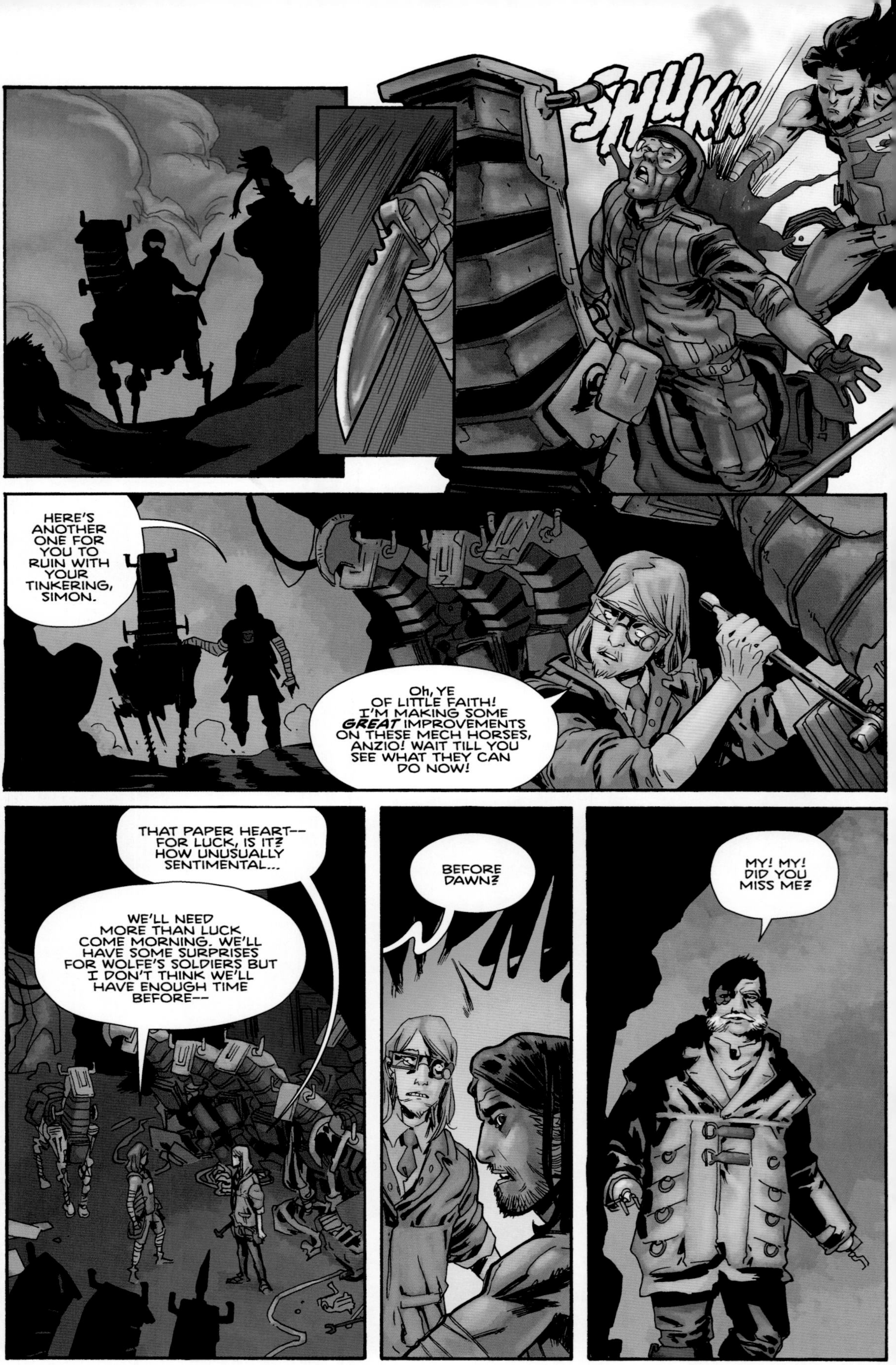
SHUKK
HERE'S ANOTHER ONE FOR YOU TO RUIN WITH YOUR TINKERING, SIMON.
Oh, YE OF LITTLE FAITH! I'M MAKING SOME GREAT IMPROVEMENTS ON THESE MECH HORSES, ANZIO! WAIT TILL YOU SEE WHAT THEY CAN DO NOW!
THAT PAPER HEART-- FOR LUCK, IS IT? HOW UNUSUALLY SENTIMENTAL...
WE'LL NEED MORE THAN LUCK COME MORNING. WE'LL HAVE SOME SURPRISES FOR WOLFE'S SOLDIERS BUT I DON'T THINK WE'LL HAVE ENOUGH TIME BEFORE--
BEFORE DAWN?
MY! MY! DID YOU MISS ME?

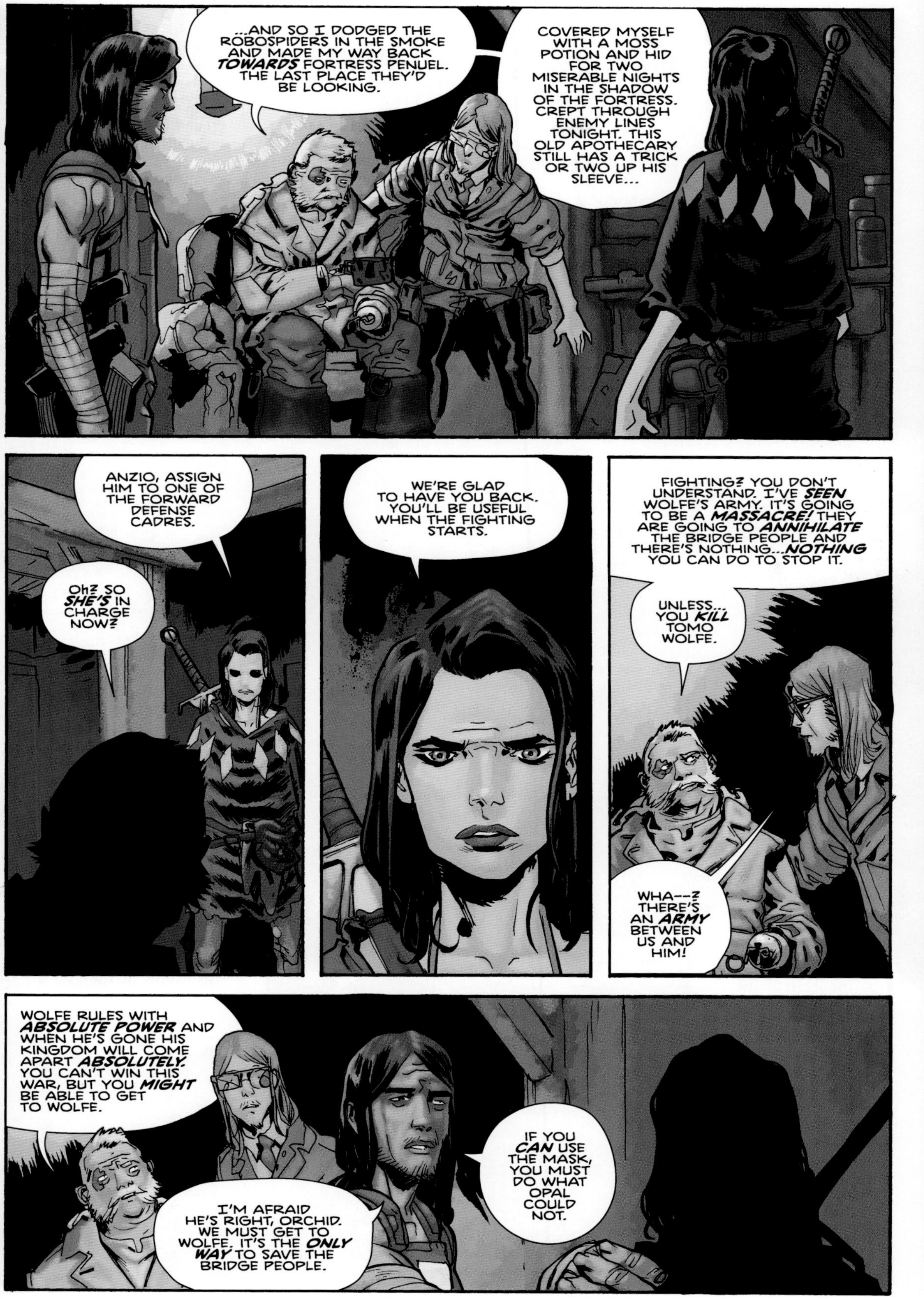
...AND SO I DODGED THE ROBOSPIDERS IN THE SMOKE AND MADE MY WAY BACK TOWARDS FORTRESS PENUEL. THE LAST PLACE THEY'D BE LOOKING.
COVERED MYSELF WITH A MOSS POTION AND HID FOR TWO MISERABLE NIGHTS IN THE SHADOW OF THE FORTRESS. CREPT THROUGH ENEMY LINES TONIGHT. THIS OLD APOTHECARY STILL HAS A TRICK OR TWO UP HIS SLEEVE...
ANZIO, ASSIGN HIM TO ONE OF THE FORWARD DEFENSE CADRES.
OH? SO SHE'S IN CHARGE NOW?
WE'RE GLAD TO HAVE YOU BACK. YOU'LL BE USEFUL WHEN THE FIGHTING STARTS.
FIGHTING? YOU DON'T UNDERSTAND. I'VE SEEN WOLFE'S ARMY. IT'S GOING TO BE A MASSACRE! THEY ARE GOING TO ANNIHILATE THE BRIDGE PEOPLE AND THERE'S NOTHING...NOTHING YOU CAN DO TO STOP IT.
UNLESS... YOU KILL TOMO WOLFE.
WHA--? THERE'S AN ARMY BETWEEN US AND HIM!
WOLFE RULES WITH ABSOLUTE POWER AND WHEN HE'S GONE HIS KINGDOM WILL COME APART ABSOLUTELY. YOU CAN'T WIN THIS WAR, BUT YOU MIGHT BE ABLE TO GET TO WOLFE.
I'M AFRAID HE'S RIGHT, ORCHID. WE MUST GET TO WOLFE. IT'S THE ONLY WAY TO SAVE THE BRIDGE PEOPLE.
IF YOU CAN USE THE MASK, YOU MUST DO WHAT OPAL COULD NOT.

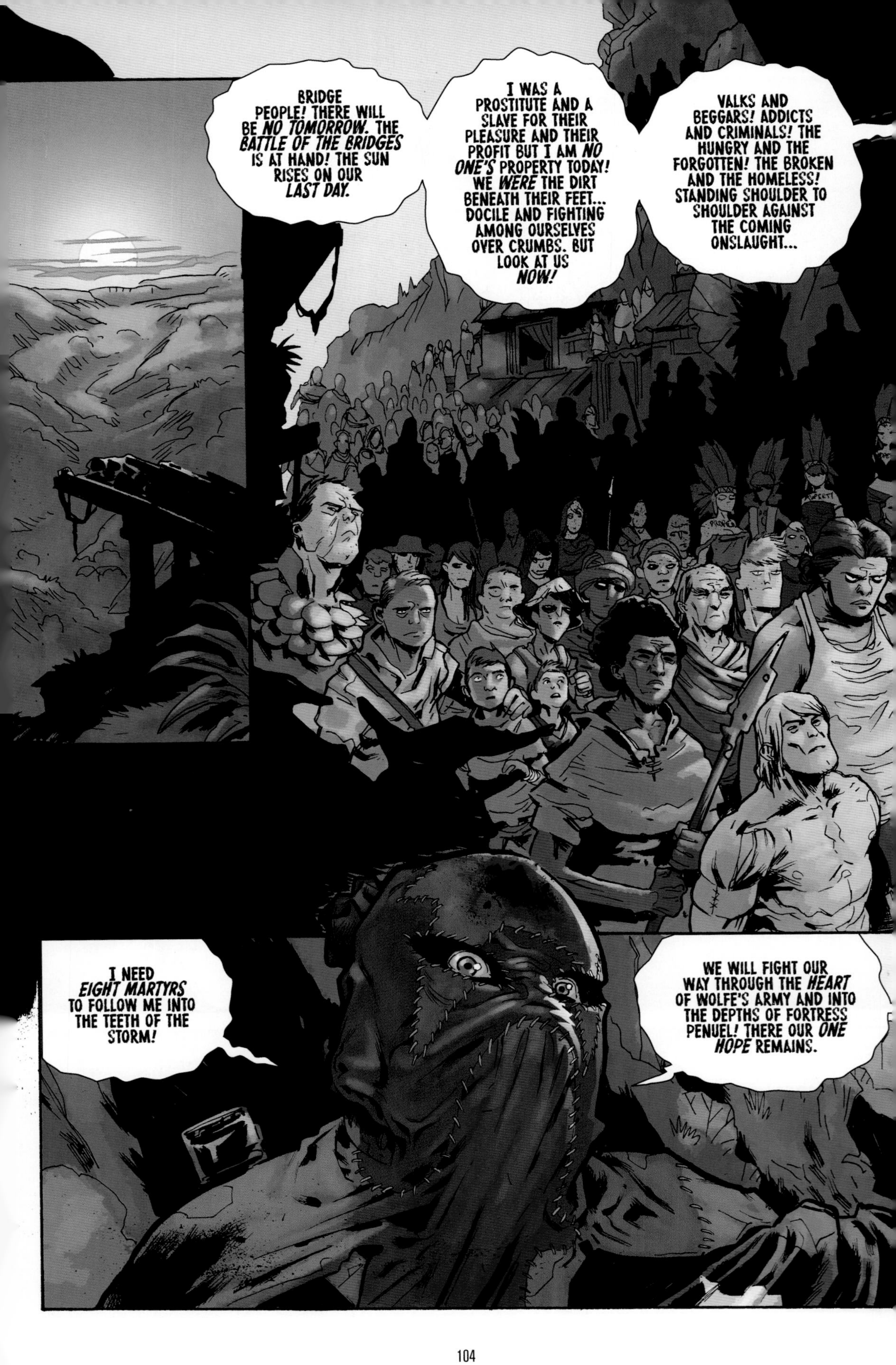
BRIDGE PEOPLE! THERE WILL BE NO TOMORROW. THE BATTLE OF THE BRIDGES IS AT HAND! THE SUN RISES ON OUR LAST DAY.
I WAS A PROSTITUTE AND A SLAVE FOR THEIR PLEASURE AND THEIR PROFIT BUT I AM NO ONE'S PROPERTY TODAY! WE WERE THE DIRT BENEATH THEIR FEET... DOCILE AND FIGHTING AMONG OURSELVES OVER CRUMBS. BUT LOOK AT US NOW!
VALKS AND BEGGARS! ADDICTS AND CRIMINALS! THE HUNGRY AND THE FORGOTTEN! THE BROKEN AND THE HOMELESS! STANDING SHOULDER TO SHOULDER AGAINST THE COMING ONSLAUGHT...
I NEED EIGHT MARTYRS TO FOLLOW ME INTO THE TEETH OF THE STORM!
WE WILL FIGHT OUR WAY THROUGH THE HEART OF WOLFE'S ARMY AND INTO THE DEPTHS OF FORTRESS PENUEL! THERE OUR ONE HOPE REMAINS.

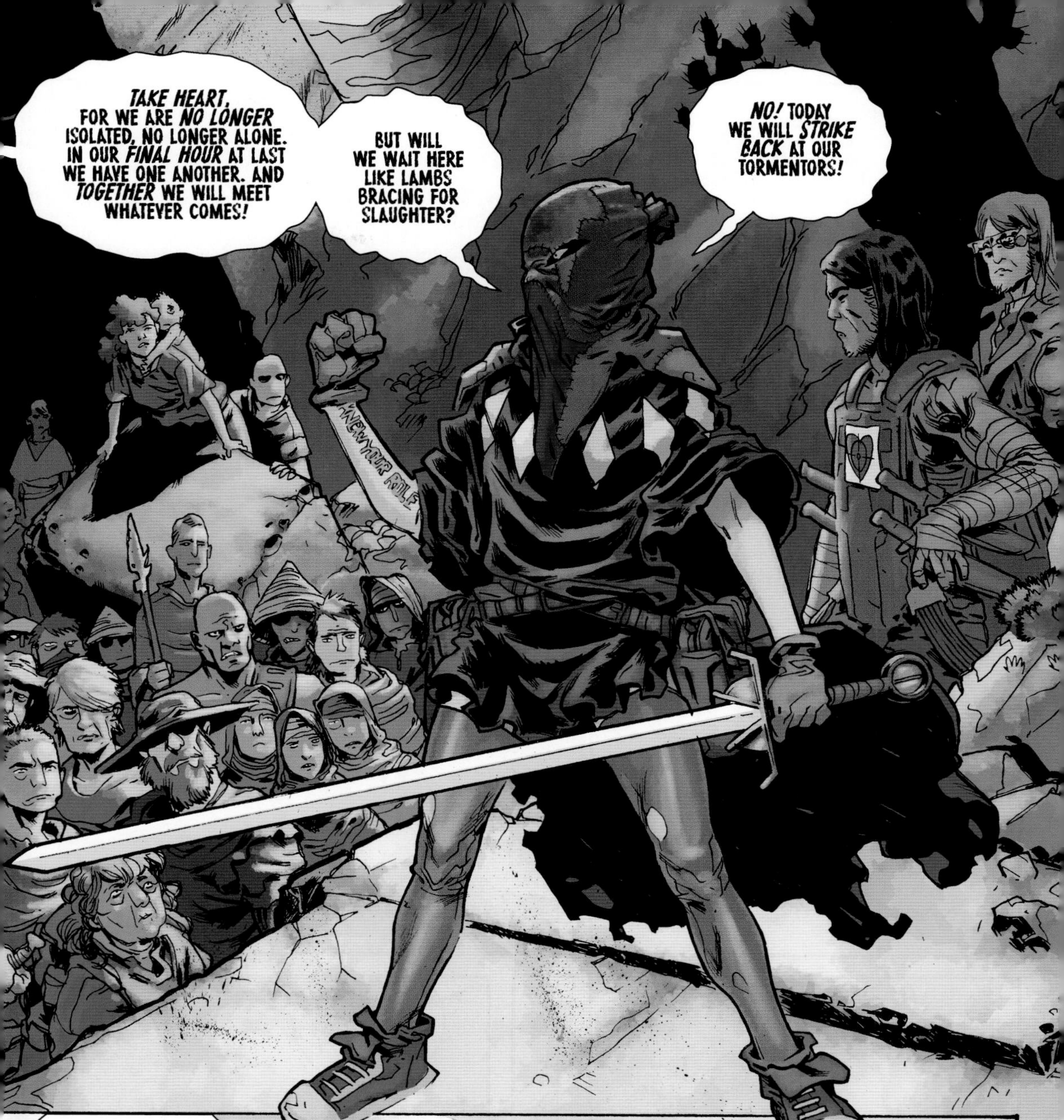
TAKE HEART, FOR WE ARE NO LONGER ISOLATED, NO LONGER ALONE. IN OUR FINAL HOUR AT LAST WE HAVE ONE ANOTHER. AND TOGETHER WE WILL MEET WHATEVER COMES!
BUT WILL WE WAIT HERE LIKE LAMBS BRACING FOR SLAUGHTER?
NO! TODAY WE WILL STRIKE BACK AT OUR TORMENTORS!
KNEW YOUR ROLE

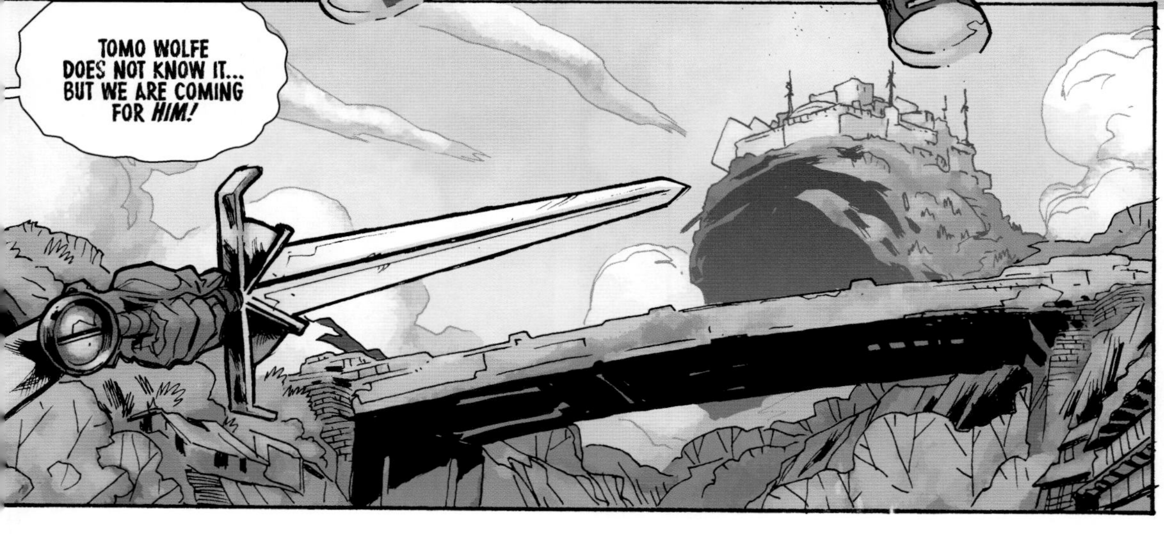
TOMO WOLFE DOES NOT KNOW IT... BUT WE ARE COMING FOR HIM!

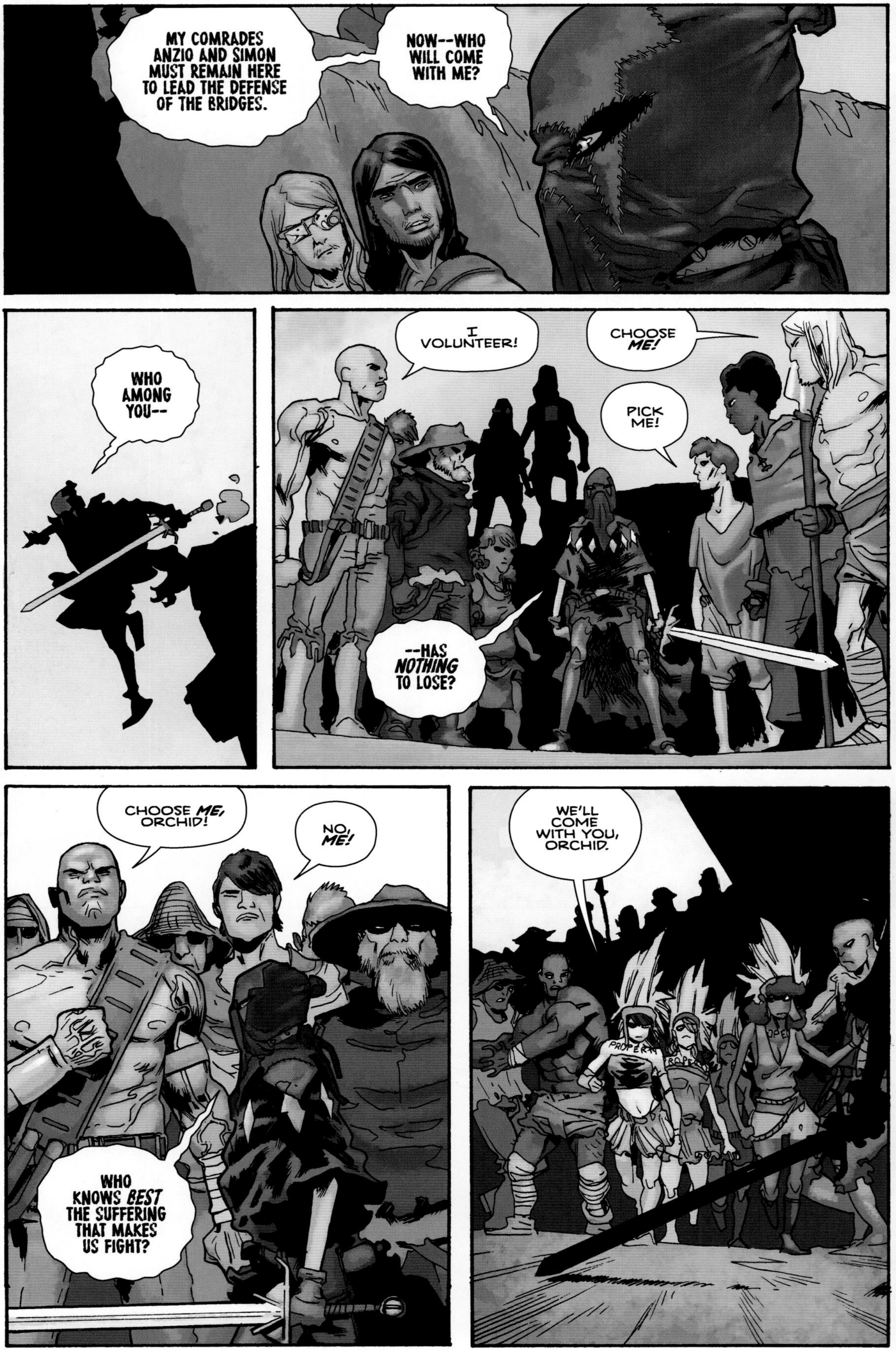
MY COMRADES ANZIO AND SIMON MUST REMAIN HERE TO LEAD THE DEFENSE OF THE BRIDGES.
NOW--WHO WILL COME WITH ME?
WHO AMONG YOU--
I VOLUNTEER!
CHOOSE *ME!*
PICK ME!
--HAS *NOTHING* TO LOSE?
CHOOSE *ME,* ORCHID!
NO, *ME!*
WHO KNOWS *BEST* THE SUFFERING THAT MAKES US FIGHT?
WE'LL COME WITH YOU, ORCHID.

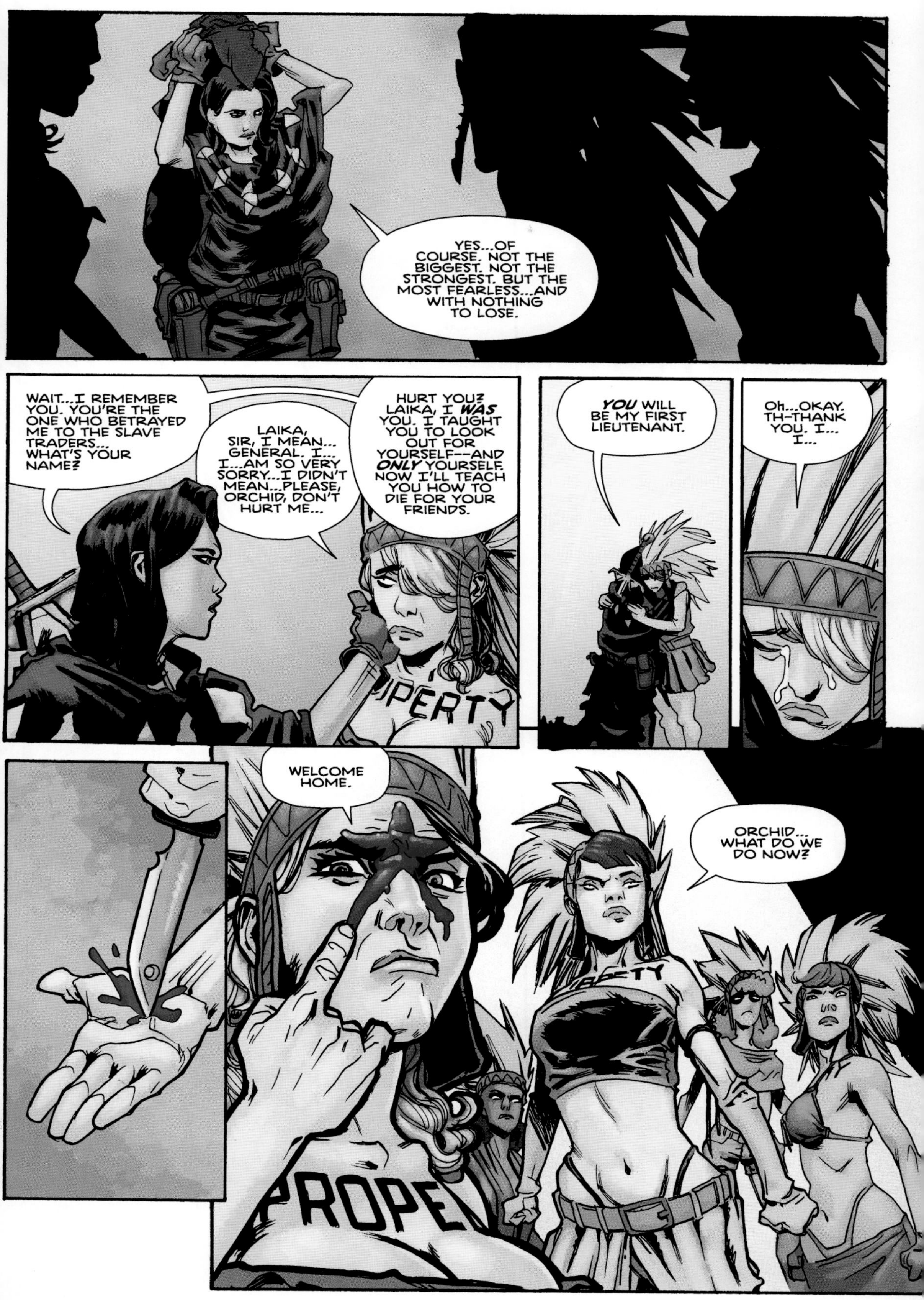
YES...OF COURSE. NOT THE BIGGEST. NOT THE STRONGEST. BUT THE MOST FEARLESS...AND WITH NOTHING TO LOSE.
WAIT...I REMEMBER YOU. YOU'RE THE ONE WHO BETRAYED ME TO THE SLAVE TRADERS... WHAT'S YOUR NAME?
LAIKA, SIR, I MEAN... GENERAL. I... I...AM SO VERY SORRY...I DIDN'T MEAN...PLEASE, ORCHID, DON'T HURT ME...
HURT YOU? LAIKA, I WAS YOU. I TAUGHT YOU TO LOOK OUT FOR YOURSELF--AND ONLY YOURSELF. NOW I'LL TEACH YOU HOW TO DIE FOR YOUR FRIENDS.
YOU WILL BE MY FIRST LIEUTENANT.
Oh...OKAY. TH-THANK YOU. I... I...
WELCOME HOME.
ORCHID... WHAT DO WE DO NOW?

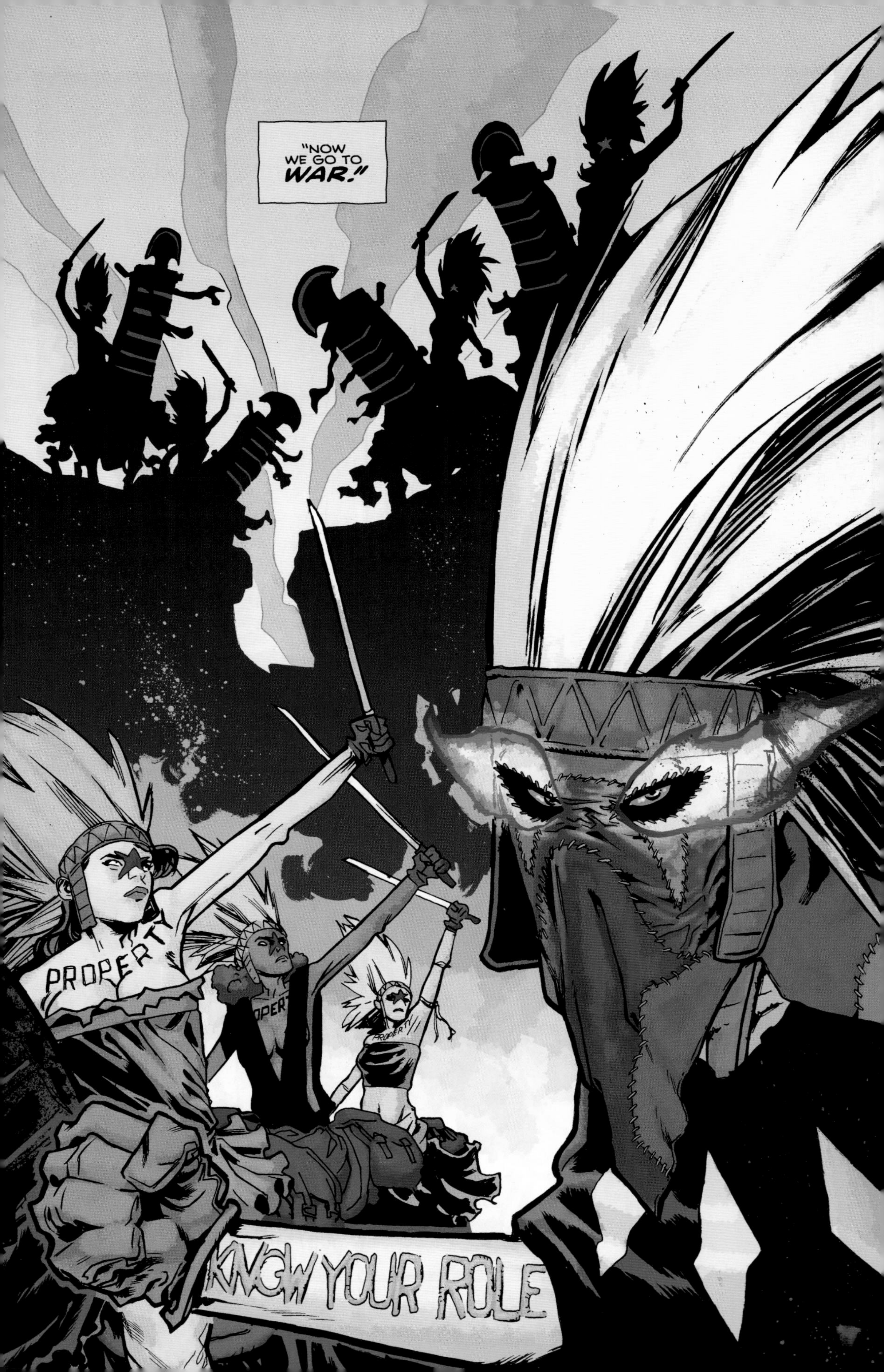
"NOW WE GO TO WAR."
PROPERTY
PROPERTY
PROPERTY
KNOW YOUR ROLE

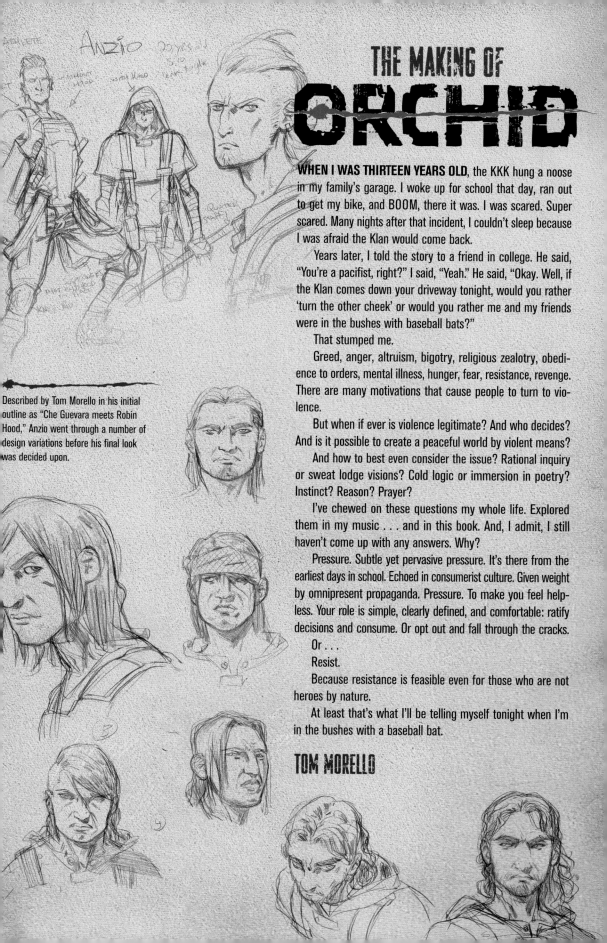

THE MAKING OF
ORCHID

Described by Tom Morello in his initial outline as "Che Guevara meets Robin Hood," Anzio went through a number of design variations before his final look was decided upon.

WHEN I WAS THIRTEEN YEARS OLD, the KKK hung a noose in my family's garage. I woke up for school that day, ran out to get my bike, and BOOM, there it was. I was scared. Super scared. Many nights after that incident, I couldn't sleep because I was afraid the Klan would come back.

Years later, I told the story to a friend in college. He said, "You're a pacifist, right?" I said, "Yeah." He said, "Okay. Well, if the Klan comes down your driveway tonight, would you rather 'turn the other cheek' or would you rather me and my friends were in the bushes with baseball bats?"

That stumped me.

Greed, anger, altruism, bigotry, religious zealotry, obedience to orders, mental illness, hunger, fear, resistance, revenge. There are many motivations that cause people to turn to violence.

But when if ever is violence legitimate? And who decides? And is it possible to create a peaceful world by violent means?

And how to best even consider the issue? Rational inquiry or sweat lodge visions? Cold logic or immersion in poetry? Instinct? Reason? Prayer?

I've chewed on these questions my whole life. Explored them in my music . . . and in this book. And, I admit, I still haven't come up with any answers. Why?

Pressure. Subtle yet pervasive pressure. It's there from the earliest days in school. Echoed in consumerist culture. Given weight by omnipresent propaganda. Pressure. To make you feel helpless. Your role is simple, clearly defined, and comfortable: ratify decisions and consume. Or opt out and fall through the cracks.

Or . . .

Resist.

Because resistance is feasible even for those who are not heroes by nature.

At least that's what I'll be telling myself tonight when I'm in the bushes with a baseball bat.

TOM MORELLO

AT RIGHT: Scott Hepburn's designs for some of Tomo Wolfe's fearsome machines–the steeds used by Don Gletkin and the gargoyles that adorn Fortress Penuel.
BELOW: Hepburn's design work on Gletkin's loyal half-machine, half-monster Sire Varesh.

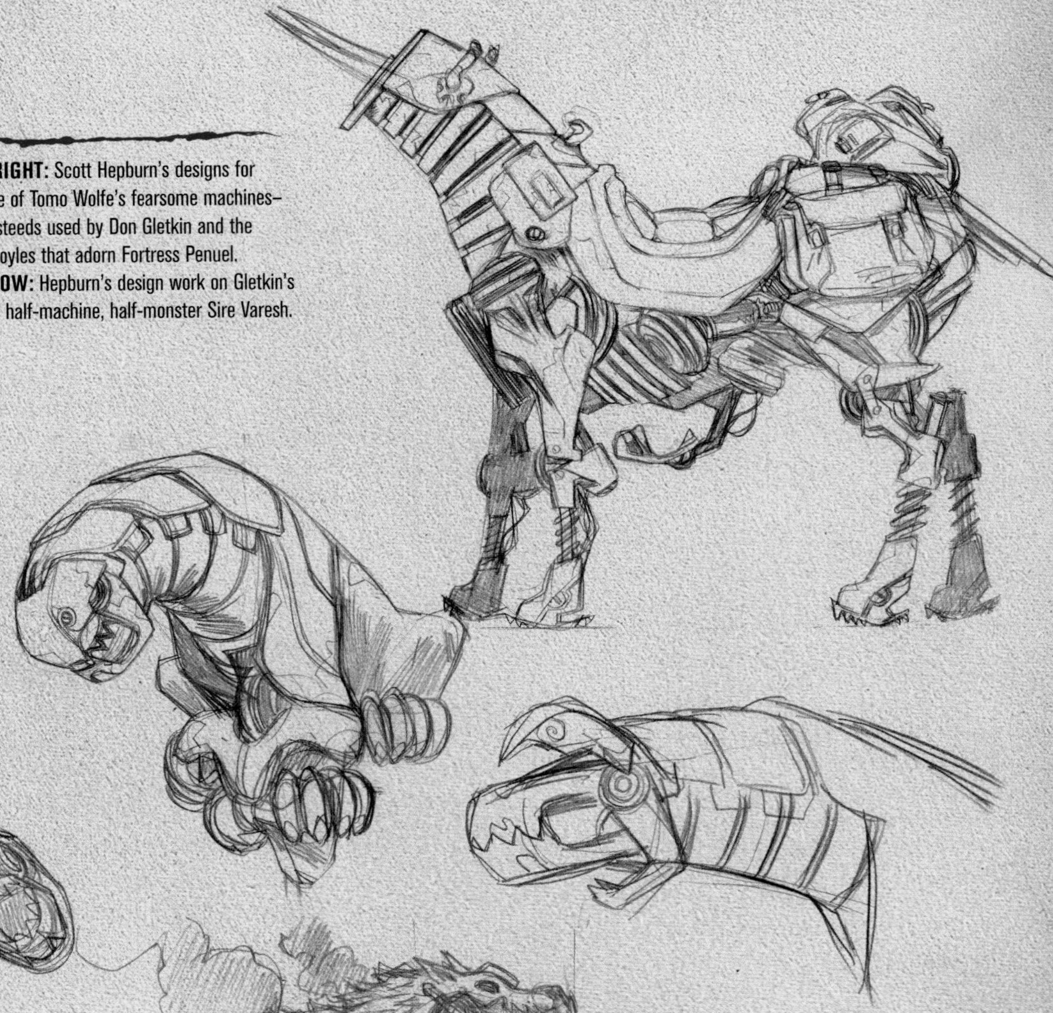

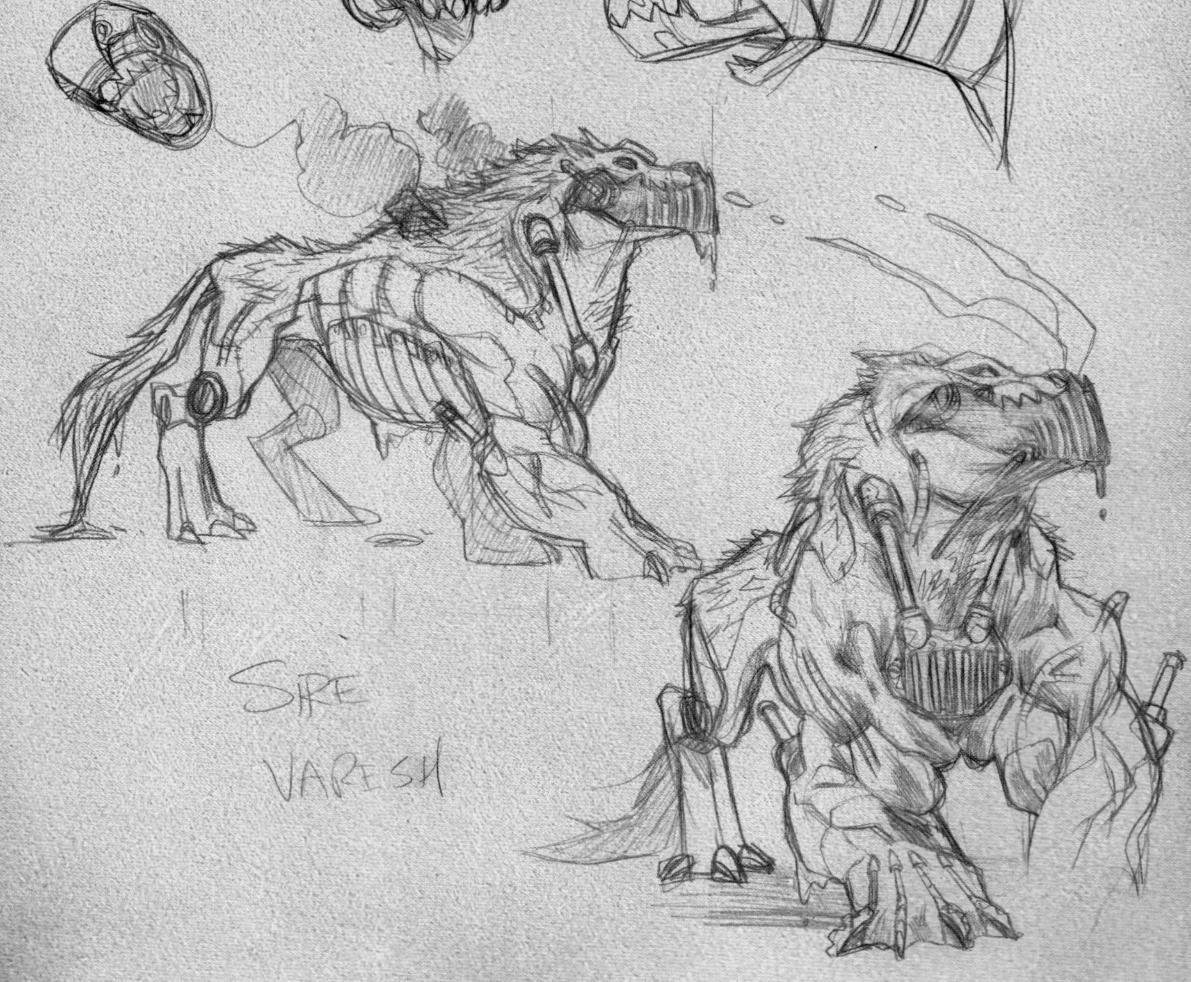
SIRE
VARESH